AGAINST

THE

GRAIN

The
Writings of
Professor
Revilo Pendleton Oliver

Volume I

1995
Liberty Bell Publications

AGAINST THE GRAIN
The
Writings of
Prfessor
Revilo Pendleton Oliver

Volume 1

Reprinted 2004 by
Liberty Bell Publications
PO Box 890
York, SC 29745
www.libertybellpublications.com

ISBN: 1-59364-002-1

Printed in the United States of America

CONTENTS

CHRISTIANITY AND THE SURVIVAL OF THE WEST

Revilo P. Oliver

Christianity And The Survival of the West

1973 Printing
by Sterling Enterprises

1978 Printing
by Howard Allen Enterprises, Inc.
by arrangement with Sterling Enterprises

1995 Printing in
AGAINST THE GRAIN:
The Writings of Professor Revilo P. Oliver
Volume I
by Liberty Bell Publications

International Standard Book Number: 0-914576-12-7
Library of Congress Card Number:73-77357

For information write to Liberty Bell Publications
P.O. Box 21, Reedy WV 25270-0021 USA

Printed in the United States of America

A return will set in of the re-active pressure of nature upon mankind. Mankind will again be restive under it.... But woe to that people which has not men that will stand up and fight without flinching. Those countries where the moral decay shall have gone deepest, where the proved stock shall have died out and given way to poor stock, where the greatest effeminisation of men shall have taken place (for the masculinisation of women will be no compensation), where the strong and the wise and the shrewd shall gain no more of wealth, power, and influence than the weak, silly, and incompetent, all being equal, those will go to the wall. And when this fate shall have overtaken most of our western white men's countries, our cycle of civilization will be completed.

-Correa Moylan Walsh(1917)

Glücklich wird niemand sein, der heute irgendwo in der Welt lebt.

-Oswald Spengler(1918)

Jamais comme aujourd'hui les peuples n'ont eu la sensation d'être menés par les événements. Jamais ils n'ont été plus impuissants, plus *volontairement* impuissants devant eux. ...Et c'est bien ce qui me parait le plus tragique dans l'aspect du monde de 1932: on n'y voit qu'une civilisation qui tombe et la nuit qui approche.

-Pierre Loewel(1932)

The mission of this generation is the most difficult that has ever faced a Western generation. It must break the terror by which it is held in silence, it must look ahead, it must believe when there is apparently no hope, it must obey even if it means death, it must fight to the end rather than submit.... The men of this generation must fight for the continued existence of the West.

-Francis Parker Yockey (1948)

CHRISTIANITY AND THE
SURVIVAL OF THE WEST

CHAPTER ONE

THE RELIGION OF THE WEST

YOU, WHO ARE now reading these lines, and I are strangers. I have no means of knowing whether you are a Christian or an atheist. That, however, will not matter, so long as we talk about facts and not wishes.

The observed and verifiable facts of the world about us are not affected by religious faith or the lack of faith. Christians and atheists must find themselves in perfect agreement when they affirm that lead is more malleable than steel, that the earth is an oblate spheroid rotating on its axis, that whales are mammals, that Germany was defeated and devastated by the many nations allied against her in 1945, and that the Chinese are Mongolians. About such matters there can be no dispute among Western men, who instinctively accept the reality of the world about us and cannot believe, as do many Orientals, that it is merely an illusion in the mind of a dreamer.

If we would salvage and restore our civilization—the Occidental culture that is peculiarly our own and that now seems to be disintegrating and rotting before our very eyes—we must do so as Western men, by observing reality objectively and by reasoning from it dispassionately. And when we try to compute what resources remain to us, we need first of all to determine the actual strength of the Christian tradition at the present time.

It is a fact, which Christians will regard with satisfaction and some atheists may deplore, that Western civilization, for about half of its recorded history, has been a Christian civilization in the

5

sense that the great majority of the people belonging to it (though never, at any time, *all* of them) believed implicitly in the truth of the Christian revelation. That religious unanimity was for a long time so nearly complete that, after the fall of the Roman Empire and the evanescence of hopes for its restoration, we of the West regarded our religion as the bond that united us and distinguished us from the rest of the human species. During the Middle Ages, our ancestors occupied the greater part of Europe, and, until they discovered the American continents, they lived only in Europe, but despite that geographical unity, they did not generally refer to themselves as the Europeans. For all practical purposes, furthermore, our ancestors belonged to the same division of the white race: they, like the true Greeks and the true Romans before them, were all members of the great race that we now call Indo-European or Aryan, but they had in their languages no word to designate their blood relationship and biological unity. Thus, when they referred to the unity of which they were always conscious as something transcending the constantly shifting territorial and political divisions of Europe, they called themselves Christendom. And for many centuries that word was adequate and misled no one.

For many centuries the West was Christendom and its civilization was indubitably Christian: that, whether you like it or not, is an historical fact. There is a complementary historical fact that was less obvious at the time and that even thoughtful men overlooked or tried to ignore until the events of the past two decades made it indubitable: Christianity is a religion of the West, and, for all practical purposes, *only* of the West. It is not, as its polemical adversaries so often charge, a Semitic cult, for it has never commanded the adhesion of any considerable number of Semites, and it is not, as Christians once generally believed, a universal religion, for experience has now proved that it cannot be successfully exported to populations that are not Indo-European.

Experience has also proved that it does not do the slightest good to deny ascertained facts. The men of Classical antiquity knew, of course, that the earth is spherical, and Eratosthenes in the third century B.C. calculated its circumference as 24,663 miles. But the early Fathers of the Church, living in the age of growing ignorance that shrouded the last century of the Roman Empire, decided, on the basis of some statements in the Old Testament, that the earth ought to be flat or, at least, no more curved than a shield. Lactantius was the most eloquent and probably, therefore, the most influential of the many who assiduously demanded that the earth be flat and so imposed on their contemporaries the conviction that it was. In the Middle Ages, to be sure, there were some learned men, such as Buridan, who knew that the globe is a globe, but they, like learned men today, who all know very well that talk about the equality of races is utter nonsense, usually refrained from publicly denouncing fashionable delusions. It was not until the Fifteenth Century that the truth became again inescapable, but when it did, the Christians, being men of the West, who do not deny the lessons of experience, surrendered the comfortable error in which they had once generally believed; and since that time, no rational Christian has doubted that the earth is spherical.

Today, as in the Fifteenth Century, Western men have had to discard a congenial assumption to bring their conception of the world into conformity with observed reality. So long as we of the West held unquestioned dominion over the whole earth, we permitted ourselves to assume that our civilization in general, and our religion in particular, could be exported and made universal. We did not sufficiently observe that talent for mimicry is common to all human beings and indeed to all anthropoids; that all human beings stand in awe of those who have power over them; and that a genius for dissimulation and hypocrisy is hereditary in the most intelligent Orientals. Even with these oversights, the evidence against our assumption was fairly clear, but in the pride of our power we felt that we could indulge an assumption that was so congenial to the romantic generosity that is a peculiarity of our race. But the events of half a century, and especially of the past two decades, have shown us, beyond peradventure of doubt, the shape of the world in which we live. We now know what our prolonged missionary effort, cultural as well as religious, accomplished—and how its visible effects were produced.

When Cortés and his small but valiant band of iron men conquered the teeming empire of the Aztecs, he was immediately followed by a train of earnest missionaries, chiefly Franciscans, who began to preach the Gospel to the natives and soon sent home, with naive enthusiasm, glowing accounts of the conversions they had effected. Their pious sincerity and innocent joy still lives in the pages of Father Sahagun, Father Torquemada, and many others. For their sake I am glad that the poor Franciscans never suspected how small a part they played in the religious conversions that gave them such happiness. Far, far more persuasive than their sermons and their book had been the Spanish cannon that breached and shattered the Aztec defenses, and the ruthless Spanish soldiers who slew the Aztec priests at their own altars and toppled the Aztec idols from the sacrificial pyramids. The Aztecs, Tepanecs, and other natives accepted Christianity, not because their hearts were touched by alien and incomprehensible doctrines of love and mercy, but because it was the religion of the white men whose bronze cannon and mail-clad warriors were invincible.

That was early in the Sixteenth Century and even then there were not wanting indications that should have given pause to a critical mind, but we of the West went on repeating that fond mistake for four centuries, as the missionaries whom we sent to all parts of the world wrote home glowing reports of the number of "hearts" they had "won for Christ." It was only after our enemies' campaign of "anti-colonialism" really got under way that most of us realized that what had won all those hearts was primarily the discipline of British regiments and the manifest power of the white man.

We now know what happened. On many a shore of Africa, for example, missionaries eager to "win souls for Christ" ventured to land alone, and the aborigines, after mutilating and torturing them for a good communal laugh, ate them, cooked or raw according to the custom of the local cuisine. Usually, a few weeks or a few months later, a British cruiser hove to off shore and lobbed half a dozen 4.5 shells into the native village, and, if not pressed for time, landed half a company of marines to beat the bushes and drag out a dozen or so savages to hang on convenient trees. Consequently the tribe, if not very obtuse, took the hint and respected the next bevy of missionaries as somehow representing the god of thunder and lightning. And if the men of God distributed enough free rice and medical care with their sermons, they were able to make "converts," as the natives learned to utter the words that Christians like to hear.

That is, in essence, the whole history of "winning souls" among the savages. There were, of course, many local variations. If the first missionaries were preceded by troops or white settlers, the blacks had already been convinced of the virtues of Christian rifles and had learned that white men should not be regarded as esculent comestibles. It often happened, however, that the natives, even after many years of preaching and conversion, rejected the white man's odd rites very emphatically, and a fresh supply of missionaries was needed. In 1905, for example, the Maji-Maji conspiracy in Tanganyika murdered all the missionaries and almost all the white men and women in the entire territory, and it required a German regiment and several companies of marines to restore the teaching of the Gospel. That was done by giving some forty or fifty thousand demonstrations that a Mauser bullet could penetrate even a black hide that had been most carefully anointed with the grease of a boiled baby.

The Christian missionaries did teach a ritual and often inculcated a superstition that had some superficial resemblance to their religion, but as for teaching the spiritual substance of Christianity, they might as well have followed the example of St. Francis and preached sermons to the birds. That is why the many, many thousands of devoted Christians who expended their whole lives to "save souls" built only an edifice of cardboard and tinsel that is now gone in the wind.

What the vanishing of that flimsy façade has made obvious was predictable from the first. The religion of the West has *never* been comprehensible to the rudimentary minds of Congoids, Capoids, and Australoids, races so primitive that they were congenitally incapable of inventing a wheel and even of using one without supervision—races that could not develop for themselves even the first and simplest preliminaries of a civilization. When the missionaries invented systems of writing the crude languages of the primitives, they had also to invent words to express such concepts as 'God,' 'soul,' 'justice,' 'morality,' and 'religion'—invent them by either creating new words or by perverting to such meanings sounds that in the native jargons conveyed impressions that were faintly and remotely analogous. That fact alone should have made us think. It was clear, furthermore, that the "converts," even those who had been most thoroughly imbued with an awe of the god of repeating rifles and locomotives, would conform to the white man's morality only under coercion, and that whenever they escaped from the white man's supervision they spontaneously reverted not only to their own *mores* but also to whatever form of voodoo they had practiced before. Even if earlier experience had not been conclusive, what happened in Haiti at the very beginning of the Nineteenth Century should have removed the last lingering doubt. But the missionaries did not learn, and the "Ladies' Missionary Society" went on contributing their mites, plying their needles, and glowing with tender emotion for the sweet little savages depicted by their romantic imaginations.

Although it is true that in some places in the former colonial possessions missionaries are still tolerated, if they are obsequious to the natives and pay very well, we have at last learned that the Gospel follows the British regiments in the white man's ignominious and insane retreat from the world that was his.

CHAPTER TWO

THE ORIENT

WE INDO-EUROPEANS have been for about half of our recorded history, and our whole culture was so intimately connected with our religion that we called our world Christendom. Today, however, our religion and hence our understanding of ourselves and the world about us have been drastically affected by three distinct developments that have no necessary relation to one another and that we should be careful not to confuse, viz.:

(1) The catastrophic decline of religious faith and belief among our own people during the past century and a half or two centuries. That is a phenomenon which, although perhaps slightly accelerated by alien influences, arose within our culture and was simply a revival of the tendency of our Western philosophy before the appearance of Christianity. It is therefore a separate topic that we must postpone for later consideration.

(2) The now obvious failure of our efforts to communicate Christianity to the primitive races, which we discussed briefly in our opening chapter.

(3) The futility of all our efforts to export our Occidental religion to the old and civilized nations of the Orient. This is really the most striking phenomenon of all.

Among the biologically and mentally primitive Congoids, Capoids, and Australoids, Christian missionaries attained for a while some specious semblance of success. One can only marvel, however, at the illusions that Christendom obstinately entertained, century after century, despite its constant and virtually total failure to win converts among the highly intelligent and subtle Orientals, both white and yellow, who had elaborate cultures of their own.

Since we are, on the whole, a rational race, there was *some* basis for those illusions. The sacred books of Christianity did not originate in the West. The Old Testament deals almost entirely with the activities of Israelites and Jews. The events of the New Testament, to be sure, took place in a Roman province in Asia Minor, and largely in Galilee, a small territory inhabited by a conglomerate population that the Jews despised as inferiors, but the first apostles, whatever their race, were certainly not Europeans, and Paul was admittedly a Jew. It was known, furthermore, that in the early centuries there had been some small Judaeo-Christian sects,* and that it was not until later that the new religion attracted votaries that could be identified as authentically Greek, Roman, and Celtic. Although Europeans knew the Christian scriptures only in Greek and Latin, and during the Middle Ages only in Latin, the Asiatic origins created a supposition that Christianity, the religion of Europe, was not European, even when everyone knew that it had no adherents outside Europe except in the territories of the Byzantine Empire, and that Byzantine Christianity was so adulterated with Levantine elements that it was unacceptable to the West.**

* The Ebionites and the Cerinthians were the most important of these sects, but there were others, most of which are catalogued in, the seven-volume edition of Adolf von Harnack's *History of Dogma*. I need scarcely add that the term "Judaeo-Christian" is correctly used *only* with reference to these sects and their antecedents.

** The differences between Western and Oriental Christianity were so profound and fundamental that repeated attempts made before 1453 to effect a union of the two churches were utter failures despite the Byzantines' desperate need for military aid from the West, despite the West's idealistic notion that its religion was "universal," and despite a generous amount of hypocrisy on both sides. After the capture of Constantinople by Mohammed II, most of the surviving Byzantines devoutly thanked their god that they had fallen under the rule of Moslems (with whom they had much in common) instead of European Christians, who would have tried to impose on them an alien religion. It is significant that the abyss between the two religions that called themselves Christian was too wide to be bridged, even though the conglomerate and partly Levantine population of the Byzantine Empire had inherited the culture and learning of the ancient (and extinct) Greeks.

We cannot here analyze the effects of that supposition on Mediaeval Christendom. A concise and incisive treatment of that subject may be found in Lawrence R. Brown's brilliant work, *The Might of the West* (New York, 1963). It will here suffice to note that even during the high-tide of Christian faith marked by the Crusades, that supposition prevented our ancestors from drawing the correct deductions from their manifest and perpetual failure to extend Western Christianity beyond the borders of the West.

Ever since it was founded, the Christian Church has labored incessantly to convert Jews, using every method from flattering exhortations and cash rewards to legislative pressure and armed coercion, and it has failed utterly. That failure, furthermore, was conspicuous in every city and almost every town of Christendom, year after year and century after century. It was known even to the most ignorant and isolated peasant.

In Christendom, as elsewhere, the international race planted its colonies wherever there was money to be got from the natives, and it always followed the standard procedure that it used, for example, in Alexandria in the fourth century B.C. The colonists filtered in in small groups until their numbers were sufficient to take over a part of the city for themselves to establish their own ghettos, from which the natives of the country were informally, but effectively, excluded. But the main body of colonists, ostentatiously exclusive, was usually or always accompanied by a number, smaller or greater as the occasion demanded, of *Marranos*, i.e., Jews who feigned conversion to the religion and culture of the nation in which they had come to reside. As they had professed Greek philosophy in Alexandria, so in Mediaeval Europe they professed Christianity. They, so to speak, covered the flanks of their less versatile congeners.

Here and there in Europe, Christians sometimes tried to dislodge and expel the Jewish colonies, but they never succeeded. By violence or threats of violence some cities and territories were able to drive Jews from their ghettos for a few years, but invariably, except in Spain and Portugal, the ostentatiously alien Jews returned sooner or later and industriously restored their ghettos. The *Marranos*, sheltered by their professed "conversion," eluded all efforts to control them, and in Spain and Portugal, at least, they not only entered the highest offices of the state but, despite the frantic efforts of the Inquisition, they filled even the Church with nuns, priests, bishops, and archbishops who solemnly celebrated in public the rites of a religion they despised and, when they met in their secret conclaves, laughed at the stupidity of the gullible *goyim*.

The amazing versatility and subtlety of the *Marranos*, especially in "most Christian" Spain and Portugal, has been described by many distinguished Jewish scholars. *A History of the Marranos*, by Professor Cecil Roth of Oxford, is a concise survey; the recent work by Haim Beinart, *Anusim be-Din ha-lnqwizisiah* (Tel Aviv, 1965), unfortunately not available in English, is a highly detailed study of a single community at one point in its history.

Was a Jew ever converted to Christianity? The learned and candid Rabbi Solomon Schindler,* addressing a Christian audience in Boston, was certain that *no* Jew could "submit conscientiously" to so inferior a creed. "There never was a Jew," he said, "converted to Christianity who conscientiously believed in the doctrines of his adopted religion. They were all hypocrites, who changed their creed for earthly considerations merely." And the acute, sagacious, and earnest Maurice Samuel,** after diligent and conscientious study, concluded that "Obviously you do not make a gentile of a Jew by baptizing him any more than you would make an Aryan of a negro by painting him with ocher." Such sweeping generalizations may be too absolute, and there seem to be some certain instances of Jews who sincerely defected to Christianity, but they are few. On the whole, the failure of Christians to allure or compel Jews has been total and spectacular.

Christians often explain that failure by attributing to the Jews

* Solomon Schindler, *Messianic Expectations and Modem Judaism*, with an introduction by [the Reverend] Minot J. Savage. Boston, Cassino, 1886.

** Maurice Samuel, *You Gentiles*. New York, Harcourt-Brace, 1924.

some peculiar perversity or malevolence, the result of either a divine curse or of conscious collaboration with Satan. But in the interests of both fairness and objectivity, we should consider respectfully and dispassionately the testimony of the erudite and discerning Jews who have earnestly studied and pondered the many and profound differences between their people and ours, and who assure us, as courteously as they can, that to *their* minds *our* religion and most of the standards of *our* culture appear ludicrous or repulsive and sometimes utterly incomprehensible. How can we expect or require a man to believe what is to *his* mind mere nonsense? Would not that be as absurd as to expect the Jews who reside in our country to consult our interests rather than their own?

So long as Christendom knew only the Jewish colonies in its territory and the Semitic and Hamitic Moslems on its southern borders, some theory of an obduracy or perversity peculiar to Jews and Moslems could perhaps be maintained, but surely Christians should have perceived, as their geographical horizons expanded, that their religion had no appeal for *any* Oriental people.

The name of Christ, to be sure, is used by certain Monophysite cults in the Near East and Malabar and by other sects in Egypt and Abyssinia, of which vague rumors reached Mediaeval Europe and inspired the romantic legends of Prester John. But actual contact with those sects in the Sixteenth Century brought disillusion; the reading of their sacred books in Syriac, Coptic, and Geez showed how vastly those conceptions of religion differed from the European; and missionaries were dispatched to convert those "Christians" to Western Christianity—efforts that always ended in failure and sometimes in bloody failure.

With the exception of such isolated and minor cults as the Mandeans and the Yezidis, the Semitic peoples of Asia have found *their* aspirations and *their* religiosity fully satisfied by Islam, and all the exhortations of our missionaries for a millennium induced only a handful of Moslems to profess Christianity. In India, where the blood of the Aryan conquerors was blotted up long ago, a few outcasts and famished drudges became "rice Christians," and some educated babus said they were converts so long as "conversion" seemed likely to expedite their advancement in the bureaucracy of British India; and the Hindus sent us in return hundreds of sloe-eyed swamis to convert us and care for our souls—especially the souls of wealthy dowagers. In China and Japan the seeds of the Gospel, though sown over and over again by generations of earnest and often martyred missionaries, produced no better harvest.

In sum, experience has shown us that the Jews, though unique as an international race, do not differ from other Orientals in their resistance to the "glad tidings" (*euangelion*) of Christianity. In Asia, as in Africa, though for far different reasons, Christianity is evaporating as rapidly as dew in the morning sun, and there is every reason to believe that, with a few possible exceptions, the remaining Asiatic "Christians," including native clergymen and bishops, are simply Arab, Hindu, Chinese, or Japanese Marranos and profess a Western religion for business or diplomatic reasons.

We have an unbroken record of failure in all our efforts to export Christianity to other peoples. That failure has nothing to do with the decline of faith among our own people in very recent times as a result of a skepticism based on *our* science and technology. Uniformly since the foundation of the Western Church, Christianity failed to attract and convince other races, and in the great Age of Faith in Europe that failure was as complete as it is today. Christendom should have understood the reasons for that inevitable failure long ago.

For centuries our clergymen had the strange custom of looking through all the other religions and cults of the whole world to find superficial similarities that they would then adduce as somehow corroborating our religion. They clutched eagerly at every ghost story in the world and used it to "prove" that a belief in immortality was "universal." What all the other doctrines and myths really proved was that *our* belief in immortality was something peculiar to ourselves and probably incomprehensible to other races.

We Aryans have a deep and innate longing to endure forever. But the immortality of which the atheist despairs and for which the Christian hopes is a *personal* immortality the survival of the individual consciousness complete with all its memories of life on earth. For each of us, immortality is the prolongation of *his* consciousness after the death of his body. Although we, if not spiritually sick, desire the survival of our race and culture, that is not what *we* mean by immortality; even if we felt assured that our people would eventually own the whole earth and all the other peoples in it, that would seem to *us* to have nothing to do with the question whether or not you and I as individuals will live after death. Again, we can believe that at death a man will be either annihilated or become a single disembodied consciousness: we cannot believe that he will become five or six different and widely scattered pieces of a ghost. Again, if some psychic spark of ourselves should survive death but be unconscious, having no knowledge or memory of what we were in life, to *us* that fate would be annihilation, not immortality. Again, if I am to live after death, so must my wife: no number of houris could reconcile me to a Paradise attained by many millions of men but only four women and one dog. Furthermore, we can imagine reincarnation, but only reincarnation as ourselves. If my wife has been Napoleon and Richard the Lion-Hearted, she is nothing that I have ever known or loved. And if I was ever Aspasia and Nell Gwyn, then I do not exist even now: I am just an illusion.

The kinds of "immortality" posited by the other major religions are inacceptable to us: meaningless, absurd, or repulsive to our racial instincts. But obviously such notions of a future life are not only satisfactory to other peoples but represent what *they* instinctively desire. To the great majority of the world's inhabitants our conception of immortality is meaningless, absurd, or repulsive. That is simply a fact that we cannot change.

Christianity embodied all the moral instincts of our race, such as our concepts of personal honor, of personal self-respect and integrity, of fair play, of pity for the unfortunate, of loyalty—all of which seem preposterous to other races, at least in the form and application that we give to them. They simply lack our instincts.

We think that it makes a great difference whether we kill a man in a fair fight or by treacherously stabbing him in the back or by putting poison in the cup that he accepts from our friendly hand; to at least one other race, we are simply childish and irrational: if you are to kill a man, kill him in the safest and most convenient way. Again, we, whether Christians or atheists, have an instinct for truth, so that if we lie, we have physical reactions that can be detected by a sphygmomanometer (often called a polygraph or "lie detector"). When officers of American military intelligence tried to use that device in the interrogation of prisoners during the Korean War, they discovered that Koreans and Chinese have no reaction that the instrument can detect, no matter how outrageous the lies they tell. We and they are differently constituted.

We can no longer be so obtuse as to ignore the vast differences in mentality and instinct that separate us from all other races—not merely from savages, but from highly civilized races. The differences are innate, and to attempt to change their way of thinking with argument, generosity, or holy water is as absurd as attempting to change the color of their skins. That is a fact that we must accept. However one may relate that fact to Christian doctrine, if we, a small minority among the teeming and terribly fecund populations of the globe, call all other peoples perverse or wicked, we merely confuse ourselves. If we are to think objectively and rationally, we must do so in the terms used by Maurice Samuel, who, after his discerning and admirably candid study of the "unbridgeable gulf" that separates Indo-Europeans from Jews, had to conclude that "This difference in behavior and reaction springs from something more earnest and significant than a difference of beliefs: it springs from a difference in our biologic equipment."

We cannot reasonably expect beings differently constituted to have our instincts or to believe as we do, any more than we can expect dogs to climb trees or cats to bark at intruders. And let us beware of the word "superiority." If it means that we are superior in terms of our own values, it is a mere tautology; if it has an objective and practical meaning, it poses a question that can be answered only when the future has proved which peoples will survive and which will go under in the proximate struggle for possession of an overcrowded globe.

This is not a matter of doctrine or wishes, and it does not depend on our faith or lack of faith. Whatever may be the meaning of certain passages in the Old Testament, the earth is not flat. Whatever may be the meaning of certain passages in the New Testament, Christianity was not for "all the world." The earth is spherical. Christianity is an Indo-European religion.

CHAPTER THREE

CHRISTIANITY TODAY

IF YOU DESIRE TO PRESERVE our country and our civiliza-tion, you must face two fundamental facts.

The first of these is that 90% of all the active support of pro-American efforts has come from Christians.

Of that, there can be no doubt. Almost without exception, all of the thousands of "conservative" and "anti-Communist" organizations that have come and gone during the past fifty years have been specifically Christian, proposing to defend Christianity and the Constitution simultaneously. Many of the most active organizations today are evangelical and try to revive Christian faith by holding meetings in which the Gospel and patriotism are inseparably blended. Some organizations specifically established to resist or promote certain legislation do not explicitly raise religious issues, but they take Christianity for granted. The only patriotic organizations that are explicitly non-Christian are a small periodical, *The Truth Seeker*, which, having spoken disrespectfully of Jews, is now being forced to the wall, and one small "activist" group in California.

It is true that a very successful promotion was founded by a master-salesman who began by admitting, with a show of candor, that he rejected belief in a personal god as childish and preferred a vague pantheism that recognized an "upward reach" in "all mankind" that was similar to the upward reach of growing plants. But after testing the market, he began to claim that he was purveying a doctrine that was a kind of pep pill good for all religions and guaranteed to make the purchaser a better Christian, better Pharisee, or better Moslem, as the case might be. (There are no Buddhists,

Parsees, Yezidis, Jains, Saivites, or Tantrists with large bank rolls in the United States at the present time, nor are they represented by oil-rich governments abroad.) The only point that need concern us now is that the promoter accurately gauged his market. Of all the members who passed through his organization in its heyday, at least 80% were Christians—probably 90% of those who really worked and gave money to the limit of their resources.

You have only to attend *any* "anti-Communist" meeting, including both the most sincere efforts and the most fraudulent promotions, and talk to the persons who attend and contribute to convince yourself that almost all of them are Christians, and by that I mean persons who really *believe* in Christ, as distinct, of course, from the many persons who attend Sunday-morning clubs because they think it good for business, politically expedient, or socially amusing. Whether you like it or not, you must accept the fact that 90% of the active support for patriotic and pseudo-patriotic efforts comes from men and women who have a sincere faith in Christ.

During more than two decades, the active Defense of the West has rested almost entirely on the shoulders of Christians in all Occidental nations. And that has been true on all levels. I know that comparisons are invidious, but to make my point I will say that if I had to pick one periodical on our side as having the highest literary finish and intellectual content, I should have to name *Découvertes*, the monthly publication of a highly cultivated group of staunchly Christian Frenchmen now in Lisbon.

That is not astonishing. For almost fifteen centuries Occidental civilization was Christendom, and, as is shown by the data that we have already examined, Christianity as we know it is, and always has been, an Indo-European religion, incomprehensible to the rudimentary minds of the primitive races and unacceptable to the subtle minds of the Orientals who have civilizations of their own. If that seems to you negative proof, consider the conversion of the Norse peoples during the early Middle Ages. They were not subject to a Christian government that could coerce them and they needed no Christian support against anyone; the Christians whom they plundered on occasion were certainly not militarily superior, nor were the institutions and culture of the Dark Ages anything that Vikings and Varangians might have envied and wished to imitate. Their only reason for abandoning the bleakly pessimistic religion of Thor and Odin must have been that Christianity was more congenial to their minds.* Such *spontaneous* conversions are rare phenomena in the history of the world's religions; the closest parallel is the adoption of decadent Buddhism by the Chinese who found it congenial to their mentality.**

There is a second fact that you must also face. The Western world is no longer Christendom. The religion that once united us has become the faith of a minority.

That is obvious from what has been happening here and in every country of Europe except Spain and Portugal. The real question is how small a minority are Christians in the United States.

---

* One factor often overlooked was Christianity's appeal to the historical sense of our race. Norse theology was a collection of inconsistent tales, admittedly mythical since the skalds could revise or elaborate them at will, about the adventures of various gods in Niflheim, Jotunheim, Asgard and other realms outside the known world and inaccessible to men, at dates no more specific than "once upon a time." Christianity offered a circumstantial and realistic narrative of events that had taken place in remote but specific and well-known towns and geographical areas at precisely stated times during the reigns of known Roman Emperors; the historicity of the narrative was further guaranteed by the generally consistent and apparently independent statements of four eye witnesses, whose veracity was further guaranteed by the official reports of Roman governors who had themselves participated in the climactic scene (i.e., the *Acta Pilati, Epistula Lentuli,* and other forgeries that were accepted as genuine during the Dark Ages). It may be relevant that the *Epistula Lentuli* certifies Christ as unmistakably Nordic: tall, fair-skinned, with blonde hair and blue eyes.

** Note, however, the very important difference that although the Chinese adaptation of the Buddhist religion eventually made a large number of converts, it never supplanted Taoism and other native cults, to say nothing of the widely-held doctrine of Confucius (which virtually ignores the supernatural) and the more restricted philosophy of the Fa Chia (which regards all religions as myths useful for governmental purposes). It would *never* have been proper to speak of China as a Buddhist country.

In 1942, after a very careful study of the situation in England, Professor A.N. Whitehead concluded that "in the whole country far less than one-fifth of the population are *in any sense* Christians today." There is very little difference in this respect between England and the United States. And today?

Let us transcend all the doctrinal differences, important as they are, that divide the Christian churches. The absolute minimum requirement of a Christian is faith that Christ was literally the Son of God. Of course, persons who do not have that faith may have the impudence to call themselves Christians, just as they may call themselves elves, Martians, or pterodactyls, but if they do, they are obviously intending some hoax or fraud.

How many adult Americans today really believe that Christ was God Incarnate? I have consulted discerning Christians of indubitable piety and zeal who have had exceptional opportunities to observe in all parts of the country. The lowest estimate was 9%. The figure that was best supported was approximately 12%.

Of the 12% of adult Americans who truly believe in Christ, not all, by any means, are active in efforts to defend our nation and civilization. Of true believers, some also believe that the End of the World is at hand; others believe that the destruction of the Western world has been ordained as condign punishment for its sins, and that it would be impious to resist the manifest Will of God; and others quite logically regard the events of the brief life on earth as merely preparation for the salvation of their souls. I should be astonished if more than half of the remaining Christians are actively committed to the preservation of our country. And yet this 6% has provided almost all of the support for anti-Communist causes. That is something to think about.

We must specifically notice that the minority that still believes that Christ was really the Son of God does not include the majority of the persons who now talk from the pulpits of Sunday-morning clubs, including the propaganda chain operated by the National Council of Churches. The majority of professional clergymen were trained in theological seminaries in which they were taught that the Christian Bible is an agglomeration of forgeries perpetrated by persons too ignorant to write coherently and patched together by persons too stupid to make a consistent story out of it. They were further taught that Christ, *if* he existed and was not merely a myth created by awkward revision of the Essene story about the Teacher Yeshu, was a crack-pot agitator to whom were attributed, long after his death, some nice remarks about ethics and "social justice."*

Believing this but lacking the courage to seek honest employment, the poor wretches are ordained and find themselves in a business in which their income depends on their ability to keep congregations awake or, at least, in a donating mood each Sunday, while they must curry the favor of both their atheistic superiors and of the Lords of the Press and Radio. It is no wonder that they preach the "social gospel." Some of them, no doubt, really believe it, for it is a fact that the loss of religious faith merely leaves many minds morbidly susceptible to the contagion of the most grotesque superstitions. Some see no reason why they shouldn't peddle the brand of buncombe that pays the best. Some doubtless thirst for revolution and chaos to avenge themselves on the society that makes them exert themselves in pulpits, and, like the Vicar in Daphne du Maurier's memorable novel, *Jamaica Inn,* picture themselves as clever wolves preaching to congregations of uncom-

* Christians who have the courage to contemplate the present status and the now inevitable future of all the large organized denominations must read a recent book by a highly reputed "Biblical scholar" whose works have long been respected as authoritative in ecclesiastical seminaries: Dr. Hugh J. Schonfield's *The Passover Plot* (1965). Although his reconstruction of the way in which a crack-brained Jewish agitator named Jesus tried to stage a fake miracle is admittedly conjectural, his interpretation of the character and motives of that man (assuming that he ever existed) is now accepted in all of its essentials by virtually all educated clergymen, although, understandably, they may prefer to envelop it in clouds of misty verbiage when they harangue the persons who fill the collection-plates each Sunday. *That* Jesus, although an ignorant blunderer, is thought admirable because he was an early Bolshevik who tried to incite a revolution to destroy our race's Classical civilization and realize the old Jewish dream of One World ruled, of course, by God's Own People.

prehending mutton-heads. That is the real explanation of what has happened to most of our churches, and there is no need to imagine some fantastically large and cunning conspiracy of Illuminati or other Supermen to account for the behavior of clergymen who do not believe in Christianity.

The catastrophic decline of Christian faith is the most important, the crucial event of our recent history. Even the dullest members of Sunday-morning clubs know that it has happened, but they will try to deny it by informing you that the Seventh Baptopistical Church has just moved to a wonderful new edifice that cost half a million dollars and is architecturally indistinguishable from a night club, and that St. Olaf's Presbutheran Church has just added a hundred-thousand-dollar gymnasium to its sacred facilities. Believing Christians, on the other hand, know what has happened and deplore it. When they try to account for the catastrophe, however, they, if they recognize a natural cause at all, most commonly blame the Jews. That, I think, is unfair and, what is much worse, incorrect and therefore dangerous.

The most comprehensive and scholarly survey of Jewish pressures on, and infiltration of, Christianity from the earliest times is the work of one of the most learned ecclesiastical historians of our day and is now available in a passable English translation: *The Plot Against the Church* by Maurice Pinay. The virtual capture of the Catholic Church in recent years, which has been celebrated in articles in *Look* and other periodicals, is ably described by Vicomte Leon de Poncins in his *Judaism and the Vatican*. No Protestant scholar, so far as I know, has made a comparable study of Protestant denominations. It would be difficult to take exception to the reporting of historical facts in the two books that I have cited, and let us not question the authors' conclusions. Do they adequately explain the decline of Christianity?

I have no wish to defend the Jews, and I shall not ask whether it is entirely reasonable to blame them for forwarding their own interests by their own methods wherever they have planted colonies among populations whom they regard as inferior, much as our ancestors regarded the aborigines of North America. Let the Jews be as wicked and diabolical as you wish, but let us consider the religious question objectively, lest error delude us with fallacious hopes.

If we, from our vantage point in the present, look back over the history of our religion dispassionately, we can discern, at a distance of a thousand years and more, the origins of our plight today. I do not refer to sectarianism and heresies: they are simply normal in all evangelical religions. In Islam, for example, the multiplicity of sects is proverbial, and by the time that Buddhism became a religion in the second century B.C., there were already eighteen major sects, each claiming, of course, to be the sole repository of the true doctrine. Christianity is exceptional only for its relative stability. Over a period of twelve centuries, from 325 A.D., when its doctrine had taken form in all essentials, to the Protestant Reformation in the Sixteenth Century, the religion of the West was an effective unity, not seriously disturbed by such sporadic heresies as the Albigensians, and Waldenses, the Patarini, and the Hussites.*

Christianity is, as we have said, an Indo-European religion and it was therefore accepted and understood in terms of the mentality and thought-processes peculiar to our race. Our minds, unlike those of other races, demand that all the elements of a doctrine be logically consistent with one another and in conformity with observed reality. The intellectual efforts of the early Fathers of the

* We are not here concerned with the theological convulsions of the Byzantine ("Orthodox") Church, which, as we observed earlier, was a radically different kind of religion, imbued with Levantine elements rejected by the West, and thereby appealing to a racially different people. A discussion of the origin, incidence, and relative importance of Jewish and other Levantine elements in the early Christian doctrines, the progressive supersession of such elements in the West, and their recrudescence in some heresies would necessarily be long, involved, and somewhat abstruse. We cannot touch upon that topic here, where our concern is with Christianity as it was generally understood and accepted by our race. Debates about whether our distant ancestors understood it correctly or should have accepted what they did would be, for our present purposes, irrelevant and otiose.

Church, who labored to establish texts and resolve contradictions, have some analogies in other religions, but the Scholasticism of the Middle Ages is unique. This great philosophical effort to understand the world about us has nothing to do with heresies or even scepticism; it was, as one of the Scholastics defined it, *fides quaerens intellectum*, it was carried on by churchmen, and, as we too often forget, accompanied by mathematical investigations and empirical observation of nature. There are many histories of Scholasticism, and a good outline may be found in the second volume of Ueberweg's standard *History of Philosophy*. There are some very stimulating observations on late Scholasticism in the first volume of Egon Friedell's *Cultural History of the Modern Age*. The histories of science by Sarton and by Thorndike cover the Mediaeval period fairly well. The reader, however, will find the essentials most clearly presented in the brilliant work of Lawrence R. Brown, *The Might of the West*, which not only brings together facts that are artificially separated in other works, but identifies in its Mediaeval origins the great tension of modern thought. Christianity brought with it from Asia Minor alien elements that were generally ignored but remained latent in its sacred books and dogmas, incompatible at the limit with Western man's innate need to know and master the physical world, and further complicated by historical accidents. That is what gave us, as Mr. Brown observes, "a society whose inward convictions have been at hopeless variance with the outward professions that the events of history have forced it to make." We need only add that the conflict became even more acute with the Renaissance and became one of the hidden causes of the Reformation and Europe's first Civil War.

From the Renaissance to the present, we of the West have had to observe an ever increasing discrepancy between the tenets of our religion and the observed phenomena of the world in which we live, and during the past century the discrepancies became catastrophic.

One can enumerate sixteen intellectual factors that have contributed to the decline of Christianity, but the four most important, all of which took effect during the past hundred years, are:

(1) The recovery by archaeological excavation of much of the history of the Near East.

(2) Perception of the great physiological and anatomical similarity of human beings to extinct sub-human species and to existing anthropoids, the whole forming a neat evolutionary sequence.

(3) Determinations that the earth is at least a billion years older than the Creation posited by Christian doctrine.

(4) Most important of all, perhaps, perception of the size of the universe. It is one thing to call it infinite; it is another to know that there are galaxies so remote that light from them, traveling at more than eleven million miles a minute, has taken eight billion years to reach us.

Christian theologians, to be sure, have offered innumerable explanations of these discrepancies. Some are forthright efforts to meet the issues squarely, of which the best that I have seen is *The Genesis Flood*, by Professor John C. Whitcomb, Jr., of Grace Theological Seminary, and Professor Henry M. Morris, of the Virginia Polytechnical Institute. Some are bizarre efforts to conjure a god from the Planck constant or squeeze him out of the (hypothetical) Lorentz contractions. And some reach the level of the books that Teilhard de Chardin must have written with tongue in cheek. But we are not here concerned with the validity of any of these Christian explanations. The important fact is that they convince no one except Christians. Perhaps they should, but they do not.

That is the *principal* cause of the recession of Christian faith, and you cannot blame the Jews for it. It is most unlikely that the Jews planted every inscribed tablet found by excavators in Asia Minor, and it is quite certain that they did not create quasars or even the great galaxy in Virgo. The blame, if any, must fall entirely on our race—on the philosophical mentality and Faustian will that distinguish us from all other races and that alone made possible the abstruse and complex determinations of fact that undermined our faith. The four intellectual factors that I listed above and eleven of the twelve that I did not have space to enumerate all depend on data that *no* other race had either the capacity or the wish to ascertain—data, furthermore, that all other races either cannot comprehend or regard as insignificant and irrelevant to their racial mentality.

To repudiate the science of the West is simply to blow out our brains figuratively, as our fetish-men, witch-doctors, and other "Liberal intellectuals" would have us do. And if we of the West do it figuratively, we may as well all do it literally, too, and so escape the ultimate misery and degradation in store for us.

I began this cursory discussion by saying that it did not matter whether we were Christians or atheists so long as we faced facts and reasoned objectively about them. As rational men, all that we can do is measure the consequences of the disastrous decline of faith—for it is a disaster even greater than most Christians suppose—and ascertain by what means (if any) we can hope to survive it.

CHAPTER FOUR

THE PREDICTABLE FUTURE

CHRISTENDOM IS NO LONGER Christendom. The faith that Christ was literally the Son of God, which dominated the Western world for fifteen centuries, and effectively united all the men of our race for ten, has become the faith of a minority.

It is vain to wish that this calamity had not happened, and nugatory to try to blame our enemies for it, however cunning and malevolent they may be. For it is our destiny—the destiny that is biologically innate in our race and the only source of our greatness and of the power that enabled us thus far to survive in a world in which we are a small and universally hated minority to think philosophically about the external and physical world, and to seek objective truth, at whatever cost to our vanity or comfort. As Lawrence R. Brown says, in the book that I quoted before, "Whatever has been easier to believe than to discover has never been what created the unique greatness of our society. Not the comforting satisfaction of inward belief, but the potential humiliation of outward fact has been the last standard of truth in the West." And that has been the *principal* cause of the waning of what was once our common faith.

We cannot expect, therefore, within the foreseeable future any increase in the number of believing Christians, who now number about 12% of adult Americans; on the contrary, a gradual decrease is possible and in some circumstances likely, since the majority of them are now in or past middle age.*

* I need not remark that no one should take seriously the little bands of hysterical adolescents who occasionally try to attract attention by emerging

We have no reason to anticipate a drastic and revolutionary change in the scientific evidence—a discovery, for example, that the earth ceased to rotate on its axis for a day or two when the Israelites invaded Canaan, or that stars outside the solar system are optical illusions. Rightly or wrongly, a great many men of intellectual integrity can now discern no evidence of the existence in the universe of a *conscious* power superior to man, and, precisely because they are men of intellectual integrity, they are not going to change their deductions in the absence of radically new evidence that is intellectually cogent to them. And precisely because they are men of our race, who reason from dispassionately ascertained data, they are not going to be swayed by the emotions of orating evangelists, and they will be simply disgusted by attempts to equate "atheism" and "Communism."

No one doubts but that the power of man—which, for all practical purposes, means the power of our race—is small indeed. We and our planet and our whole solar system are infinitesimal motes in a galaxy that is itself an insignificant part of the known universe. No one doubts, furthermore, but that for many phenomena we have no satisfactory explanation. But knowledge can

---

from the communal squalor of their *kibbuzim* and yelling "Jesus!" instead of "Peace in Vietnam!" Although some enterprising operators in the evangelical business advertise such outbreaks as harbingers of a "revival of faith," it is quite clear that the young derelicts, insofar as they are not indulging in mere exhibitionism, are actuated by the hallucinations that normally occur in minds that have been rotted by the drugs now commonly used by children in the public schools, chiefly marijuana, mescaline, lysergic acid diethylamide, and heroin. The febrile excitement of derelicts "hooked on Jesus" is merely a variation of their feeble-minded enthusiasm for every kind of occult posturing and mystery-mongering, including witchcraft, black magic, Satanism, astrology, oneiromancy, necromancy, and innumerable adaptations of various Oriental cults. More disturbing are the reports of colonies of youngsters who, reportedly without the help of hallucinatory drugs, exchange thoughts with a superior race on Jupiter, chat with visiting spooks, or have at the top of their skull a psychic opening through which the Holy Ghost whispers instructions. Like the "hippies," these unfortunates are commonly graduates of the cut-rate diploma-factories that are still called "universities." That is a fact that will be terribly significant to those who are not afraid to think about it.

not be derived from what is not known, and to deify known natural forces is to resort to a mocking evasion, not unlike that of Epicurus. In the 1930's, Leopold Ziegler thought that the Second Law of Thermodynamics was a quite satisfactory "god" and others have applied that term to biological evolution toward more complex organic forms, to the fact of human consciousness, to instincts found in one or more races that seem analogous to a growing plant's heliotropic striving for sunlight, to the theories of indeterminacy or of parity in sub-atomic physics, and a wide variety of other phenomena. But no alert Christian will be deceived. His God is a *conscious* being, a *personal* God, a God who is aware of, and has concern for, the *individual;* He is a God to whom one can pray.

Men prayed to the Sun when they believed that that incandescent globe was a conscious being who could hear them; but nobody ever prayed to the Great Mystery that $dS = \frac{dQ}{T} + \frac{dH}{T}$.

Christians rightly regard the difference between an atheist and a "pantheist" today as the difference between six apples and half-a-dozen. They can derive no comfort from the prudential evasions of some writers.

Christians are demonstrably right when they insist that if we and the other nations of the West were still Christian nations, we should not find ourselves in our present plight. We should have other difficulties, of course; we should, no doubt, continue to quarrel among ourselves, and we should have to face, as now, the open hostility or covert hatred of the rest of the world. But if we Occidentals were still Christian nations, we should have no need to worry about International Bankers, Illuminati, Bolsheviks, Jews, "Liberals," or any other *internal* menace that you may choose to name or imagine. Recognition of that fact, however, will not produce a religious revival. It is a peculiarity of our Indo-European mind that for us truth is not demonstrated by either comfort or self-interest. We *cannot* believe a proposition to be objectively true just because we wish that it were or because our personal safety depends upon it. No exposition of present danger, therefore, can create faith.

Is there *any* hope of a significant increase in the minority that now believes that Christ was the Son of God?

Some Christians anticipate that the trend will be reversed by divine intervention, but there is little agreement about the nature of the expected miracle. Some expect the Second Coming of Christ, which will provide visible evidence of the truth of Christian doctrine and thus start a wave of conversions, while others count on God's application of a psychological force that will change men's minds and force them to believe what now seems unreasonable. Others as positively expect a virtually total loss of faith with miraculous suddenness. Not infrequently one encounters a Christian, usually a lady, who is quite certain that on a day in the very near future she and 499 other persons will soar aloft into the atmosphere, apparently to a level above the cumulus and below the cirrus cloud-formations, and there float in ecstasy while the rest of the earth's population is condignly destroyed in a succession of catastrophes. But the majority of Christians, I am sure, do not count on impending miracles.

One common ground for hope is, at best, uncertain. We Americans, thanks to our folly, will soon undergo a considerable amount of physical suffering: domestic violence, economic collapse, probably some starvation, quite possibly conquest by foreign invaders and resident revolutionists. It is true that, as history shows, such afflictions usually induce a revival of religion, and many Christians expect such an effect here. That is not likely in the future that we can foresee. For one thing, the historical effect requires an unremitting and prolonged suffering—thirty years or more. The Crusade to Save the Soviet in 1939-45 inflicted great suffering on many nations of Europe, especially Germany and Poland, but produced no significant religious revival. Secondly, if there should be such an effect, it probably would not benefit Christianity. The Protestant Churches as a whole have long been disgraced by the pinks and punks of the National Council. The Catholic Church is now committing suicide by repudiating its own doctrines and burlesquing its traditions. In the eyes of non-believers now, the religion has been compromised by the antics of the greater part of the professional clergy, and despite the admirable loyalty of "traditionalist" and "fundamentalist" minorities, it is likely that the coming disasters will—unjustly, but understandably—make Christianity seem a religion that failed. Thus any revival of religiosity will benefit cults that will have the attraction of novelty and a new "revelation," possibly including some doctrine of metempsychosis.

We are left, therefore, with the present situation and very little hope that it will or can be soon altered. So we had better reckon with it, whatever our personal desires or convictions.

The visible consequences of the withering of our religion are enormous, overshadowing, frightening. Christianity was much more than a religion comparable to the religion of Osiris in early Egypt, the worship of the Olympian gods, the Orphic mysteries, or Mithraism. Unlike those cults in their time and place, Christianity for a large part of our history was the whole formal basis of our entire culture, the absolute from which were deduced our moral codes, our laws, and our political systems; it largely informed our art, inspired our literature, animated our music, and sustained our men of science. The void that has been left is so great that few can peer into the dark abyss without vertigo.

There is, however, no rational escape from a question to which there can be *only* two answers. Was Christ the Son of God?

Christians answer Yes. And on that faith they found their lives.

The majority of adults today, including most of the persons who are doing business in the pulpits, answer No. The negative answer cannot be covered with verbiage about "great Teacher," "social vision," "moral earnestness," and the like. There is no escape from logic.

If Christ was not the Son of God and an Incarnate God, then he was, on the record, a lunatic with delusions that he was. And a lunatic's views on morality and justice are simply worthless. From this simple alternative our "modernist" clergy try to escape by claiming that all the passages in which Christ speaks of his own divinity, or miraculous proof of it is given, are forgeries concocted by clumsy interpolators, but if that is true, there is no passage that is exempt from the suspicion of forgery, and we have to conclude, as did Father Loisy in his famous work on *Le mystère chrétien* (1930), that there is *no* authentic record of what Jesus said—and, indeed, no certainty that He is not, like the words attributed to him, merely an invention of the clumsy "interpolators." At the very best, if Christ was not literally the Son of God, his opinions are of infinitely less value than the opinions of learned, earnest, and thoughtful men, such as Aristotle, Cicero, and Marcus Aurelius in antiquity, and in modern times, David Hume, Schopenhauer, and Renan. From that clear alternative there is no escape except in the kind of patter and chatter that stage magicians use to distract the attention of the audience from a trick of prestidigitation.

If Christ was not literally the Son of God, the *entire* morality on which our civilization was *consciously* based for so long seems to collapse, to vanish as an illusion, to be as unfounded as the old notion that the earth was flat. And this apparent dissolution includes all of the ancient Indo-European morality that guided our peoples in the many centuries that preceded our adoption of Christianity.*

* Christianity, of course, introduced very little that was novel in the practical ethics governing human conduct in society, most of which were not only traditional in our race but were common to most civilized societies, including the oldest of which we have adequate knowledge. (Clergymen who impudently talk of "Judaeo-Christian ethics" try to give the impression that the prohibition of theft, adultery, etc. in the Ten Commandments was some kind of dazzling and miraculous invention, but if they were honest they would speak of "Sumerian-Christian ethics" in that connection.) About the only element that can fairly be called a Christian innovation was the great emphasis on forgiveness as a duty rather than an act of unnecessary generosity. (Its doctrine of rewards and punishments after death tended to enforce observance of the whole moral code, but that is another matter.) The historical antecedents, however, will not help us now, for our religion was so long re-

That is obviously what is happening—has happened today, when we witness everywhere tacit and explicit repudiation of all morality—not only Christian teaching, but the antecedent and basic morality without which civilization is flatly impossible. And, what is even more disheartening, there seems to be no basis left for *any* morality.

For a long time, men, except a few romantic and evangelical atheists, have agreed that a viable morality must be based on a religious faith. Hesiod, whom some scholars place in the ninth century B.C., warned the judges of his day that Zeus had 30,000 invisible and immortal observers who go through the whole earth and report the evil deeds of men. A discerning correspondent, whose letter reached me yesterday, remarks that "unfortunately, most people need to feel that they are watched by a superhuman power."

For Aristotle, Plato, and Cicero, civilized society must be based on a generally accepted and uniform religious faith. And, with few exceptions, the thoughtful non-Christians of our world have held the same opinion. Renan, for example, took leave of Christianity with elegiac sadness and deep apprehension: "What is ominous is that we cannot foresee for the future any means of giving men a code of conduct that they will generally accept...I frankly admit that I cannot imagine how it will be possible to restore, without the ancient illusions, the foundations of a noble and serene life."

On a quite different level, the pragmatic and cynical Augustus believed religion the indispensable basis of political stability, and many rulers and statesmen, before him and after him, had the same conviction. And some of the world's most acute minds have drawn the conclusions that Machiavelli, perhaps, stated most bluntly:

Principalities and republics that would save themselves from

---

garded as the one and *only* basis for morality and the *unique* source of all right conduct that the earlier traditions have vanished except insofar as we still instinctively regard certain actions as dishonorable. Even those feelings, however, may be consciously repressed as "relics of superstition" by persons who have reacted strongly against the religion and are proud of having "emancipated" themselves from it.

decadence must above all other things keep uncorrupted the ceremonies of their religion, and hold it always in veneration: for there can be no greater symptom of the ruin of a state than to see divine rites held in contempt....They should therefore use every opportunity to foster and augment their religion, even though they perceive it to be false; and the more prudent they are and the more they know about natural phenomena, the greater their obligation to do this.

It is now too late to heed Machiavelli's warning. The disaster that he apprehended has come upon us.

It is vain to dream of a religion to replace Christianity. Comte's notion of a "Religion of Humanity," whereby congregations would throng temples to venerate Henry Ford, Thomas Edison, and Werner von Braun as "benefactors," was one of the ideas that occurred to him when he was out of a straight-jacket, but it should have suggested to his friends and keepers the need to hustle him into one. True, there have been serious proposals by eminently sane men, who, however, seem to forget that a religion must be based on faith, not speculation or psychological peculiarities. Captain Ludovici is a highly intelligent and earnest man, and when he wrote his *Religion for Infidels* (1961), he must have known that his "rational religion" could appeal only to a few, and had no chance whatsoever of meeting our society's need for a unifying faith.

If the faith of Christendom was an error, alien gods can command no true piety—not even in the little circles where they may enjoy a passing vogue. The Oriental cults that make wealthy dowagers beam and write cheques are not for men. Christianity is irreplaceable.

THE CONSEQUENCES

NO MORE THAN 12% of adult Americans believe that Christ was the Son of God. No more than half of this minority has thus far provided from 80% to 90% of all the support given to "conservative" and "anti-Communist" efforts. So there is another fundamental fact that you must face, if you desire to preserve our country and our civilization.

If most of the men included in that 6% were physically robust and vigorous, disciplined and well trained in the techniques of guerrilla warfare, equipped with the necessary weapons (including, in addition to automatic rifles, machine guns, and land mines, such devices as infra-red projectors), and willing to fight ruthlessly under a unified command, they could recapture the United States.

If the 6%, though not capable of military action, formed a group that would not only contribute money and work to the very limit of their powers and vote as a solid bloque, but would also, at the command of their leaders, endorse and propagate the propaganda line that those leaders judged most expedient at any given time, even though that line was patently mendacious and contrary to all that they as individuals believed, and would furthermore, at command, work politically for candidates whose political patter suggested the very opposite of what they as individuals want, it might be possible for them, by persistent effort over many years, to recapture the country with conspiratorial tactics. Obviously, however, the active Christian minority is incapable of either of the only two kinds of action that could bring success. It is, furthermore, incapable of even sentimental agreement, for it is fragmented by real and important doctrinal differences, and any

39

accord that may be established among Christians can always be quickly disrupted by even the crudest incitation of sectarian emotions. Even now, one of the most influential of the Christian "anti-Communist" preachers varies his message from time to time with clear intimations that the Pope is the Antichrist. The remaining Christians in the Catholic Church, having faith in its traditions, are more sensitive than ever to Protestantism now that they see their church resorting to cheap parodies of Protestant services as part of its effort to commit suicide. "Fundamentalist" Protestants frequently quarrel over the question whether or not certain tribes of Israelites migrated to northern Europe or the British Isles after they were supposedly captured by the Babylonians. And one evangelist with a very well-known name and small following is currently urging that all the Jews residing in the United States be killed "county by county" without delay, and most vehemently denounces all who have so little faith in Scripture that they have doubts about the feasibility of carrying out the proposed purification successfully this year.

Seeking the most inclusive definition, we defined Christians as persons who have an abiding faith that Christ was in fact the Son of God. But each Christian necessarily believes more than that, and the diversity of faith in other tenets reduces the Christian minority to a multiplicity of groups that are incapable of sustained unity of purpose and could not act effectively, even if they had the means of action. Crusades were possible in ages in which Faith in Christ could bring together large and well-equipped armies of veteran warriors ready to smite and slay the paynim and to vindicate their faith with the sword, but today a suggestion that Christians could launch a Crusade is simply ludicrous. If Christians and other Americans really want to survive as Americans rather than as brutalized and stultified fellahin, the despised slaves of an alien and international super-state, they had better think seriously about the 88% of non-Christians of their race in the United States. We are here concerned only with Christians who are willing to make that effort, and we are well aware that many will find it much more entertaining to continue orating to one another, pounding their typewriters, quoting Scripture and wrangling about what it means, and contributing their money to every clever promoter who promises to produce with talk precisely the kind of miracle that would make them happy.

So what of the 88%?

The most logical alternative to Christianity is obviously atheism, by which we mean the belief that, in all probability, there does not exist in the universe a personal god to whom one can address prayers and who has conscious purposes. If the faith that was well nigh universal among members of our race for so many centuries was a fiction and delusion, then it is *a priori* highly improbable that Apollo, Odin, Vishnu, Dionysus, or any other Savior God is less of a myth and fantasy than the Christian God. If the faith that inspired our race for so large a part of its recorded history was merely a figment of overwrought imaginations, it is highly probable that faith in any substitute for Christianity is likewise a product of the same overheated fancy. He who finds Christianity unbelievable should at least equally suspect all other revelations, and conclude that, so far as we can ascertain, there is no god, no conscious power in the universe superior to man. That is only reasonable.

It is odd, therefore, that we hear so little of atheism today. There is, to be sure, a small number of evangelical atheists, who devote themselves to spreading the glad tidings that there is no god. They are best represented by the little periodical, *The Truth Seeker*, that does not enjoy enough support to continue publication in conventionally set type and has had to resort to photo-offset reproduction from copy prepared on a quite ordinary typewriter. It would be a gross exaggeration to estimate the avowed and active atheists at one-half of one percent of our adult population. And one suspects that their number is steadily dwindling.

It is true, nevertheless, that doubt and denial of religion is a long-standing and ancient tendency in our race, and is very closely connected with our peculiar capacity to think objectively about the world in which we live and our experience of it.* I shall not argue that atheism is distinctively Indo-European like Christianity, for I doubt that such an argument could be maintained, nor shall ι advance the more defensible claim that the atheism of Occidental minds differs generically from the manifestations of irreligion in other races, for that would entail a long excursus on China, with particular consideration of the doctrines of Confucius, Mencius, Hsün Tzu, and, most important of all, the Fa Chia;** a second excursus on the *falasifa* who flourished briefly in the world of Islam and included true Semites from southern Arabia; and, at least, a third excursus on the atheism that is so wide-spread among the Jews today. I shall, merely remind you of two items in the history of India, and suggest that you reflect on their significance.

If you search the annals of mankind for a parallel to the strict materialsim and concomitant atheism that is the premise of a very large part of the dominant thought of our time and simply taken for granted by many of our best minds, you will find the closest parallel in the philosophy called Lokāyata, of which traces remain in the next-to-the oldest parts of the Mahābhārata, in the Arthasastra, and in a few other ancient works in Sanskrit. It is quite clear that this virtually scientific materialism flourished while

* It may be pertinent to recall that during the Viking Age many men, including even some kings, confessed that they were atheists (*goδlauss*) and openly derided the Norse theology; many more, no doubt, were content to keep their opinions to themselves.

** I remark in passing that although the Fa Chia, which I mentioned in an earlier note, was a political philosophy confined to an intellectual elite in positions of power, it effectively dominated the practice of Chinese governments from the third century B.C. to the present, except for comparatively brief intermissions. It appears to be totally unknown to the journalists, both "Liberal" and "anti-Communist," who manufacture books about the present régimes in Formosa and on the mainland, ignoring the racial determinants of the Mongolian mind and pretending that the Chinese have a yen for "democracy" and the other abstractions that are effective bait for voters in this country. The best thing to do with such books is to drop them in the wastebasket unopened; that saves time and eyestrain.

the Aryan conquerors of India were in the plenitude of their power, and vanished as completely as though it had never been when the natives of that sub-continent succeeded, by such devices as miscegenation, military imitation, and exploitation of rivalries, in breaking the Aryan power and racial consciousness.

Late in the sixth century B.C. a young Aryan prince named Siddhartha, doubtless influenced by the Lokayata prevalent in intellectual circles, evolved an atheistic pessimism that differed from a strict materialism only in the assumption that an individual's will-to-live (as distinct from his mind and personality) could survive his death. This palingenesis of the will (which must be sharply distinguished from the reincarnation of a soul) strikingly resembled the basis of the modern philosophy of Schopenhauer, and Siddhārtha, yielding to our racial instinct to deduce and formulate universal laws, presented it as true for all men. His doctrine therefore appealed to sentimental Aryans who were concerned for "all mankind" and had an itch to "do good" to the lower races by pretending that those races were their equals. They accordingly preached the philosophy of Siddhārtha and gradually transformed that bleak pessimism into a religion complete with gods, saviors, and innumerable angels and demons, and they called Siddhārtha "the Enlightener of Mankind" (*Buddha*). As an odd mixture of philosophy and religion, Buddhism became the Established Religion of India, consummated the mongrelization of the Aryans and their submergence in the prolific native races, and then, its work of subversion accomplished, it disappeared from India and survived only as a grossly superstitious religion in Tibet, China, Japan, and adjacent Mongolian territories, and, with many doctrinal differences, in Ceylon and Southeast Asia, where it appears to have become as decadent as Christianity among us.*

* When Arnold J. Toynbee visited Burma he was impressed by the "spiritual light" that is particularly radiant in Buddhist friars who assemble in mobs and, when the spirit moves them, start killing people with the clubs, revolvers, and hand-grenades they carry under their sacred yellow robes. This social gospel, however, is a very recent innovation. On the other hand, much that is old survives, as was evident a

If we consult the direct tradition of our civilization, we find from the earliest recorded times to the present eminent men who reject the popular religion of their day and the god or gods of that religion, believing that the world is uncreated and eternal and holding, in keeping with the mentality of our race, that the world operated by natural law, that is to say, the uniform and automatic processes of a nature that is independent of supernatural intervention. What is rare is not thinking that dispenses with gods, but proselytizing atheism. That rarity cannot be entirely explained by fear of persecution, and it must be attributed in part to a reluctance to destroy the religion of the people.

In the seventh century B.C., Thales, who was regarded as the founder of both astronomy and natural philosophy, and is believed to have been the first who could predict eclipses of the sun by mathematical calculation, appears to have identified the gods with what we should call kinetic energy, gravitation, magnetic force, and, perhaps, chemical properties. Such a definition cannot have been either instructive or encouraging to persons intent on praying for mercy or favor from Zeus or one of his divine associates or subordinates, but Thales was not technically an atheist, and he disturbed established beliefs less than did Xenophanes, whose rigorous monotheism required him to ridicule all anthropomorphic gods. Democritus, one of the greatest minds of antiquity, explained all phenomena in terms of atoms governed by uniform natural forces, and he left nothing for gods to do, although he cheerfully conceded, for the benefit of those who felt strongly about the matter, that the same natural forces that produced man could have produced superior races, more perfectly formed of a more tenuous matter and so possibly exempt from some of our ills and limitations. Epicurus argued, perhaps sincerely, on the basis of epistemological considerations, that gods probably existed, but

few years ago when our propaganda machine for political purposes exhibited on television the spectacle of some Buddhists who incinerated themselves. The yokels who gawked at the exhibition did not know that it was merely the observance of an ancient custom, much older than Christianity and even older than Buddhism itself.

must dwell outside our world and must, by their very nature, have no interest in or concern for human beings. It is obviously folly to try to attract the attention of such superior beings, and it is preposterous to think that a god would have cared who won the Trojan War, or that a son of God (Diosnysos, i.e. Dionysus) could have suffered, been slain, and have arisen from the dead to save mankind, but Epicurus was not technically an atheist. Euhemerus blandly devised evidence and argument to show that Zeus had been a King of Crete and that the notion of worshipping gods was merely a development of men's natural tendency to venerate the memory of great men after they are dead. Many an ancient writer explained religion in the terms most generally accepted by modern anthropologists: *primus in orbe deos fecit timor.* Primitive men personified and tried to placate forces of nature that they did not understand. Intelligent readers could draw their own deductions, but ancient writers refrained from preaching atheism as such, and addressed themselves only to very limited and select audiences.

There may have been an intermission of such scepticism during the Roman Decadence and the darkest part of the Dark Ages, but by the Thirteenth Century men knew of the famous book *De tribus impostoribus* that is now lost. (The extant work is a forgery produced in the Eighteenth Century.) The three impostors, of course, were Moses, Christ, and Mahomet, charlatans who imposed on the credulity of their ignorant contemporaries, but so far as we can tell, the author of that doctrine did not specifically deny the existence of a god. From the Thirteenth Century to the present, the chain of such thinking is unbroken, and it is easily recognized under the various forms that it successively assumed. During the Renaissance, for example, a favorite precaution was the doctrine of "two truths," which enabled a philosopher, such as the most illustrious of the Paduans, Petrus Pomponatius, to affirm that by faith he believed to be true precisely those propositions (e.g., the immortality of the soul) that he had just demonstrated to be false in the light of reason and observation. After the Reformation, the modern method appears. For example, Sir Walter

Raleigh's friend, Thomas Hariot, now chiefly remembered for his work on the mathematics of navigation and cartography, simply ignored Christianity (except that he thought it good for the American Indians); his contemporaries suspected him of atheism, but they couldn't prove it. Today, you may pick up any serious treatise on astronomy, geology, biology, or almost any science, and you will find that the author simply ignores religion as irrelevant and does not even take the trouble to mention as curious myths the Christian beliefs that are tacitly refuted by his findings. Authors today have nothing to fear from the rage of Christian divines, but they are content to let intelligent readers draw their own conclusions. A formal profession of atheism would be in bad taste, and, what is more, many of the authors really do not want to destroy what religion is left to our people.

Our whole tradition, therefore, deprecates gratuitous and unnecessary offense to religious beliefs, and one of the strongest reasons for that restraint is, and long has been, a conviction that a belief in gods who punish moral transgressions is the most efficacious, and possibly the unique and indispensable, means of maintaining in a large population the morality without which a civilized society would become impossible. Machiavelli did not originate the doctrine that he expressed with brutal frankness in the passage from his *Discorsi* that we quoted above. The idea is ancient; it appears in Herodotus, the "Father of History," and was probably old in his time. It is not even confined to Aryans. Although he was doubtless influenced by Greek thought, the great Arabian poet, Abu'l-'Alá al-Ma'arrí, gave the idea an epigrammatic expression in verses that may be translated thus:

The Moslem stumble; Christians are astray;
The Jews are mad, and Magians grope their way.
We mortals are composed of two great schools—
Enlightened knaves or else religious fools.

"Enlightened knaves" will flout and circumvent the ethics imposed by religious sanctions, and no society can support more than a small proportion of them. Such, at least, has been the conclusion of careful observers of human society.

An infidel, to be sure, is not necessarily a scoundrel, but even if we claim that a system of ethics can be so logically deduced from objectively ascertained data that it will be cogent to every rational reader, we cannot reasonably expect that the demonstration will sway any very large part of the population. How many persons, for example, would be willing to read the *Nicomachean Ethics* or the *De officiis*, or would understand them, if they did read them? Even if we could construct an intellectually irrefragable code of morality, we should still find religion indispensable, as Aristotle said, "in order to persuade the majority." Or as James Burnham, who is certainly one of the best minds in conservative circles today, expresses it: "The political life of the masses and the cohesion of society demand the acceptance of myths. A scientific attitude toward society does not permit belief in the truth of the myths. But the leaders must profess, indeed foster, belief in the myths, or the fabric of society will crack."

That conclusion always has been widely accepted by men who, naturally, refrain from proclaiming it in public. I knew a gentleman who, although not wealthy in the usual sense of that word, contributed some five thousand dollars a year to his local church. "Of course, I don't believe in immortality and the rest of that bunk," he told me, "but belief in a hereafter is the only thing that will keep most people straight, so I do what I can." That opinion was based, not on reading, but on his own observation of men. Essentially the same opinion is held by some clergymen. I have conversed with one, who is certainly not one of the "social gospel" shysters. He is a very well educated and thoughtful man, who believes religion necessary for social stability, although he regrets that a series of historical accidents made so confused and vulnerable a cult as Christianity the religion of the West instead of the form of Buddhism found in the *Milinda-pañha* (c. 125 B.C.), which, incidentally, he has read in the original Pali. That, of course, is not what he tells his congregation, but he holds that since a belief in the supernatural must be fostered for the comfort of the majority, it is best for society that the doctrine be dispensed by men who can take an honest and coldly rational view of their task and will not be carried away by fanaticism or exhibitionism. That view is not unique, and we should remember, for example, that in this century the staunchest and most eloquent defender of the Christian faith in France was the genial Charles Maurras, who, perhaps indiscreetly, confessed that he personally was an atheist.

One of the most striking proofs of the extent of irreligious support of religion as a social utility is the current rash of books and articles that urge Christians to unite with all other religions in "combating scepticism," because the important thing is to have "*a* faith," chosen from the contemporary flowerbed that provides nosegays to match any complexion or ensemble. That, of course, is the equivalent of saying that it does not matter what you believe, provided that you believe it hard enough. Just as the antithesis of love is not indifference but hate, so the opposite of a true religion is not scepticism but a false religion. So far as there is any honesty in this campaign to "save religion"—so far as it is not a swindle— it must be based on the premise that the beliefs of all Christians, Pharisees, Kabbalists, Theosophists, Moslems, Buddhists, etc., are equally false, but should be encouraged because such superstitions may serve to restrain men's natural propensity to crime. Obviously, the "interfaith" cuddling that is so much in the vogue among professional clergymen these days is possible only for those who have no faith in their own religion, and we can only hope that some of them are thinking in terms of social utility rather than promoting a racket—or a conspiracy.

The incidence of disbelief in a personal god—atheism, although many atheists escape social disapproval by using such euphemisms as agnosticism and pantheism—cannot, therefore, be estimated, even roughly. It is not limited to strict materialism. The structure of the human consciousness is at present so little understood, and so many psychological phenomena (e.g., hypnotism, the effects of hallucinogenic drugs, possible instances of telepathy, certain instincts of civilized men, many of the mental peculiarities of our race) remain unexplained that a belief that we have an immaterial and spiritual component is widely held, often associated with hypotheses concerning a fourth (or, if time is the fourth, a fifth) dimension. This spiritual element, though yet mysterious in the way that the observed effects of radioactivity were mysterious before radium was isolated and identified, is regarded as subject to natural laws yet unascertained, and therefore as involving no presumption that a deity is responsible for those phenomena. Some of our contemporaries, indeed, consider probable a doctrine similar to that of the "godless" Yogins of India (Nirisvara-samkhya) and posit cycles of reincarnation governed by moral laws that are as automatic and impersonal as gravitation. And Captain Ludovici, in his well-known *Religion for Infidels*, believes in the efficacy of prayer even in the absence of a god or other conscious force to hear it.

For many earnest Americans, religion has become a private matter, a system of ethical conduct reposing on metaphysical premises, hopes, or conjectures that they are unwilling to discuss and might have difficulty in defining precisely even to themselves. All that is certain is that there must be the greatest variety in their conceptions of the praeterhuman. It is impossible, therefore, to estimate the persistence in our time of the Stoic conception of a deity that is the Soul of the Universe, which reappeared in the Deism of the late Eighteenth Century, which was professed by some of the founders of the American Republic—just as it is difficult to be certain to what extent that Deism was more than a way of rejecting Christianity without incurring the stigma of atheism. Many of its pronouncements, indeed, such as Voltaire's famous dictum, *si Dieu n'existait pas, il faudrait l'inventer* (particularly when read in context), suggest much more concern for the stability of society than faith in the unnamed god.

One suspects that a numerical majority of our population has simply lost interest in religion as such and does not think about it at all, except as a kind of social convention, regarding the existence or non-existence of a god as something that probably cannot be determined, so that thought about it is impractical and profit-less—a waste of time that can be used more advantageously in thinking about how to get a raise in salary, and more pleasurably in watching a baseball game or a prize fight. The conventions must, of course, be observed; indeed, some corporations when they send an "executive" into a new territory, perhaps as District Sales Manager for Charnel House cosmetics or Bloaters' beer, that he must promptly join a country club, a church, and a local business men's association. I am told that at least one corporate monstrosity has thoughtfully compiled a catalogue of the churches that are best for business in each section of the country, so that its "executives" and their wives (who must be "college graduates without intellectual interests and active in community work") won't have to worry about a choice. "Fundamentalist" churches, I hear, are *streng verboten*: being suspected of taking Christianity seriously would be, like atheism, bad for sales. And that, I fear, is symptomatic of what religion has become for a large section of our people: not a matter of belief or disbelief, not a subject that excites either emotion or thought, but just a social gesture, to be made perfunctorily and with indifference.

All this, I know, is acutely painful for Christians, but it will do them no good to weep or to curse infidels or to hire an evangelist to tell them that they must "fight atheism" by booking him for a return engagement. The facts are but little less distressing to non-Christians who want to preserve what is left of our culture and our race, and who desperately wish that there were some way to restore the faith that was our bond of unity when the West was Christendom. But we were born into the Twentieth Century, not the Eleventh or the Thirteenth, and, unless we prefer to retreat into a dreamworld or passively await our doom, it is with the realities of the present that we must cope, if we can.

CHAPTER SIX

SUCCEDANEOUS RELIGION

LOSS OF CHRISTIAN FAITH as the West's bond of union was a disaster; the spiritual vacuum thus created was a catastrophe.

Since the later part of the Eighteenth Century, we have had among us bands of evangelical atheists, numerically small but at times very influential, who, either openly or under the euphemistic appellation of "anti-clericals," worked to destroy Christianity. Although they were used by political conspiracies with which they sometimes knowingly collaborated, and although they were certainly encouraged and often subsidized by the Jews, who always profit from the misfortunes of the peoples among whom they have planted their colonies, most of the polemists against our religion were quite sincere and many were men of good moral character. Let us, for our own instruction, disregard here the scabrous plotters who appear so often darkly in the background, and let us disregard also the often funeste consequences of the anti-religious agitation. Let us reduce to the simplest terms the principles of every society for the promotion of atheism, whatever it was formally or informally called.

There are just three basic propositions. Let us examine them, remembering that we are trying to reason about a desperate situation in which we find ourselves, whatever our beliefs. If we feel a need to indulge orgiastic emotions, let us do that elsewhere and after we have concluded our serious business.

(1) Christianity is false. This conclusion is drawn from (a) a critical examination of the Christian Scriptures to discern the innumerable internal inconsistencies and contradictions, and to

weigh the innumerable and equally contradictory attempts of theologians to explain them away; (b) comparison of Scriptural accounts, so far as possible, with historical records; (c) examination of Scriptural statements in the light of known natural laws; and (d) consideration of the discrepancies between Biblical statements about the world and the observed nature of that world. Obviously, we cannot here consider the data and arguments adduced by the atheists under each of those four headings, but the important point is that, with no exceptions worth mentioning, this first step is *intellectually* sound. Each writer reports the facts correctly (except insofar as they were supplemented by later discoveries) and reasons from them with strict logic to rigorously drawn conclusions. Christians, to be sure, surmount those conclusions by various acts of faith, and their faith is entitled to every respect, but although it is asking much of them—as it is asking much of any man to ask him to be objective and just to his opponent—I hope that they will be able to admire the intellectual processes by which the conclusions were obtained. They cannot deny the facts without lying; to throw themselves on the floor, kick with their heels, and scream "blasphemy!" is unworthy of adults.

(2) Religion is therefore an imposture on the ignorant perpetrated by priests for their own profit. This conclusion is drawn from (a) the long, long history of fraudulent simulation of supernatural phenomena, from the witch-doctors among the Congoids, who excite the awe of their tribesmen with some of our simpler parlor-tricks, to the elaborate machinery and drugs used in ancient Egypt, Asia Minor, and even Greece to show the ways of god to the suckers; (b) the manufacture of relics and the forgery of decretals and donations in Christianity; (c) the power-politics of the established clergy in many historical periods; and (d) the corruption and scandalous profligacy or dishonesty of many churchmen of exalted rank, including some Popes. Here, however, we have gone a little fast, haven't we? There is no conduct attributed to the clergy, even to its worst members, that is not at least matched by conduct that is common enough among laymen, including rulers

and members of a nobility or aristocracy, and while believers may be distressed that their religion does not transform men, how can atheists think it very significant that ecclesiastics are human beings? And have we not *excluded* some data here? Does not the record show a very large number of well educated and highly intelligent men, both churchmen and laymen, who, if not insane, *must* have held the faith they professed? And can we suppose that religion answers no natural need or desire in men? That it serves no purpose in civilized society? That it would never have existed, if the equivalent of our stage magicians and our confidence men had not imposed on the credulity of our ancestors?

(3) Let us, therefore, destroy religion, that monstrous engine of deception and exploitation—*écrasez l'infâme!*—and men, governing their conduct by clear-sighted reason alone, will enjoy the infinite progress that Science makes possible. This conclusion is based on—what? History provides no example of a people that governed itself by cold reason, and, for that matter, not many examples of leaders and governors who behaved reasonably even in terms of their own personal advantage or the advantage of their family or other small group. It provides no example of a civilized people without a prevalent religion.* If, in our society, religion is a fraud, it is only one of the hundreds of frauds currently playing

* I speak, of course, of nations as a whole. It is true that small and essentially aristocratic groups, delimited by birth and education, such as Victorian gentlemen, found in a code of personal honor an adequate substitute for religion, and there have been times when incredulity was normal among an upper and politically dominant group, but it may be significant that the incredulity was most open and notorious in the periods that immediately preceded a great national catastrophe. Even during those periods, however, the mass of common people remained religious. In Eighteenth Century France, 95% of the population practiced Christianity until the Revolution. In the late Roman Republic, before the great Civil Wars, the Capitoline gods suffered some neglect, but the religiosity of the populace was increasing as shown by the importation and spread of various Oriental cults, and the local deities of the countryside seem to have enjoyed about as much veneration as ever. We shall come to the situation in the United States today below.

on ignorance and emotions, usually with appeal to such constant human incentives as greed and malice. So what is the basis of the atheists' third proposition? Faith. Faith in a statement that is completely unsupported by objective thought—unsupported by data or by logical deductions, and even contrary to the indications of all the relevant evidence that can be found.* It is a faith that can be based on no revelation other than the effervescence of an overheated imagination, and that can have been accepted for no reason other than that it promises a miracle that seems delightful.

What has happened to the evangelical atheists without their being aware of it is clear. When they expelled their faith in Christianity, they created within themselves a vacuum that was quickly filled by another faith. And the fervor with which they hold that faith is of religious intensity. They preach the joyful tidings that there is no God with as much ardor and sincerity as ever a Christian preached his gospel. They sacrificed themselves, and some even underwent martyrdom, for their faith. If we wanted to indulge in paradox, we could describe them as the zealots of an antireligious religion, but it is more accurate to say that their faith in a religion, which was rational in that it expected miracles only from the supernatural power of its invisible deity, was replaced by a

* For example, Robert G. Ingersoll was a very intelligent and well-read man, but readers of his famous orations and of his collected letters (which will guarantee the candor of the speeches) can only marvel at the facility with which his evangelical eloquence disregards the French Revolution, which should have provided him with an unforgettable lesson of what Gibbon termed "the danger of exposing an old superstition to the contempt of the blind and fanatic multitude." Ingersoll must have read, in one of the three historians whom he most highly esteemed, the passage from which I have quoted, and he must have read many reports, written by non-Christians and so acceptable to him, of the orgy of sadism, savagery, and homicidal mania in France, but the lesson was evidently lost on him, perhaps because he had faith in institutions that have now disappeared in all but name from the United States—and yet he had himself fought in the fratricidal madness commonly called the Civil War, and he had himself witnessed the sadistic reprisals carried out by hate-crazed fanatics on the civilized inhabitants of the conquered and helpless Confederacy!

superstition that expects miracles from natural causes that have
never produced such effects—a superstition that is totally irrational.

Societies for the promotion of atheism as such are relatively
innocuous and merely exhibit on a small scale a psychological
phenomenon that has catastrophic effects when it occurs on a
large scale, much as sand spouts and dust devils are miniature
tornadoes. When religious faith is replaced by materialistic superstition on a large scale, the consequences are enormous dev-
astation.

The great wave of anti-Christian evangelism swept over
Europe about the middle of the Eighteenth Century, and its
natural results were most conspicuous in France, where decades
of strenuous social reform imposed by a centralized government under a king whose mediocre mind had been thoroughly
addled by "Liberal" notions, naturally triggered the outbreak of
insanity and savagery known as the French Revolution. Since
the shamans and fetish-men of the new superstition control
our schools and universities today, the history of that event is
little known to the average American, who is likely to have derived his impressions, at best, from Carlyle's novel, *The French
Revolution,* and, at worst, from the epopts and fakirs of Democracy. Obviously, we cannot here insert an excursus of a
thousand pages or so on what happened in France at that time,
nor need we. The efforts at social uplift through economic and
political reforms during the reign of Louis XVI are well summarized by Alexis de Tocqueville in *The Old Régime and the
French Revolution.** The best short account in English of the
underlying forces of the disaster is the late Nesta Webster's *The
French Revolution,* supplemented by the two volumes of her bi-

* The reader should remember that de Tocqueville wrote at a time
(1856) when the recrudescence of religion that followed the French
Revolution permitted him the illusion that Christianity had been
"definitely reëstablished" and that the climate of his time was "highly
favorable to Christianity."

ography of Marie Antoinette and Louis XVI and by the pertinent chapters of her *World Revolution.**

We need not here concern ourselves with the sinister and mephitic conspiracies that clandestinely incited and contrived so much of the disaster, for our interest is not in the manipulators but in the men of our race who were manipulated. Our problem is not what was done to them, but why they let it be done. Adam Weishaupt, the founder and titular head of the homicidal conspiracy of the Illuminati,** was undoubtedly a cunning creature, who was able to enlist some of the kings and princes of Europe in a conspiracy to abolish monarchy, to enlist Christian clergymen in a conspiracy to destroy Christianity, and to enlist tender-hearted sentimentalists in a conspiracy to murder thousands of cultivated men and women, but however subtle his methods of deceit, his success argues some fundamental weakness, mental or moral, in his victims.

* Mrs. Webster wrote as a Christian and so, although she was a woman of great learning and penetrating mind, her interpretations of the facts that she correctly reports are colored by (a) failure sufficiently to allow for the fact that while the publication of the great French Encyclopaedia was undoubtedly subversive of both church and state, it was nevertheless an accurate report of the science, technology, and historical knowledge of the time, so that if we deplore the publication of encyclopaedias, we must logically demand that accumulated knowledge be made accessible only to a restricted and small élite; and (b) the Christian conception of a universal connection between God and Satan, whence it follows that whatever is anti-Christian is morally evil and wicked. Many of the early colonists in North America, especially the English, accordingly thought that the Indians must have been incited by the Devil not to surrender their hunting grounds to the Christians, and today many think that the Jews are Satanic and wicked because they act in conformity with the interests, instincts, and beliefs of their race. Non-Christian readers should make allowance for this tendency without illogically rejecting Mrs. Webster's report of the facts.

** We must, of course, be careful to avoid exalting Weishaupt to the rank of Satan by making him and his scabrous crew responsible for the whole of the catastrophe to which they (and many others) undoubtedly contributed. In my *Conspiracy or Degeneracy?*, note 19, I commented sufficiently on the notion, popular in some circles, that the Illuminati were and now are an incredibly powerful gang of mysterious Master Minds

No historical period is more instructive than the half-century in France during which the yet numerous members of the hereditary aristocracy and the more numerous *nouveaus-riches* with their purchased titles worked so assiduously to produce the catacylsm in which they perished. They spoke proudly of their time as the Enlightenment, the Siècle des Lumières, the Age of Reason. Most of them saw the light at last when they faced a new humanitarian machine for amputating their heads; and many did not live until 10 November 1793, when they could have seen Reason finally enthroned and incarnate in the person of a nude whore seated on the high altar of Notre Dame. The results proved that, taken as a whole, the French aristocracy, which included much of the best (and some of the worst) blood in the nation, was the most spectacular collection of boobs seen anywhere before Twentieth-Century America.

The Eighteenth Century saw great and solid achievement in all the basic sciences, in industrial technology, and in historical scholarship. It is indubitable that almost all of those brilliant achievements in science and scholarship directly or indirectly impugned the tenets of Christianity. Although comparatively few men had a thorough understanding of those discoveries, a superficial knowledge of their implications was communicated, usually by witty popularizers, to the entire educated class. That sufficed to destroy their religious faith, which was accordingly replaced by the

who have conspired and labored for hundreds or thousands of years, and have caused all the woes of the world for some purpose of their own. The underlying premise, sometimes explicit but often left latent these days, is that the terrible but unidentified Illuminati are engaged in a Conspiracy Against Christianity, presumably with the active coöperation of the Devil. If those diabolic conspirators had not done their dirty work, there would now be no nasty skeptics and awful atheists, and everyone in the whole world—well, everyone in the United States, at least, would believe every word in the Bible and conduct himself accordingly. Now, as I have indicated above, if you accept that idea, you must accept its necessary corollary, that most of the physical world about us is an illusion that we mistake for reality—an illusion somehow contrived by the Illuminati or their immortal Superintendent. And if you believe that, the best thing to do is to retire, as did the well-known group of Byzantine monks, and contemplate your navel (assuming that it is not also an illusion).

weird superstitions of the self-styled *philosophes*. That gabbling crew could no longer believe in God, but they could believe in World Peace, which was to be magically produced by either the Abbé de Saint-Pierre's project for a "United Nations" or by tobacco, which, if smoked by everyone, would infallibly so soothe men's nerves that they would no longer lose their tempers and want to fight. They could not believe in Christ, but they could believe that an oleaginous Jew who impudently called himself the Comte de Saint-Germain had witnessed the Crucifixion and had remained in good health ever since by abstaining from all food and extracting his nourishment directly from the air—and they thought it the most natural thing in the world that such a long-lived genius should be installed in the royal palace as a personal adviser to the king. They could not believe in the immortality of the soul, but they could believe that a sleazy Jew named Balsamo, alias Mr. Bacthymore, alias Comte Pellegrini, alias Comte de Cagliostro, etc., could conjure up the dead, foresee each person's future, make diamonds grow bigger, and distill an elixir that would rejuvenate old men and convert young men into infants.*

If there is any one individual who can be regarded as a perfect representative and, as it were, archetypal symbol of the Enlightenment, it is the famous Marquise d'Urfé. She was a high-born, wealthy, and intelligent woman who evidently had a serious interest in chemistry and is credited with the invention of a self-regulating laboratory furnace for use in her experiments. She also believed that it would be much nicer to be a young man than an old woman, and accordingly she took steps to have herself transformed. She took one important step on the advice of Querilin-

---

* In this connection, we should perhaps mention the Cardinal de Rohan, a model ecclesiastic who was so intellectual that he discovered how profitable it was to collaborate with the Cerf-Beers and other Jewish banking houses. He knew, of course, that Christianity was a "silly superstition," but after he saw the "Comte de Cagliostro" manufacture a potful of gold out of dross, he logically concluded that the conjurer was Divine and perhaps an incarnation of God, and must therefore have the power to help the Cardinal seduce Marie Antoinette and cuckold the King.

thos, a Genius then residing in the Milky Way, and at the exactly calculated astrological moment she, after a solemn prayer to Selenis, the Spirit of the Moon, cast into the Mediterranean a casket which she had filled with fifty pounds of gold, silver, mercury, and other metals, and diamonds, rubies, emeralds, sapphires, chrysolites, topazes, and opals. (Casanova, of course, had thoughtfully substituted fifty pounds of lead before the lady cast into the waves her offering to the Seven Planets.) This devotion so moved Selenis that she sent from the Moon an immortal Undine (one of Casanova's mistresses in green tights) to give the Marquise a ceremonial bath. The Marquise d'Urfé, I need not say, was a true intellectual, who had emancipated herself from vulgar prejudices.

It is not astonishing that a society of such intellectuals took seriously a crack-brained vagabond who was given to sniveling ecstatically as he meditated on the Virtue that filled his Pure Heart, and to denouncing the corruption of the Christian Churches that maintained the orphan asylums at which his bastards were surreptitiously abandoned. Rousseau, unfortunately for us, had the ability to write an emotional prose that gave spice to his balderdash, and he seems on occasion to have been capable of a forced lucidity (as in his *Considérations sur le gouvernement de Pologne*), but he himself summed up his whole career when, in a moment of candor, he told Boswell, "I live in a world of fantasies, and I cannot tolerate the world as it is."*

We should not damn Rousseau for his influence. The real gravamen of guilt falls on the educated, sceptical, intellectual society that did not laugh at his fantasies about the innate Virtue of hearts uncorrupted by civilization, the Noble Savage, the Equality of all human beings, who can become unequal only through the wickedness of civilized society, the sinfulness of owning property of

* Not by any means his only confession; cf. his letter to Malesherbes, 4 January 1762: "Je trouve mieux mon compte avec les êtres chimériques que je rassemble autour de moi qu'avec ceux que je vois dans le monde." One could collect at least a dozen more or less candid admissions that he could not bear to think about the real world.

any kind, and the rest of the tommyrot that you will find in the thousands of printed pages of Rousseau's whining and ranting. You can read all of it—if you grit your teeth and resolve to go through with it—and you really should, for otherwise you will not believe that books so widely read and rhapsodically admired can be so supremely silly and so excruciatingly tedious.

What Rousseau's fantasies produced is an amazing superstition. It is not exactly an atheism, for a vague god was needed to create perfectly noble savages to be corrupted by civilization, and to inspire perfectly pure hearts, like Rousseau's, that overflow with Virtue and drip tears wherever they go; but for all practical purposes, Rousseau's creed substituted "democracy" for God, and put civilized society in place of the Devil. It replaced faith in the unseen and empirically unverifiable with faith in the visibly and demonstrably false.

We cannot afford to smile at poor Mme. d'Urfé. Her instructions came from Querilinthos, but that great Spirit had been conveyed to the Milky Way by seven salamanders, so naturally she could not expect him to come in person for her to see. You may think that if the noble lady had been really shrewd at the time that the immortal and voiceless Undine was giving her a lustral scrub, she would have jabbed that Moon-maid with a pin, but, after all, a woman who has just thrown a fortune in gold and jewels into the sea is apt to be a little excited, and something must be allowed for the impatience of an old woman eager to become a young man. No such apology can be made for the mighty minds that were stunned by Rousseau's drivel. They could have tested the proposition about natural Equality by just walking down the street with their eyes open, looking inside the nearest prison, or paying a little attention to the conduct of any one of the score of really noteworthy degenerates of very high rank.*

They must have met every day military men and others who

* Including, by the way, the great Apostle of Democracy to whom we owe both the word *Sadism* and the nonsensical dictum that 'All men are created equal' ("La Nature nous a fait naître tous égaux"). This favorite dic-

had observed savages in their native habitat and could comment on the innate nobility of the dear creatures. And some conversation with a few footpads and cutpurses would have elucidated the problem whether or not Society was responsible for their having been born without a conscience, wings, and other desirable appurtenances. In fact, no rational person could have escaped a daily demonstration that Rousseau's babble was utter nonsense—except, perhaps, by confining himself in a windowless and soundproof room. But the *philosophes* were able to attain in their own capacious minds a far more total isolation from reality.

How was this possible? There are two obvious factors.

Of the first of these, let us take one of the innumerable examples that have no political or religious implications.

Many of the novels of Dickens were published serially in periodicals, and naturally each installment was published in England before it appeared in the United States. In 1840, ships arriving from Britain found awaiting them on the dock little knots of well-dressed men and women who, as soon as the vessel came within hailing distance, inquired with tearful anxiety, "Is Little Nell dead?" Now those who asked that question with bated breath were literate and presumably educated persons of what is called the leisure class. They were neither drunk nor insane, so they must have

---

tum of the Marquis de Sade is elaborated early in the first volume of his *Justine*, where he expounds the doctrine, now tacitly or explicitly espoused by our "Liberals," that the most revolting crimes are always justified as a form of social protest and receive the special approbation of Providence, since it is only through every form of criminal action that we can restore the blessed state of perfect equality intended by our Creator ("l'état où elle [la Providence] nous a créés est l'Égalité"). De Sade was twice condemned to death for revolting crimes of which it had been possible to convict him in the courts, but under the decadent government of Louis XVI, as in the United States today, political influences were always available to save the utterly depraved from execution, and De Sade was held in a comfortable prison until he was released by the French Revolution. He became one of the most fervent orators for Social Justice and Brotherhood, and continued to exercise his phenomenal ingenuity in torturing and mutilating the men and women whom he kidnapped for his private amusement, throughout the Revolution. The degenerate creature was clapped into an insane asylum as soon as Napoleon came to power.

known that Little Nell was a purely fictitious product of Dickens' imagination and that she appeared in a tale set quite some time before the present. If they had any acquaintance with human life, they must further have known that the fictitious Little Nell was a paragon that resembled no child ever born of woman. A minimal amount of reflection would have assured them that Dickens was contriving with conscious art a tear-jerking story of which the peripeties and denouement would be determined by his judgement of what would most excite the sentimentality of his readers within the limits of length that he thought most advantageous for his magazine.

The inquirers were not idiots; they knew all that. But the imaginations that Dickens had stimulated were so vivid and powerful, and were reenforced by sentiments of generosity and pity so strong, that the rational mind was, so to speak, put on a chain, like an inconvenient watchdog, and a part of the consciousness luxuriated in the illusion that Little Nell was a real being and in anxiety over her fate.

The hypostatization of Little Nell was merely an extension or, rather, perversion of a psychological process common to our race and that we all experience whenever we read a work of imaginative literature, in prose or verse. When we take up a work of poetry or prose fiction, we begin with what literary critics commonly call the poetic suspension of doubt. We resolve that during our reading we will believe that whatever the author tells us actually happened, and that we will vicariously be present when it happens and will experience the emotions that we would experience if we were physically present. That is the literary experience of great literature—and, indeed, our experience when we read any fiction that is sufficiently well written to keep us from throwing the book in the fireplace. When we read tales of the marvelous and praeternatural, we make a temporary act of faith and accept the world that the author has created. Only the poor in spirit will refuse to believe in hippogriffs when they read the *Orlando furioso* or doubt Prospero's power when they read *The Tempest*. We make what is essentially the same act of faith when we read fiction written in more realistic terms. It is a faith of strictly limited duration, and, unless our minds have slipped a cog or two, when we put down Hardy's greatest novel we no more suppose that we have read the biography of a man named Jude the Obscure than we expect to find hippogriffs mingling with the traffic on the street outside after we have read Ariosto.

Literature provides us with emotional and spiritual experience of which we have a racial need, for we Indo-Europeans inherit genetically vivid imaginations that are apt to get out of control if we try to repress or ignore them instead of exercising them rationally and thus satisfying our inner yearning for worlds brighter, more beautiful, and more dramatic than the one in which we live. Our first great literature was the poems of Homer, both the *Iliad*, with its eternal figuration of the unalterably tragic fate that only we men of the West are strong enough to meet knowingly, and the *Odyssey*, with its magic casements opening on the foam of perilous seas. And that literature we shall need so long as we endure as a race. The power of our imagination, while not, perhaps, unique, as is the capacity for philosophic reasoning that enables us to know and partly master the physical world, is a part of our racial being, and we can deny it only at our own peril.

The danger comes, of course, when imagined scenes are so vivid that we ignorantly mistake them for reality. That is what makes "historical" and "thesis" novels as dangerous as nitroglycerine and to be handled with the same caution. Many a person who has not read in the historical sources has been left with the impression that Dickens' *Tale of Two Cities* describes the French Revolution. Many readers of Cooper's *Last of the Mohicans* have thought that they had learned something about Indian tribes that had actually lived in North America. And, incredible as it seems, the sentimental drivel exuded by the infected imagination of Harriet Beecher Stowe so inflamed weak minds that it became one of the causes of national insanity and a fratricidal war that permanently impoverished our nation and may yet prove to have been suicidal.

On a vulgar and prosaic level, we see constantly cases of imaginative intoxication that match anything produced by alcohol. The good ladies of the local church's sewing circle read the prose of some missionary or journalist, and lo! each sees in her imagination sweet little black boys and girls just like her Johnny and her Mary, only a little nicer, and her heart yearns to equip them with trousers and dresses and a copy of the New Testament, and to supply them with ice-cream cones. And so she plies her needle for their sake and puts her mite in the collection box, blissfully unaware that the darling objects of her concern are no more real than Lewis Carroll's Sylvie and Bruno. It is also a commonplace phenomenon that whenever some particularly vicious young brute has rearranged his wife's anatomy with an axe, a certain number of females will generate pictures of a dear misunderstood boy and write him offers of marriage, and a much larger number of females, seeing the same vision but less impulsive in their behavior, will hope that, at the very worst, the parole board will turn the lad loose in a year or two so that he can resume his amateur surgery. The phenomenon is not by any means confined to the more lachrymose sex, and we see instances of it every day. We enact laws to discourage people who see pink elephants on the wall from driving automobiles, but we do nothing about the far graver problem of preventing people who see World Peace around the corner from voting.

Our hyperactive imaginations usually act in concert with the generous impulses that are peculiar to our race—so peculiar that no other race can understand them except as a kind of fatuity from which they, thank God! are exempt. Long before we began to indulge in international idiocy on a governmental scale, it was virtually routine for Americans to hear that the Chinese in some province were starving, and within a few weeks numerous individuals, many of them comparatively poor, made private contributions, and food was bought and shipped to the starving (if the collections were honestly made). Now I do not deprecate that exercise of charity, which is a virtue that we instinctively admire, but we should understand that although the Chinese gladly ate the food and politely said "thank you," they privately concluded that we must be weak in the head. They would never have done anything of that sort, not even for men of their own race in a neighboring province. The White Devils, they decided, must have maggots in their minds. Sympathetic generosity, however, is a virtue or vice of our race, and we shall have to live with it.

What happened in the Eighteenth Century was that Rousseau's fantasies so excited imaginations and generous impulses that the reasoning mind lost control. The nobility's collective heart bled for Little Nell.

There is, however, a second factor more important for our purposes here. You will find a clear illustration in our recent history, during the presidency of Woodrow Wilson, who appears to have been a not uncommon combination of mental auto-intoxication with corrupt ambition, and who was appointed President after the resident General Manager, Barney Baruch, and his crew had (as one of them boasted to Colonel Dall) led him around "like a poodle on a string," taught him to sit up and bark for bonbons, and made sure that he was well trained. As we all know, Baruch eventually decided that it would be good for the Jewish people to prolong the war in Europe, so that more Indo-Europeans would be killed and more of their countries devastated, and that the time had come to repay Germany and Austria for their generosity toward the Jews, who had been given in those countries more of economic, social, and political dominance than in any other European nation. It followed therefore that the thing to do was to stampede an American herd into European territory.

Our concern here is with the herd: what set it in motion? We all know how credulous individuals, many of whom had visited Germany and knew better, were impelled to imagine pictures of the evil War Lord, Kaiser Wilhelm II, and the terrible Huns-pictures that were as vivid and convincing as the vision of the monster Grendel that we see every time we read *Beowulf.* And, of course, there was much rant about supposed violations of a code of chivalry that no one even remembered a few years later. A college professor with some reputation as an historian was hired, doubtless for a small fee, to prove that wars are caused by monarchies, although he somehow forgot to mention the terribly bloody war that had taken place on our soil some fifty years before and which had obviously been caused by the dynastic ambitions of King Lincoln and King Davis. And, naturally, the press was filled with many other ravings. So pretty soon the Americans found themselves engaged in a "war to end wars" and a "war to make the world safe for democracy." It would probably have been a little more expensive—good propaganda costs money—to make them fight a "war to end selfishness" and a "war to make the world safe for goblins," but it doubtless could have been done. Green snakes are not much harder to see on the wall than pink elephants.

We must not tarry to discuss either the methods of the conspirators who so easily manipulated the American people or the folly of those who were manipulated. Let us consider our enthusiastic rush on Europe as an historical movement.

If, taking the larger view, you ask yourself what that movement most resembled, you will see the answer at once. It was a crusade—or, to be more exact, an obscene parody of a crusade. It was a mass movement inspired by a fervor of religious intensity.

The Crusades, which mark the high tide of Christianity, were (given our faith) entirely rational undertakings.* It was obviously desirable that Christendom own the territory that was a Holy Land, where its God had appeared on earth and whither many pilgrims journeyed for the welfare of their souls. The Crusades were, furthermore, the first real effort of European unity since the fall of the Roman Empire, and they were also a realistic missionary effort. It was impossible to convert Orientals to Christianity, but it was possible to make Orientals submit to Christian rulers. The Crusaders established the Kingdoms of Cyprus and Jerusalem and

* Except, of course, the so-called Children's Crusade, which is significant only as evidence that even at that early date some members of our race had a pathological propensity to have hallucinatory imaginations.

the Principalities of Edessa, Tripoli, and Antioch—and eventually they found it necessary to capture Constantinople. But they could not take Bagdad and their high emprise ultimately failed for reasons which need not concern us here. The Crusades were, as we have said, the high tide of Christianity.

Wilson's fake crusade against Europe evoked from the American people the energies and spirit that the real Crusades had aroused in Europe, and while we must deplore their delusions, we must admire the unanimity and devotion with which the Americans attacked and fought the Europeans.* The crusade was irrational, however, because it was prompted, not by religion, but by the debased and debasing superstitions represented by Rousseau.

From about the middle of the Eighteenth Century to the present we have witnessed the spread and propagation throughout the West of a superstition that is as un-Christian as it is irrational, as obviously contrary to the Scriptures and tradition of Christianity as it is a blanket denial of the reality that all men see and experience every day—a superstition by which faith in an unseen God is replaced by hallucinations about the world in which we live. After that grotesque superstition inspired the most civilized and intelligent part of France to commit suicide, and loosed the frenzied orgy of depravity, crime, and murder called the French Revolution, its influence was contracted by a resurgence of both Christian faith and human reason, but recovering its malefic power over the imagination and sentimentality of our people, it grew again and as a succedaneous religion it gradually supplanted Christianity in the consciousness of both unintelligent non-Christians and infidel Christians, paralyzing both reason and faith.

This grotesque caricature of religion is now the dominant cult in the United States: its marabouts yell from almost all the pulpits; its fetish-men brandish their obscene idols before all the children in the schools; its witch-doctors prance triumphantly through all

* Of course, we did not actually fight Great Britain, France, and Russia, our ostensible allies; they were defeated in other ways.

the colleges and universities. And virtually everyone stands in fearful awe of the fanatical practitioners of mumbo-jumbo. Both the God of Christendom and the reasoning mind of our race have been virtually obliterated by the peculiar system of voodoo called "Liberalism."

It is obvious that this mass delusion is leading, and can lead, to but one end. James Burnham named it correctly in his generally excellent book, *Suicide of the West*.

It can be argued—and argued very plausibly—that a race that could long accept the "Liberal" voodoo-cult a sa substitute for both its religion and its powers of observation and reason—a race capable of such mindless orgies as a "war to end wars"—a race that has for decades worked to commit suicide—is a race that has become too imbecile to be biologically viable. It is entirely possible that our unique capacity for science and technology will, after all, be no more effective in the struggle for life than was the vast bulk and musculature of the dinosaurs. It may be that any attempt to reason with a people seemingly in the grip of suicidal mania is itself the greatest folly, and that the vainest of all illusions is the hope that anything can save men who evidently no longer want to live.

If we permit ourselves as Christians any hope this side of Heaven, and if we permit ourselves as atheists any hope at all, we must base that expectation on the hypothesis that the collapse of Christendom, the loss of faith in the religion of the West, was a traumatic shock to our racial psyche that stunned but did not kill. If that is so, then there is hope not only that we may retrive from the shock and survive, but also that the unique powers of our unique race may again be exerted to give us a future that will be brilliant, glorious, and triumphant beyond all imagining. If that is so....

The question is one that only the future can answer. But a significant indication will be given by the attitude and action of the Christian minority that has thus far been the only defender of our race, the only champion of our embezzled heritage. Will they be willing to face, as did their ancestors in the great Crusade, the fact that wars are won only by mobilizing and directing superior *force* against the enemy; that pious sermons, Scriptural citations, and benevolent intentions never turned a single spear or blunted a single blade; and that if Christians had put their trust in miracles, they would long since have disappeared from the face of the earth? Christendom survived at Châlons, and at Tours, and at Vienna, and in many another crisis, not by book, bell, and candle, but by grace of the shining sword in a mailed fist directed by a dauntless heart.

POSTSCRIPT, 1978

The foregoing pages were written in the spring of 1969, and there is nothing that I would change in them now, except to substitute past tenses in references to persons now dead and to the periodical, Découvertes, which necessarily ceased publication when the United States financed the overthrow of responsible government in Portugal.

The developments of the past nine years that are directly relevant to the subject of this booklet fall into three categones, videlicet:

1. The occult hocus-pocus mentioned in the footnote on p. 27, which was then in its incipient stages, has become a national epidemic, propagated by lavish and intensive promotion of every imaginable kind of grotesque superstition and pseudo-scientific hoax, from witchcraft and "higher consciousness" to astrology and "pyramid power." Opportunity always brings forth swarms of fakirs to batten on ignorance and credulity, but the strident publicity and endorsement gratuitously given them by the alien-owned media of communication is proof of a conscious and concerted campaign to destroy with orgiastic irrationality what is left of our sanity.

2. Small enclaves of Christians, attached to time-honored traditions or having the biological vitality to desire the survival of their race, are still found here and there, but it is now clear that the organized churches are finished. As anyone could have predicted decades ago, when the leading holy men began slyly to substitute 'Judaeo-Christian' for 'Christian,' the religion that was once accepted by Western civilization is everywhere being progressively and rapidly reduced to the primitive "Christianity" of the Naz-

arenes and Ebionites. Unthinking Christians like to imagine that there is a "great revival of Faith" when they read about the mass "conversions" claimed by Billy Graham and the many other big-time salvation hucksters who call sinners to come to Jesus and the Jews. Christians who understand their own religion know that what the howling dervishes are peddling to the suckers is a particularly insidious and irrational form of occultism.

3. The succedaneous religion I described in Chapter VI is beginning to break up, perhaps more rapidly than I dared hope. The odd cults that call themselves "humanitarian" and "liberal" still dominate the nations of the West, and, thanks to their adroit use of the schools to implant their dogmas in susceptible and immature minds, they number their faithful and unthinking votaries by the millions. But, as always happens when men of our race find that the discrepancy between pleasing fancies and observed reality has become intolerably great, tacit doubts are being replaced by open disbelief. And the waning of the One-World faith is only advertised by the anguished howls of the shamans and boobherds, who are ever more openly demanding an Inquisition to suppress ruthlessly the infidels who dare to reject such sacred dogmas as the absolute equality of all races (except the infinitely superior Jews.)

In the past few years there has been a steady increase in the number of learned and rational men who dare publicly to deny some humanitarian fairy tale or expose one or another "liberal" hoax. Their number is yet small, but they are the most important—and the most encouraging—development of our time. And what makes it particularly encouraging is that it is the work of minds that have not been swayed by the emotional exhortations of patriotic propaganda, but have instead operated with the powers of objective observation and dispassionate reason that are peculiar to our race. (Cf. p. 27 above.)

We may also record with satisfaction another development of some significance. The comparatively small number of persons who have for so long supported a few genuine and many fraudulent patriotic organizations increasingly view with impatience or disgust the self-appointed messiahs who have for so long bilked them with "conservative" and "anti-Communist" versions of the humanitarian myths. The market for patriotic snake oil, guaranteed to "save the country" decorously and without unpleasantness, is rapidly contracting. And it is a remarkable fact that many men and women who once lavished time and money on nugatory or expertly misdirected agitations are not now much interested in determining whether the Pied Piper whom they then followed is in business for himself or the employee of secret principals: that no longer seems important. They have learned from investigation and reflection, or have been taught by personal experience, that there is only one really crucial issue: race. All else is secondary, tertiary—mere epiphenomena.

Twelve years ago I asked publicly a question that is still unanswered: Have we, the men of the West, lost the will to live? In other words, is our race biologically degenerate? Or, alternatively, is it conceivable that we, despite the unique intellectual power manifest in our science and technology, are innately too stupid to survive under the somewhat novel conditions that we ourselves fecklessly created?

The answer to that question cannot be deferred much longer. It will be decisive and irreversible.

About the author....

Dr. Revilo Pendleton Oliver, Professor of the Classics at the University of Illinois for 32 years, is a scholar of international distinction who has written articles in four languages for the most prestigious academic publications in the United States and Europe. His first book was a copiously annotated translation from the Sanskrit (Mrcchakaika, the Little Clay Cart, Urbana, 1938).

During World War II, Dr. Oliver was Director of Research in a highly secret agency of the War Department, and was cited for outstanding service to his country.

One of the very few academicians who has been outspoken in his opposition to the progressive defacement of our civilization, Dr. Oliver has long insisted that the fate of his countrymen hangs on their willingness to subordinate their doctrinal differences to the tough but idealistic solidarity which is the prerequisite of a Majority resurgence.

Christianity and the Survival of the West is the latest of several books authored by Dr. Oliver to elucidate the deliberately obscured causes of Western decline.

HISTORY and BIOLOGY

Revilo P. Oliver

HISTORY AND BIOLOGY

History is the record of what men do. Scientific discoveries and technological applications of them are often events of historical importance, but do not affect our understanding of the historical process since they shed no light on the behavior of men in civilized societies.

For example, the recent use of atomic fission to produce a more powerful explosive has no significance for a philosophy of history. Like the many changes in the technology of war that have occurred throughout history, this one will call for changes in tactics and strategy, alters to some extent the balance of power in the world, and may well occasion the fall and extinction of a world power so fat-headed that it does not understand the importance of technological superiority in warfare. But all this is merely history repeating itself. It is true that the improved weapon set bands of addle-pated neurotics throughout the country to shrieking as wildly as a tribe of banshees out on a week-end spree; but that is merely another instance of the rather puzzling phenomenon of mass hysteria. It is also true that Communist agents have been scurrying about the country to brandish the phrase "nuclear holocaust" as kind of up-to-date Jack-o'-Lantern to scare children. But while it is the historian's task to understand the International Conspiracy in the light of such partial precedents as are available, the new weapon will not help him in that. He will merely marvel that a large part of our population is not only ignorant of history

History and Biology was written by Dr. Oliver for, and published in, *American Opinion* for December 1963.

in general, but evidently had not read even the Old Testament, from which it would have learned that atomic bombs, as instruments of extermination, are much less efficient than a tribe of Israelites armed with the simplest weapons (See *Joshua* vi. 20 *et passim*).

As an exception to the general rule, however, our century has brought *one* new area of knowledge in the natural sciences that must profoundly affect our understanding of history both past and present—that is as relevant to the rise and fall of the Mitanni and the Hittites as it is to our future. Distressingly enough, the new science of genetics raises for the historian many more questions than it answers, but it discloses the existence of a force that must be taken into account in any philosophy of history.

Multiplex Man

Civilized human beings have long been puzzled by the mysterious diversity of human beings. It is possible, indeed, that perception 0f, and thought about, mystery was part of the process by which some people were able to rise from barbarism to civilization. The perception requires mental powers that are by no means universal. The aborigines of Australia, for example, who are probably the lowest form of human life still extant, have a consciousness so dim and rudimentary that they multiplied on that continent for fifty thousand years without ever suspecting that sexual intercourse had anything to do with reproduction. Most savages, to be sure, are somewhat above that level, but no tribe appears to have been aware of its own diversity, let alone capable of thinking about it.

Human beings capable of reflective thought, however, must have begun early to marvel, as we still do, at the great differences obvious among the offspring of one man by one woman. Of two brothers, one may be tall and the other short; one stolid and the other alert; one seemingly born with a talent for mathematics and the other with a love of music.

Many were the theories that men excogitated to explain so

strange a phenomenon. One of the principal grounds for the once widespread and persistent belief in astrology was the possibility of explaining the differences between two brothers by noting that, although engendered by the same parents, they were conceived and born under different configurations of the planets. In the Seventeenth Century, indeed, Campanella, whose plan for a Welfare State is the source of many of our modern "Liberal" crotchets and crazes, devised a whole system of eugenics to be enforced by bureaucrats who would see to it that human beings were engendered only at moments fixed by expert astrologers.

Again, the doctrine of metempsychosis, once almost universally held over a wide belt of the earth from India to Scandinavia, seemed to be confirmed by the same observations; for the differences between brothers were understandable, if their bodies were animated by souls that had had far different experiences in earlier incarnations. There were also some theoretical explanations, such as the one that you may remember having read in the stately verse of Lucretius, that were sound bases for scientific inquiry, but they were not followed up. Until the last third of the Nineteenth Century, men learned nothing of the basic laws of heredity. Darwin's knowledge of the subject was no better than Aristotle's, and Galton's enthusiasm for eugenics was no more firmly founded than was Plato's. It remained for a humble and too modest priest, Father Johann Gregor Mendel, to make one of the most important scientific discoveries ever made by man.

Father Mendel's *Versuche über Pflanzenhybriden* was published in 1886, but the famous professors in the great universities could not take a mere priest seriously—ertainly not a priest so impudent as to contradict Darwin—and so they went on for decades pawing over Problems that Father Mendel had made as obsolete as the epicycles of Ptolemaic astronomy. He was simply ignored and forgotten until 1900, when three distinguished biologists discovered independently and almost simultaneously some of the laws that he had ascertained and formulated.

It required some time for systematic study of genetics to get

under way, and research has been greatly impeded by two catastrophic World Wars and by the obscurantism of Communists
and "Liberal intellectuals."

In Russia and other territories controlled by the Conspiracy,
Marx's idiotic mumbo-jumbo is official doctrine and the study of
genetics is therefore prohibited. There are, however, some indications that research may be going on secretly, and it is even possible
that, so far as human genetics are concerned, the knowledge thus
obtained may exceed our own; for the Soviet, though usually inept
in scientific work, has facilities for experiments that civilized men
cannot perform. In the mid-1930's, for example, there were reports that experiment stations in Asiatic Russia had pens of human
women whom the research workers were trying to breed with
male apes in the hope of producing a species better adapted to life
under Socialism than human beings. It was reported a few years
ago that the Soviet is now trying to create subhuman mutations by
exposing their human breeding stock to various forms of irradia-
tion. One cannot exclude the possibility that the monsters who
conduct such experiments may incidentally find some significant
data.

In the United States, the situation differs somewhat from that
in Russia. Geneticists are permitted their studies in peace so long
as they communicate only with one another and do not disclose to
the public facts of which the American boobs must be kept ignorant. Since it requires rare courage to provoke a nest of "Liberal intellectuals" or rattlesnakes, the taboo thus imposed is generally
observed.

Grim Genetics

Despite the restraints placed on scientific investigation, and
despite the awesome complexity of genetic factors in so complicated a creature as man, it is now virtually certain that all of the
physiological structure of human beings, including such details as
color of eyes, acuity of vision, stature, susceptibility to specific dis-

eases, and formation of the brain are genetically determined beyond possibility of modification or alteration except by physical injury or chemical damage. Some of the processes involved have been well ascertained; others remain unknown. No one knows, for example, why the introduction of minute quantities of fluorine into drinking water will prevent development of the brain in some children and so roughly double the number of Mongolian idiots born in a given area.

It is far more difficult to investigate intellectual capacities, since these must involve a large number of distinct elements, no one of which can be physically observed; but all of the evidence thus far available indicates that intelligence is as completely and unalterably determined by genetic inheritance as physical traits.

Moral qualities are even more elusive than intellectual capacity. There is evidence which makes it seem extremely probable that criminal instincts, at least, are inherited, but beyond this we can only speculate by drawing an analogy between moral and intellectual potentialities.

Many persons find the conclusions thus suggested unpleasant, just as all of us, I am sure, would be much happier if the earth were the immobile center of the universe and the heavens revolved about it. But although vast areas in the new science of genetics remain unexplored, and although the complexity of many problems is such that we cannot hope to know in our lifetime many of the things that we most urgently need to know, the principles of heredity have been determined with a fairly high degree of scientific probability. They are, furthermore, in accord with what common sense has always told us and also with the rational perception of our place in the universe that underlies religion.

We can blind children, but we cannot give them sight. We can stunt their minds in "progressive" schools, but we cannot give them an intelligence they did not inherit at birth. It is likely that we can make criminals of them by putting them (like the somewhat improbable Oliver Twist) in Fagan's gang or its equivalent, but we cannot induce a moral sense in one who was born without it. We have always known that it is easy for man to destroy what he can never create.

One Certainty   .

The Mendelian laws and hence the finding that human beings, physically and intellectually, at least, are absolutely limited to the potentialities they have inherited — which may be impaired by external action but cannot be increased — are the accepted basis of all serious biological study today. From the standpoint of scientific opinion, to deny heredity is about equivalent to insisting that the earth is flat or that tadpoles spring from the hair of horses.

The point is worth noting, for even if you choose to reject the findings of genetics, that science will enable you to demonstrate one very important truth.

Our "Liberal intellectuals," who have done all in their power to deride, defile, and destroy all religion, are now sidling about us with hypocritical whimpers that the facts of genetics ain't "Christian." This argument does work with those whose religion is based on the strange faith that God wouldn't have dared to create a universe without consulting their wishes. But if you inquire of the "intellectual," as though you did not know, concerning scientific evidence in these matters, the chances are that he will assure you, with a very straight face, that he is, as always, the Voice of Science. Thus you will know that he still is what he has always been: a sneak and a liar.

The Warp Of Culture

Given the facts that all men are born unequal; that the inequality, apparent even among children of the same parents, increases with differences in genetic strains; that civilization, by the very fact of social organization and the variety of human activity thus made possible, accentuates such differences; and that the continuity of a culture depends on a more or less instinctive acceptance of the common values of that culture—given those facts, it becomes clear that historians who try to account for the rise and fall of civilizations by describing political, economic, philosophic, and religious changes without reference to genetic changes in the population are simply excluding what *must* have been a very important factor, however little we may be able to measure it in the past or the present.

Whatever should be true of statutory and often ephemeral enactments in human jurisprudence, it is undoubtedly true of all the laws of nature that ignorance of the law excuses no-one from the consequences of violating it. And it may be unjust, as it is certainly exasperating, that we must often act with only partial and inaccurate knowledge of such laws. But that is a condition of life. Societies are like individuals in that they must make decisions as best they can on the basis of such information as is available to them. You may have stock in a corporation whose future you may find it very difficult to estimate, but you *must* decide either (a) to sell, or (b) to buy more, or (c) to hold what you have. What you *cannot* do is nothing.

The scope of genetic forces in the continuity of a civilization, and, more particularly, of Western civilization, and, especially, of that civilization in the United States was illustrated by one of the most brilliant of American writers, Dr. Lothrop Stoddard, in *The Revolt Against Civilization* (Scribner's, New York, 1922). The book was out of print for many years, for our "Liberal intellectuals" promptly decided that the subject was one that American boobs should not be permitted to think about, and accordingly shoveled their malodorous muck on both book and author, in the hope of burying both forever. Copies of it disappeared from many libraries, and the book became hard to find on the secondhand market (I obtained my copy from a dealer in Italy). I am told, however, that the book has just been reprinted by photo-offset from the original edition (Freeland Products Co., 700 O'Keefe Avenue, New Orleans 12; c. 275 pages, $1.50).

I commend *The Revolt Against Civilization*, not as a revelation of ultimate truth, but as a cogent and illuminating discussion of some very grim problems that we must face, if we intend to have a future. The book, you must remember, was written forty-two years ago, when problems in genetics seemed much simpler than they do now in the light of later research, and when Americans felt a confidence and an optimism that we of a later generation can scarcely reconstruct in imagination. Some parts of the book will seem quaint and old-fashioned. Dr. Stoddard assumes, for example, that the graduates of Harvard are a group intellectually and morally above the average: That probably was true when he was an undergraduate and when he took his doctorate; he did not foresee what loathsome and reptilian creatures would slither out of Harvard to infest the Dismal Swamp in Washington. And when he urged, forty-two years ago, complete toleration of Communist talk (as distinct from violence), he was thinking of soap-box oratory in Bug-House Square and the shrill chatter of parlor-pinks over their teacups; he did not foresee penetration and capture of schools, churches, newspapers, and political organizations by criminals who disseminate Communist propaganda perfunctorily disguised as "progressive education," "social gospel," and "economic democracy."

But the book remains timely. What were sins of omission in 1922, when we were, with feckless euphoria, repeating the blunders that destroyed past civilizations, are now sins of commission, committed with deliberate and malicious calculation by the enemies whom we have given power over us. And we should especially perpend Dr. Stoddard's distinction between the ignorant or overly-emotional persons who "blindly take Bolshevism's false promises at their face value," and the real Bolsheviks, who "are mostly born and not made." That dictum is as unimpeachable as the *poëta nascitur, non fit,* that it echoes.

The Optimistic Pessimist

Since Stoddard wrote, the horizons have darkened around us. A recent and stimulating book is Dr. Elmer Pendell's *The Next*

Civilization (to be obtained from the author, 206 West Mountain Avenue, Jacksonville Alabama; 232 pages, $3.75). The title may remind you of an article that Arthur Koestler published in the *New York Times* on November 7, 1943 — an article whose bleak pessimism startled all but the very few readers who were in a position to surmise, from the hints which Koestler was able to smuggle into the pages of the *Times,* that he, an ex-Communist, was able to estimate the extent to which the Communist Conspiracy had already taken control of the government of the United States. Koestler, stating flatly that we would soon be engulfed in a Dark Age of barbarism and indescribable horror, called for the establishment of monasteries that, like the monasteries of the early Middle Ages, would preserve some part of human culture as seed for a new Renaissance in some distant future. Dr. Pendell, although he does not entirely deny us hope for ourselves, is primarily concerned with preserving the better part of our genetic heritage as seed for a future civilization that may have the intelligence to avoid the follies by which we are decreeing our own doom.

Dr. Pendell very quickly reviews the historical theories of Brooks Adams, Spengler, Toynbee, and others to show that they all disregard the fact that decline in a civilization is always accompanied by a change in the composition, and deterioration in the quality, of the population.

We know that such changes took place in every civilization of which we have record. The majority of Roman citizens in 100 A.D. were not related at all to the Roman citizens in 100 B.C. We know that the great Roman families died out from sheer failure to have enough children to reproduce themselves, and we have reason to believe that all classes of responsible Romans, regardless of social or economic position, followed the fashion of race suicide. Since the Romans had the preposterous notion that any person or any race imported from any part of the world could be transformed into a Roman by some magic in the legal phrases by which he was made a Roman citizen, the children that the Romans did not have were replaced by a mass of very diverse origins. Some of the importations undoubtedly brought with them fresh vigor and talent; some were incapable of assimilating civilization at all and could only imitate its outer forms without understanding its meaning; and some, while by no means inferior in intelligence and energy, had a temperament which, although eminently suited to some other civilization, was incompatible with the Roman. For some estimates of the deterioration of the population of the empire that the Romans founded, see the late Tenny Frank's *History of Rome*. (Holt, New York, $6.50) and Martin P. Nilsson's *Imperial Rome* (Schocken, New York, $4.50, cloth, $1.95, paper).

When Dr. Stoddard wrote, we were merely behaving as thoughtlessly as the Romans: *carpe diem* and let tomorrow take care of itself. But now, as Dr. Pendell hints and could have stated more emphatically, the power of government over us is being used, with a consistency and efficiency that must be intentional, to accelerate our deterioration and hasten our disappearance as a people by every means short of mass massacre that geneticists could suggest. To mention but one small example, many states now pick the pockets of their taxpayers to subsidize and promote the breeding of bastards, who, with only negligible exceptions, are the product of the lowest dregs of our population, the morally irresponsible and mentally feeble. An attorney informs me that in his state and others the rewards for such activity are so low that a female of this species has to produce about a dozen bastards before it can afford a Cadillac, and will have to go on producing to take care of the maintenance. Intensive breeding is therefore going on, and the legislation that was designed to stimulate it may therefore be said to be highly successful.

The United States is now engaged in an insane, but terribly effective, effort to destroy the American people and Western civilization by subsidizing, both at home and abroad, the breeding of the intellectually, physically, and morally unfit; while at the same time inhibiting, by taxation and in many other ways, the reproduction of the valuable parts of the population — those with the stamina and the will to bear the burden of high civilization. We, in our fatuity, but under the control of persons who must know what they are doing, are working to create a future in which our children, if we have any, will curse us for having given them birth.

When Dr. Pendell tells us what we must do, if we are to survive or even if we limit ourselves to the more modest hope that human civilization may survive on our planet, is to reverse the process -- to encourage the reproduction of the superior stock and to check the multiplication of the inferior— he is unquestionably right. He may also be right when he urges that we must do more than desist from interfering with nature for the purpose of producing biological deterioration --- that we must, instead, interfere with nature to ameliorate and improve our race. But here, I fear, Dr. Pendell, although he almost despairs of our civilization and looks to the next one, is yet too optimistic. There are two practical difficulties.

Our *coup d'état*

Dr. Pendell proposes voluntary eugenic associations and "heredity corporations," which, no doubt, would help a little, as he argues, but which, as he is aware, would not have much more effect than a few buckets — or barrels — of water thrown into the crater of Mauna Loa. At this late date, to accomplish much for ourselves or even for our putative successors, we must use at least the taxing power of government, if not its powers of physical coercion, to induce or compel the superior to have children and to prevent the inferior from proliferating. So here enters on the stage that most unlovely product of human evolution, the bureaucrat, whom we shall need to apply whatever rules we may devise. And if you can stand a moment of sheer nightmare, dear reader — imagine, just for five seconds or so, what mankind would be like, if the power to decide who was or was not to have children fell into the hands of a Senator Fulbright, a Walt Rostow, an Adam Yarmolinsky, a Jack Kennedy, or a Jack The Ripper.

For that dilemma, of course, there is an obvious solution — but, so far as I can see, only one. You, my dear reader, Dr. Pendell, and I must form a triumvirate and seize absolute power over the United States. Unfortunately, I can't at the moment think of a way of carrying out our *coup d'état*, but let's leave such details until later. Assume that we have that power, which we, certainly, are determined to use wisely and well. What shall we do with it?

Dr. Pendell is certainly right. We must breed for brain-power: We must see to it that the most intelligent men and women mate with one another and have many children. And we can identify the intelligent by testing their "I.Q." and by their grades in honest college courses (as distinguished from the childish or fraudulent drivel that forms so large a part of the college curriculum today).

Let us not digress from the subject by questioning the relative validity of the various tests used to determine "intelligence quotient." And we shall ignore the exceptions which, as every teacher knows, sometimes make the most conscientious grading misleading. Father Mendel, to whom we owe the greatest discovery ever made in biology, failed to pass the examination for a teacher's license in that field. A. E. Housman, one of the greatest classical scholars in the world, failed to obtain even second class honors at Oxford, and was given a mere "pass." But such exceptions are rare. Let us assume that we can test intelligence infallibly. *Is that enough?*

It is always helpful to reduce generalizations to specific examples. Percy Bysshe Shelley was one of the great English poets; Albert Einstein, although fantastically over-advertised by yellow journalism, was a great mathematician. Both were brilliant men in more than one field of intellectual activity (Shelley is said to have exhibited a considerable talent for chemistry, among other things, and Einstein is said to have done well in courses on the Classics). Both, I am sure, would have placed themselves in the very highest bracket of any intelligence test, and (if so minded) could have been graduated *summa cum laude* from any college curriculum that you may advise. Both were, in their judgement of social and political problems, virtually morons. Merely a deficiency of practical common sense, you say? Yes, no doubt, but both acted on the basis of that deficiency and used their intellectual powers to exert a highly pernicious influence. One need not underestimate either the beauty of Shelley's poems or the importance of the two theories of relativity to conclude that the world would be better off, had neither man existed.

But we must go farther than that. It is odd that most of the persons who urge us to foster "superior intellect" and "genius," whether they recommend eugenics or educational subsidies or other means, simply ignore the phenomenon of the mattoid (see Lothrop Stoddard, op, cit., pp. 102-106, and the article by Max Nordau there cited).

A mattoid is a person possessed of a mentality that is, in the strict sense of the word, unbalanced. He is Shelley or Einstein tilted just a few more degrees. He exhibits an extremely high talent, often amounting to genius, in one kind of mental activity, such as poetry or mathematics, while the other parts of his mind are depressed to the level of imbecility or insanity. Nordau, who was an acutely observant physician, noted that such unbalanced beings are usually, if not invariably, "full of organic feelings of dislike" and tend to generalize their state of resentment against the civilized world into some cleverly devised pseudo-philosophic or pseudo-aesthetic system that will erode the very foundations of civilized society. Since civilized people necessarily set a high value on intellect, but are apt to venerate "genius" uncritically and without discrimination, the mattoid's influence can be simply deadly. Nordau, indeed, saw in the activity of mattoids the principal reason why "people [as a whole] lose the power of moral indignation, and accustom themselves to despise it as something banal, unadvanced, and unintelligent."

Nordau's explanation may be satisfactory so far as it goes, but moral insanity is not by any means confined to minds that show an extraordinary disproportion among the faculties that can properly be called intellectual and can be measured by such things as intelligence tests, academic records, proficiency in a profession, and outstanding research. The two young degenerates, Loeb and Leopold, whose crime shocked the nation some decades ago although the more revolting details could not be reported in the ᵖress, were reputed to be not only among the most brilliant undergraduates ever enrolled in the University of Chicago, but to be almost equally proficient in every branch of study. One could cite hundreds of comparable examples.

Most monsters that become notorious have to be highly intelligent to gain and retain power. Lenin and Trotsky must have had very active minds, and the latter, at least, according to persons who knew him, was able on occasion to pass as a cultivated man. Both probably had a very high "I.Q." All reports from China indicate that Mao Tse-tung is not only extremely astute, but even learned in the Chinese culture that he is zealously extirpating. A few Communists or crypto-Communists who have been put in prominent positions may be mere stooges, but the directors of the Conspiracy and their responsible subordinates must be persons of phenomenally high intelligence.

It is clear that there is in the human species some biological strain of either atavism or degeneracy that manifests itself in a hatred of mankind and a lust for evil for its own sake. It produced the Thugs in India and the Bolsheviks in Russia (cf. Louis Zoul, *Thugs and Communists*, Public Opinion, Long Island City; $2.00, paper). It appears in such distinguished persons as Giles de Rais, who was second only to the King of France, and in such vulgar specimens as Fritz Haarmann, a homosexual who attracted some attention in Germany in 1924, when it was discovered that for many years he had been disposing of his boy-friends, as soon as he became tired of them, by tearing their throats open with his teeth and then reducing them to sausage, which he sold in a delicatessen. And it animates the many crypto-Communists who hold positions of power or influence in the United States.

It is probable that this appalling viciousness is transmitted by the organic mechanisms of heredity, and although no geneticist would now even speculate about what genes or lack of genes produce such biped terrors, I think it quite likely that the science of genetics, if study and research are permitted to continue, may identify the factors involved eventually — say in two or three hundred years. I know that we most urgently and desperately need to know *now*. But it will do no good to kick geneticists: The almost infinite complexity of human heredity makes it impossible to make such determinations more quickly by the normal techniques of research. (Of course, a brilliant discovery that would transcend those methods is always possible, but we can't count on it.)

It is quite likely that at the present rate, as eugenicists predict, civilization is going to collapse from sheer lack of brains to carry it on. But it is now collapsing faster and harder from a superabundance of brains of the wrong kind. Granting that we can test intelligence, we must remember that at or near the top of the list, by any test that we can devise, will be a flock of diabolically ingenious degenerates. And even if we could find a way to identify and eliminate the spawn of Satan, we should still have problems.

What causes genuine "Liberal intellectuals"? Many are pure Pragmatists. They have no lust for evil for its own sake; they wouldn't betray their country or their own parents for less than fifty dollars — and not for that, if they thought they could get more by bargaining. Others are superannuated children who want to go on playing with fairies and pixies, and are ready to kick and bite when disturbed at play; but they have the combination of lachrymose sentimentality and thoughtless cruelty that one so often finds in children before they become capable of the rational morality of adults. But all of our "Liberal intellectuals" were graduated from a college of some sort, and many of them, I am sure, have a fairly high "intelligence quotient" by modern tests. I do not claim or suggest that they are the result of hereditary defects; I merely point out that we do not know and have no means of finding out. We can't be sure of anything except that our society now has as many of those dubious luxuries as it can endure. And yet we are going to encourage them to raise the intellectual level.

Come to think of it, my friends, I guess we'd better postpone our *coup d'état* for a couple of centuries.

The Shape Of Things To Come

For a neat antithesis to Dr. Pendell's book and, at the same time, a very significant application of genetics, I suggest Roderick Seidenberg's *Anatomy of the Future* (University of North Carolina Press, Chapel Hill; 175 pages, $3.50). Mr. Seidenberg — I call him that because I haven't been able to find out whether or not it should be "Dr." — told us what our future was going to be in an earlier book, *Posthistoric Man* (same publisher; 256 pages, $3.50), which, according to the "Liberal" reviewers, made him a gigantic "philosopher of history." In the present volume, however, he has condescended to tell us again and in fewer pages which may make this one the better bargain.

Mr. Seidenberg, according to Mr. Seidenberg, has surveyed with his eagle eye the whole course of human history and, what is more, the whole course of biological evolution since life first appeared on this planet. That is how he knows about the "ineluctable determinism" that is going to put us in our places.

The Prophet takes his departure from the now familiar phenomenon called the "population explosion" (see *American Opinion*, April, 1960, pp. 33 f.). He says that an increase in the number of human beings automatically increases the "complexity" of society.

Of course, we have been hearing about this "complexity" for years. I am sure that you, poor harried reader, have reflected, every time that you leap into your automobile, how much simpler life would be, if you had to worry about the health of your horses, the condition of your stable, the quality of your oats and hay, the disposition and sobriety of your coachman, the efficiency of your ostlers, and the reliability of the scavengers whom you have hired to keep clean your mews. And I know that whenever you, in Chi-

cago, pick up the telephone to call your aunt in Miami, you remark, with many a bitter oath, how much less complex everything
would be, if all that you had to do was find and hire a reliable
messenger who would ride express to her house and deliver your
hand-written note in a month or so — if he was not waylaid on
the road, and if his horse did not break a leg or cast a shoe, and if
he did not decide to pause at some bowsing-ken *en route* for an in-
vigorating touch of delirium tremens. Sure, life's gettin' awfully
complicated these days; ain't it a fact?

Well, as we all know, life's getting complexer every minute
'cause there are more Chinese and Congolese and Sudanese than
there were a minute ago; and that means, according to Mr.
Seidenberg, that we have just got to become more and more organized by the minute. And the proof of this is that, if you want
to resist the ever increasing organization and socialization of society, you have to join some organization, such — I interpolate, for
I need not tell you that Mr. Seidenberg would never mention anything so horrid — such as The John Birch Society. The need to
join organizations to resist the organization of society proves the
point, for, as is obvious, if you in 1776 had wished to resist the
rule of George III, you would not have needed to join the patriots
of your colony. And if, in 490 B.C., you had wished to resist the
Persian invasion of Europe, you would have had no need to join,
or co-operate with, your fellow Athenians who marched to Mara-
thon. In those days of greater individualism, you, as an individual,
could have stood up alone on your hind legs and stuck out your
tongue — and that, presumably, would have scared Darius and
his armies right into the middle of the Hellespont. But alas, no
more! So, you see, History proves that the day of the individual
has passed forever, and the day of Organization has come.

You must not smile, for Mr. Seidenberg is in earnest, and even
if he is a bit weak in knowledge of past and present, his projection
of the future has seemed cogent not merely to "Liberals," but even
to thoughtful readers.

Forward To Irkalla!

Mr. Seidenberg bases his argument on inferences that he draws with apparent logic from three indisputably correct statements about the contemporary world and from a widely accepted biological theory.

(1) We have all observed that we are being more and more subjected to a Welfare State, which, with Fabian patience, takes away each year some part of our power to make decisions for ourselves regarding our own lives. It is perfectly obvious that if this process continues for a few more decades (as our master's power to take our money to bribe and bamboozle the masses may make inevitable), we shall have lost the right to decide anything at all, and shall have become mere human livestock managed by a ruthless and inhuman bureaucracy at the orders of an even more inhuman master.

(2) Our Big Brains agree with Mr. Seidenberg in believing, or pretending to believe, that "the kernel of Marxism ...consists in elaborating ...the social message of Christ." They assure us, therefore, that it is simply unthinkable that Americans could ever be so wicked as to fight to survive. Thus we have got to be scared or beaten into One World of universal socialism in which, as Walt Rostow, Jack Kennedy, and others now gloatingly and openly tell us, not only our nation but our race must be liquidated and dissolved in a vast and mongrel mass of pullulating bipeds.

(3) The number of human beings — anatomically human, at least — is undoubtedly increasing at an appalling rate. The United States is already overpopulated for optimum life, although no critical reduction in our standard of living would be necessary for the better part of a century, if our masters permitted us to remain an independent nation. But our increase is nothing compared to the terrible multiplication of the populations of Asia and Africa, caused, for the most part, by our export to those regions of our medical knowledge, medicines, food, and money. Although we Westerners might stave off a crisis for a few decades by working

harder and ever harder to support our betters and to speed up the rate at which they are breeding, it is clear that we (unless we do something unthinkable) must soon be drowned in the flood that we, like the Sorcerer's Apprentice, started but do not know how to stop. So, even if we did not have Master Jack and his accomplices or employers to arrange for our liquidation, the sheer multiplication of the human species would produce the same result anyway.

One has but to glance at a graph of the world's population to see that it is rapidly approaching the point at which the vast human swarm can be kept alive, even on the level of barest animal subsistence, only by the most expert management of every square inch of earth's arable surface plus expert harvest of the very oceans themselves. In that monstrous human swarm jammed together on our planet, like a swarm of bees hanging from a limb, there can be no privacy, no individuality, no slightest deviation from the routine that must be maintained just to keep alive the maximum number that can subsist at all.

Now the theory of biological evolution, as usually stated, provides that species must adapt themselves to the conditions of survival. Men, having bred themselves into a maximum swarm, become mere units of the species, and will obviously be most efficient when they perform every action of the routine by an automatic reflex. This means that thought and even consciousness will become not only unnecessary but intolerable impediments to the efficient functioning of the human animals. Obviously, the human mind must disappear in order to permit billions of human ants to make the globe an ant-hill in which they can all live in perfect socialism.

That is what "ineluctable determinism" makes ineluctable, but Mr. Seidenberg, who is as adroit in twisting words as any editor of the *New York Times*, shows you how nice that will be. The Revelations of Freud have shown that we are now just bundles of instincts. Mankind will necessarily evolve to the higher stage of what Mr. Seidenberg calls "pure reason." As he explains, "pure reason" is now found only among the forms of life that are biologically superior to us because better adapted to environment. The examples which he gives are "ants, bees, and termites," whose "essentially unchanged survival during sixty million years testifies to the perfection of their adjustment ...to the conditions of life." We must strive to become like them — nay, the "ineluctable determinism" inherent in the "population explosion"; and the need for a "more advanced society" will make us, willy nilly, just like ants and termites — intellectually and spiritually, that is, for Mr. Seidenberg does not seem to entertain a hope that human beings will ever be able to crawl about on six legs.

In this perfected socialist world there can be no change and hence no history: That is why the perfect man of the near future will be, in Seidenbergian terminology, "post-historic." Everybody will be happy, because there will be no individuals — only organisms that are part of a species and have no separate consciousness. To see how attractive the inevitable future is, you have only to reflect, dear reader, how much happier you would be, if you were an ant or a cockroach in your basement. You would operate by what Mr. Seidenberg calls "pure reason." You could not possibly be affected by religion, art, literature, philosophy, science, capitalism, racial discrimination, or any of the other horrid things that will have to be blotted out anyway in the interests of Equality and Social Justice. You could never have a thought to trouble you. You would have no consciousness; hence you would not know that you exist, and would have no organ that could feel pain when somebody steps on you. What more could you want?

If you are so reactionary as to prefer to be conscious, even at the cost of being unhappy from time to time, you may be amused by the similarity of Mr. Seidenberg's vision of the future to the scene described in one of the oldest of the Babylonian tablets, on which the cuneiform characters represent an oddly sibilant and staccato language: *a-na māt lā tāri kak-ka-ri-i-ti-e ila ištar mārat ilu sin u-zu-un-sa iš-kun,* etc.

"To the land whence none return, the place of darkness, Ishtar, the daughter of Sin, her ear inclined.

"Then inclined the daughter of Sin her ear to the house of darkness, the domain of Irkalla; to the prison from which he that enters comes not forth; to the road whose path does not return; ...to the land where filth is their bread and their food is mud. The light they behold not; in unseeingness they dwell, and are clothed, like winged things, in a garment of scales...."

Of all of mankind's nightmarish visions of a future existence, that Babylonian conception of the dead as crawling forever, like mindless insects, in a fetid and eternal night has always seemed to me the most gruesome.

Joy Is Not Around The Corner

Mr. Seidenberg's ecstatic vision of the New Jerusalem has, I am sorry to say, imposed on at least two men of scientific eminence who should have known better. They permitted themselves to be confused by the theory of biological evolution. If man evolved, over a period of 500,000 years or more, from an ape (*Australopithecus*) that discovered that by picking up and wielding a long bone it could increase its efficiency in killing other apes, is it not possible that our species can go on evolving and become, in another 500,000 years or less, the perfectly adjusted biped termite that Mr. Seidenberg predicts? Heavens to Betsy, I'm not going to argue that point. Granted!

And isn't the "population explosion" a fact! Sure it is, but don't overlook one detail — the time factor. At the present rate, the globe, sometime between 2000 and 2005 A.D. — that is to say, *within forty years* — will be infested by 5,000,000,000 anatomically human creatures, the maximum number for which food can be supplied by even the most intensive cultivation. And then, to keep the globe inhabitable at that bare subsistence level, it will be necessary to kill every year more people than now live in the whole United States — kill them with atomic bombs or clubs, as may be most convenient.

I shall not argue about what human beings could or could not become by biological evolution in half a million years: We all know, at least, that there is going to be *no* biological evolution in fifty years. And, if we stop a moment to think about it, we also know that the world is not going to have a population of five billion. Not ever.

The population of the world is going to be drastically reduced before the year 2000.

The reduction could come through natural causes. It is always possible — far more possible than you imagine, if you have not investigated the relevant areas of scientific knowledge — that next week or next year may bring the onset of a new pestilence that will have a proportional mortality as great as that of the epidemic in the time of the Antonines or the Black Plague of the Middle Ages. Alternatively, the events described in John Cristopher's brilliant novel, *No Blade of Grass*, could become fact, instead of fiction, at any time. And there are at least three other ways, all scientifically possible, in which the world could be partly depopulated in short order by strictly natural forces beyond our control.

But if Nature does not act, men will. When things became a bit crowded in east Asia, for example, the Huns and at a later time, the Mongols swept a wide swath through the world as locusts sweep through a wheat field. And wherever they felt the inspiration, they were every bit as efficient as any quantity of hydrogen bombs you may care to imagine. In the natural course of human events, we shall see in the near future wars of extermination on a scale and of an intensity that your mind will, at present, refuse to contemplate. The only question will be what peoples will be among the exterminated.

If the minority of the earth's inhabitants that is capable of creating and continuing (as distinct from aping) a high civilization is exterminated (as it now seems resolved to be), or if for some reason wars of extermination fail to solve the problem, civilization will collapse from sheer lack of brains to keep it going, and the consequent reversion to global savagery will speedily take care of the excess in numbers. In a world of savages, not only would the intricate *and hated* technology of our civilization be abolished, but even the simplest arts might be forgotten. (Every anthropologist knows of tribes in Polynesia and Melanesia that forgot how to make canoes, although without them it became almost impossible to obtain the fish that they regard as the most delicious food, or how to make bows and arrows, although they needed them for more effective hunting and fighting.) A world of savages in 2100 probably would not have a population more numerous than the world had in 4000 B.C.

The ordinary course of nature and human events (separately or in combination) will, in one way or another, take care of the much-touted "population explosion," and *Mr. Seidenberg knows it.* You have only to read him carefully to see that all his talk about history, biological evolution, and "ineluctable determinism" is strictly for the birds — or, at least bird-brains.

Do-It-Yourself For Socialists

Like all internationalists, Mr. Seidenberg envisages a One World of universal socialism.

Every student of history and mankind (as distinct from the ignorant theorists who prefer to chirrup while hopping from cloud to cloud in Nephelococcygia) well knows what is needed for a successful and stable socialism. And our intelligent socialists know it, too. There are two essentials, viz.: (1) a mass of undifferentiated human livestock, sufficiently intelligent to be trained to perform routine and often complicated tasks, but too stupid to take thought for their own future; and (2) a small caste of highly intelligent planners, preferably of an entirely different race, who will direct the livestock and, with the aid of overseers who need be but little more intelligent than the overseen, make sure that the livestock work hard and breed properly and do not have unsocial thoughts. The owners must be so superior to the owned that the latter will not regard themselves as of the same species. The owners must be hedged about with a quasi-divinity, and their chief, therefore, must be represented as an incarnate god.

Mr. Seidenberg knows that and tells us so. Our blissful future, he says, is assured by the emergence of "administrators [whose] special talents place them above other men." The most important of these special talents is enough intelligence to understand that "moral restraints and compassions [and]... the attitudes and values upon which they were based have become obsolete. On the basis of such progressive thinking, "the relatively small élite of the organizers" will manipulate the "overwhelming social mass" and guide it toward its destiny, "the mute status of unconscious organisms."

The Chosen Few will do this by promoting "the spiritual and psychological dehumanization of man" and "a vast organizational transmutation of life." For this glorious purpose, various techniques are available; for example, as Mr. Seidenberg tells us, "there is, plainly, *more* than a nihilistic meaning in the challenging ambiguities of modern art." And, in a masterfully managed society, "the gradually *inculcated* feeling of helplessness... will make the mass of humanity ever more malleable and dependent upon the complex functioning of society, with its ensuing regimentation under organized patterns of behavior." But the Supermen will use, above all, "*a scientific program of genetic control* to assure the complete adjustment of the human mass to its destiny" and "the final elimination of the socially maladjusted," such as Right-Wing Reactionaries and other American swine, whose "anachronistic stance" and silly efforts to avoid "the mute status of unconscious organisms" show that they "belong essentially to the past."

As for the Supermen, who form "the nucleus of an élite of administrative functionaries and organizers ruling over the vast mass of men," you can bet your bottom dollar (so long as Master Jack permits you to have one) that that Master Race has no intention of becoming like the bipeds that it will supervise and selectively breed for more and better mindlessness until it has attained its "historic" goal, "the settling of the human race [as distinct from its owners] into an ecologic niche of permanent and static adjustment," which, as Mr. Seidenberg says in a moment of candor, is simply "living death." Obviously, when this goal has been achieved, human beings, deprived of mind and even consciousness, will differ from the Master Race as much as ants and bees now differ in intelligence from human beings. Glory be!

To any attentive reader of the book it is clear that the author, under the guise of a transparently inconsistent prophecy about a distant future, is presenting a plan for a near future that is to be *created*, in spite of history, in spite of nature, and in spite of mankind by the purposeful and concerted action of a small band of "élite" conspirators, comparable to, if not identical with, the directors of the International Communist Conspiracy.

To publish such a plan in a book sold to the general public seems a fantastic indiscretion, even when one allows for the breath-taking effrontery that our Internationalists are now showing in their confidence that Americans have already been so disarmed and entrapped in the "United Nations" that, for practical purposes, it's all over except for the butchering. When I first read these books, therefore, I was inclined to believe that the author was trying to warn us.

The Veiled Prophet Of Doylestown

My inquiries, necessarily hasty and perfunctory as I write this article to meet a deadline, have elicited almost no information about Mr. Seidenberg. I do not know what region on earth was blessed with his nativity, what academic institutions bestowed the benison of their degrees upon him, or even what may be his liaison with the University of North Carolina. He is said to be an architect, but he is not listed in the 1962 edition of the *American Architects' Directory*. He is said to practice that art in Doylestown, Pennsylvania, but an informer in that town reports that he is not listed in the telephone directory as an architect, although there is listed under his name, without indication of profession or occupation, a telephone which did not answer, when called on successive days.

I do not have the facilities of the FBI, so all that I really know about Mr. Seidenberg, apart from his books, is that he surfaced momentarily on February 22, 1962, in the pages of the *New York Times*, to emit a yip for the abolition of the House Committee on Un-American Activities. (And if you wonder why anyone should now yip against a Committee that appears to have been virtually silenced by the concerted howling of our enemies after the release of *Operation Abolition*, I can only tell you that, according to persons who should know, the Committee has amassed in Executive Sessions testimony which, if published, would expose some of the most powerful anti-humans in Washington.)

Mrs. Sarah Watson Emery, in her excellent book, *Blood on the Old Well* (Prospect House, Dallas; cf. *American Opinion*, October, 1963, pp. 67 ff.), reports that the elusive Seidenberg, in a conversation with her, "clearly implied that he wrote the books in order to bring about the ghastly future" that he "so confidently predicts." If Mrs. Emery is right, Mr. Seidenberg's books are inspirational literature for the Master Race of "administrators," who are now taking over the whole world. They can own and operate the world forever in perfect Peace, if, by a scientific application of genetics, they reduce human beings to the status of mindless insects.

Is One World Feasible?

You, my patient reader, may be a member of the Radical Right and hence unenthusiastic about the happiness that is being planned for you. If so, I confess that I, whom a learned colleague recently described as a "filthy Fascist swine," share your misgivings. But let us here consider the Seidenbergian ideal exclusively as a problem in genetics. Is it possible?

Probably not, by the hit-and-miss methods that the Conspiracy has thus far employed.

As Mr. Seidenberg carefully points out, "Russia [under Lenin, Stalin, and Khrushchev] and America [under Roosevelt, Eisenhower, and Kennedy] are basically akin by reason of the dominance of their organizational trends," but — *hélas!* — even today "the collectivization of society is *only in its incipient stages in Russia.*" And the reason is obvious. Although Ulyanov (alias Lenin) and Bronstein (alias Trotsky) butchered millions of reactionary Russians who wanted to be individual human beings, and although Dzhugashvili (alias Stalin) butchered millions more, and although Saint Nick (formerly Khrushchev) shot, hacked to pieces, or starved seven million in the Ukraine alone when he was just a local manager for the Communist Conspiracy, the nasty Russians are still unregenerate. Although the world's vermin have had absolute control of Russia for almost half a century and have certainly worked hard to exterminate every Russian who had in himself a spark of self-respect, human decency, or even the will to live, observers agree that the recent failure of crops would have precipitated a crisis and possibly even a revolt of blind desperation, if Master Jack had not ordered his American cattle to provide the wheat that Comrade Nick needed to keep his own restive cattle fairly quiet. And it is quite likely that if the Conspiracy were to lose control of the United States and so be forced to retreat somewhere in the world, the Russian people would revolt anyway. The most systematic butchery has not destroyed the genetic transmission of human instincts. And it is unlikely to do so for centuries, at least.

Americans are apt to be even more refractory, and I am sure that One Worlders, now that they think their final victory almost achieved, must be giving thought to the problem of what to do with them. (And I need not remind you that advanced minds are not troubled by "moral restraints" and the other "attitudes and values.") The American kulaks were useful and even necessary to fight wars "to make the world safe for democracy" and to finance with "foreign aid" the Communist conquest of the world, but when that goal has been achieved, they are likely to be a real nuisance.

There are rumors, for example, that Master Jack is planning to send the U.S. Army — which as purged by Yarmolinsky and his stooges will presumably be a docile instrument for the abolition of the nation it established to defend — to seal off one area of the country after another, drive the white swine from their homes, and search them to confiscate such firearms or other weapons as they may have in their possession. It may be necessary to beat a few hundred of the white pigs so that their squealing will teach the other livestock to obey their owner, but, according to the rumors, nothing more than that is contemplated. But even if the operation is successful, one can foresee endless trouble. Human instincts are more or fixed by heredity.

It is no wonder, therefore, that Mr. Seidenberg foresees "long-range genetic manipulation designed not only to improve the human stock according to the social dictates of [the proprietors of] a collectivized humanity, but *above all* to eliminate, in one manner or other, any traces of anti-social deviation."

Those are, doubtless, sound general principles, but what, specifically, is to be done with the Americans when the "United Nations" takes them over? One could, as Mr. Seidenberg delicately hints in one passage, just castrate all the males. (If the idea seems shocking to you, remember that that's just your "anachronistic stance.") Or one could adopt the policy which the Soviet, according to a report that was leaked "from U. N. official sources" and reported in the now defunct *Northlander* (September, 1958), uses in Lithuania, where all potentially troublesome males were rounded up and shipped to Siberia and then replaced in their own homes by public-spirited Mongolian males eager to improve the quality of the Lithuanian population. A Baluba or a Bakongo thus installed in every American home would not only effectively end "discrimination" and promote the "world unity" desiderated by Internationalists, but would also — according to a "scientific" study made by a Professor of Sociology in a tax-supported American university and reported both in his classroom lectures and in his broadcast over a radio-station entirely owned by that university — fulfill the secret yearnings of all American womanhood.

This may seem a perfect solution (if you have a "One World" viewpoint), but it has, I fear, its drawbacks. Balubas and such are just fine for exterminating white men in Africa and creating chaos under direction from Washington and Moscow, but I suspect that anyone who tries to regiment them to do work is in for a powerful lot of trouble. After they have served their purpose, it will be necessary to exterminate them, too. And the Masters, after they have blotted out the civilization they hate, are going to need workers, not cannibals and other savages, if, in keeping with the Seidenbergian vision, they are to rule the world forever.

Now Americans and Europeans are excellent workers. What is needed, obviously, is not to destroy them but to convert them, as Mr. Seidenberg predicts, into true zombies, that is to say, creatures that have no will or personality of their own and therefore do whatever they are told. But that transformation, so far as I can learn from geneticists whom I have consulted, is genetically impossible by any process of selective breeding within any reasonable length of time — say a thousand years or less. This, I am sure, our author realizes, for after admitting that "the art of brain-washing and, even more so, the *science of controlling society by pharmaceutical manipulation*, are in their infancy," he places his hope for the future in "the ever increasing techniques and the ever more refined arts of mental coercion." Presumably, the human mind and will can be destroyed by drugs, or perhaps by an improved technique of lobotomy, to produce the kind of "mental health" requisite in the zombies who, like mindless insects, are to work to support the Master Race of the future. But this is not genetics, and the qualities thus induced in individuals can not be transmitted genetically. The Masters, therefore, will be put to the trouble of operating on each generation of biped insects as it is produced—and, what is even worse, there is some reason to doubt that the zombies would or could reproduce themselves.

So, you see, the New Dispensation of which Internationalists dream is by no means assured, either historically or biologically. For that matter, it is even possible that enough Americans may ob-

ject in time to frustrate the "determinism" that only their ignorance, apathy, or cowardice could make "ineluctable." But I cannot speculate about that possibility here. I have sought only to
show you, as dispassionately as possible, what kind of thoughts
very advanced minds are thinking these days.

THE JEWS
LOVE CHRISTIANITY

THE JEWS
LOVE CHRISTIANITY

Our contemporaries are coming to a radically new understanding of the Jewish problem. One by one, and independently of one another, several of our best minds have re-examined the historical record or analyzed the forces that are today driving our race to suicide. And each of them has come spontaneously to the conclusion that Christianity was a Jewish invention, devised for the specific purpose of enfeebling and paralyzing the civilized peoples of the world, on whom the Jews were preying in antiquity and have preyed ever since.

A century ago, Nietzsche perceived that our civilization, although it seemed to have an absolute mastery of the whole world, was infected by a degenerative disease, a cancer of the spirit that would destroy it, if our people did not have the intelligence and the fortitude to excise the malignancy. He came to the conclusion that Christianity was a "transvaluation of values," a mental virus cunningly invented and propagated by the Jews to implement "Jewish vengeance and hatred—the deepest and sublimest hatred in human history." Our contemporaries, whether or not they have read the *Genealogy of Morals,* reason largely from events that have occurred or from historical evidence that became available since Nietzsche's day. They come to substantially the same conclusion.

The origins of Christianity are extremely obscure. No histori-

The Jews Love Christianity was (under the pseudonym of Ralph Perier) Dr. Oliver's first contribution to, and was first published in, *Liberty Bell* for August 1980. This article evoked many responses—pro and con—which are reproduced in Appendix B.

cal record of its beginnings has survived, and scholars can only draw deductions from the earliest historical references to it and inferences from its confusing and incoherent mythology.

One thing is certain. Christianity was originated by Jews and based on oral traditions about one or, more probably, several of the Jewish agitators and miracle-mongers who bore the extremely common Jewish name of Jesus and called themselves christs. The word 'christ' comes from a Greek word that means 'oil, grease,' but which was used in the Jews' uncouth dialect of Greek to mean 'a messiah,' that is, a man appointed by the Jews' tribal god to lead his Chosen barbarians to a definitive victory over the civilized peoples, whom they implacably hated. One of the cleverest tricks of the Fathers of the Church in promoting their cult was to give to non-Jews the impression that 'christ' was the name of a person, and even to this day many Christians ignorantly believe that their god was a man who was baptized "Jesus Christ."

Nietzsche saw that successful promotion of Christianity depended on a pretence of reciprocal hostility between Christians and Jews. It depended on making the Jewish cult, when peddled to the *goyim*, seem non-Jewish and even anti-Jewish. "Was it not," he asked, "a necessary feature of a truly brilliant politics of vengeance, a far-sighted, subterranean, slowly and carefully planned vengeance, that Israel had to deny its true instrument publicly and nail him to the cross like a mortal enemy, so that 'the whole world' (meaning all the enemies of the Jews) might naively swallow the bait!" This policy, however, produced an unexpected backlash, which was only with difficulty brought under control.

It would take a volume even to summarize the scandalous and scabrous history of Christianity from its known beginnings around the middle of the second century to the triumph of a particularly shrewd and aggressive sect in the fifth century. There were hundreds of sects, each with its own bundle of gospels, peculiar doctrines, and adroit theologians, but among them there were dozens of sects that took seriously the purported antagonism of the Jews to the new religion.

One of the earliest of the Christian sects of which we have some record, and for almost two centuries one of the largest, was the Marcionites. It is noteworthy, by the way, that until quite recently, the earliest extant inscription from a Christian church came from a Marcionite church that was built in 318 and, of course, destroyed when the victorious sect got the power to persecute.

The Marcionites believed that the Jews really were "the synagogue of Satan." They denied that their Jesus had been a Jew. They saw that it was preposterous to claim that an incarnate god could die or would foolishly have himself crucified. They held that it was outrageous to identify the supreme god, who was a just god and loved all mankind, with the capricious, ferocious, and highly immoral god described in the Jews' story-book, which Christians now call "the Old Testament." The Marcionites naively thought those stories historical, but regarded them as a chronicle of the crimes perpetrated by the Jews and their supernatural accomplice, a much inferior deity whose abused power the supreme god had justly revoked. Other Christian sects took the logical step of frankly identifying the Jews' god with Satan. This plausible identification commended itself to *goyim* who had to live with Jews and suffer their depredations.

We have no means of estimating numbers, but it is possible that early in the third century, taking the numerous sects as a whole, a majority of the Christians repudiated the notion that the wily Jews were God's People and that the Jesus who was divine could have been a Jew. The anti-Jewish sects, however, appear to have thought of themselves as merely religions and to have believed what was said in their scriptures about love, faith, and peace. Content to believe certain dogmas and to observe rules that would assure them postmortem bliss, they seem to have had no interest in political intrigue and conspiracy, for which they had no talent. So they eventually fell victims to a gang of crafty, ruthless, and tightly-organized theologians, who are now known as the Fathers of the Church and given a prominence they cannot have had in their own time, when they must have appeared to be just another clique of salvation-hucksters.

When the Fathers of the Church finally got their hands on the police powers of the state, doubtless with much covert help from the Jews, they extirpated the anti-Jewish Christians with fire and sword, the natural instruments of Christian love as understood by ambitious holy men. Despite all the pious massacres in the fifth century, the anti-Jewish "heresy" has appeared from time to time in later ages. It is found today in certain "fundamentalist" churches and, most clearly, in the group of loosely affiliated sects called "British Israel," whose members probably have never even heard of the Marcionites or their other ancient precursors.

"British Israel" may be another ploy that backfired. It began in England at the time when Disraeli was crawling up to the British Prime Ministry and peerage. In its original form, it taught that the "ten lost tribes" supposedly taken captive by the Assyrians had been Anglo-Saxons, who migrated *en masse* from Assyrian territory to the British Isles. A handsome geneology was concocted to show that Queen Victoria was a lineal descendant of a bandit chief named David. It followed, therefore, that God's Own People, to-wit, the Anglo-Saxons and the Jews, reunited at last after many centuries, should jointly rule the world. That notion, however, imposed too great a strain on even Christian credulity.

Today, the "British Israelites" accept the story that the "ten tribes" were Anglo-Saxons or, at least, Nordics, and hotfooted it from Assyrian territory to the British Isles or, at least, northern Europe. They further claim that the Jesus of Holy Writ was an Aryan, despite his distinctively Jewish name and the distinctively Jewish (or conceivably Egyptian) name of his supposed mother. They rely principally on some of the early Christian forgeries which explicitly describe that Jesus as having had blue eyes and blond hair and beard. They do not use, and seem not to know, the tradition, attested as early as any of the other Christian tales, that one of the Jesuses was the son of a Jewess by a soldier named Pandara/Panthera, who probably was not a Jew and could well have been a Macedonian or other Greek in a Seleucid or Roman army.

We must feel a considerable sympathy for the "British Isrealites" of the present. They candidly recognize the Jews as the eternal enemies of our race. They are the best of the Christians and are making a valiant effort to free their religion from its Jewish trammels and make it conducive to the survival of our race. Unfortunately, their doctrine is historically preposterous and, what is even worse, demoralizing. It makes our race the accomplices and beneficiaries of the ferocious god, Yahweh, who, according to the "Old Testament," helped his pets swindle, plunder, torment, and butcher their betters in Egypt and Canaan.

THE FATHERS OF THE CHURCH

Christianity today, including all of the many minor sects, is what it was made by the patient and subtle work of the Fathers of the Church. They were a knavish lot. There is no way of knowing how many of them were actually Jews on duty for God's Race. It is highly unlikely that any one of them was a Greek or Roman. Most of them were probably Semites or descendants of one of the other Oriental peoples that swarmed into the mongrelized Roman Empire and displaced or replaced the Romans. Whatever their racial antecedents, it is clear from their own writings, despite much later whitewashing, that they were a motley crew of shysters, psychopaths, and other misfits. They were calculating or compulsive liars and forgers; see the able review of their record by Joseph Wheless, *Forgery in Christianity* (New York, 1930).

One of the Fathers' most audacious and successful hoaxes certainly emits a Jewish odor. By brazen affirmation constantly repeated, they put over the claim that the wicked Romans, beginning in the time of Nero, persecuted Jesus's little lambs because the innocent creatures wanted to worship "the true God." Nothing could be more absurd historically. The Romans, aside from their typically Aryan obtuseness to the facts of race, were an admirably practical people and knew how to govern. It was their fixed policy never to interfere with the superstitions of their subjects. They impartially tolerated the most grotesque rites and obscene religions. Some of the disgusting cults that flourished among the dregs of society practiced human sacrifice, but so long as they were content to sacrifice their own members, the Romans took no action: they knew that nothing should be done to save fools from the consequences of their folly. It was only when religious zeal inspired the murder of Romans or of the subjects entitled to their protection that the Romans drew a line beyond which their toleration would not go. Even then, they punished, not the pernicious faith, but only violence and conspiracy to commit violence.

The vermin executed by Nero were Jewish terrorists from the rabble of the huge ghetto that the Jews had planted in Rome. They were accused of having set the great fire that destroyed the greater part of Rome in 64; they confessed and were executed—cruelly, it is true. When one considers the appalling outbreaks of Jewish nihilism that occurred throughout the world from time to time, whenever a christ stirred up the rabble, one sees that it is highly probable that the terrorists were guilty of the crime to which they confessed. It is true that Nero's political opponents, who were conspiring to overthrow him, preferred to accuse him of the crime; and the young egomaniac's arrogant folly, when he expropriated the devastated center of the city for an extravagant new palace, seemed to confirm the political propaganda. That was what enabled the Fathers, when they began to impose their hoax on the ignorant more than a century later, to pretend that the ferocious terrorists had been persecuted for wanting to love everybody.

When historical criticism became feasible in our eighteenth century, the Fathers' clever hoax long escaped detection: thirteen centuries of Christianity had so accustomed our people to the practice of torturing and killing men for their thoughts and superstitions that the story seemed plausible enough.

After the middle of the third century, when the successors of the extinct Romans tried desperately to shore up the crumbling empire, a few of them are known to have taken some action against Christians as such, but we do not know under what provocation and, of course, no reliance can be placed on the tales told by the Fathers. The usual policy, however, was toleration, and we know that Diocletian admitted Christians to positions of high trust and responsibility in his own palace until 303, when the Christians' piety got the better of them and they tried to murder him by burning him alive in his own bedroom. That made him angry.

At the end of the fourth century, St. Jerome, who was much better educated than most of the Fathers and probably the best of a bad lot, was the real founder of a new type of short story that became immensely popular: tales about the "martyrs" who "suffered for their faith." There is extant a letter by Jerome in which he bitterly reproves some Christians who thought that it mattered that the hero of his first fiction had never existed. That, Jerome indignantly said, was irrelevant, since his tale edified the clergy's customers, who knew no better. And Jerome went on concocting the tales with such brilliant success that he soon had a host of imitators, all trying to invent more grisly plots.

Jerome, as you see, was an accomplished theologian. He is now best remembered for his revision of the Latin text of the Bible, which he carried out with the help of kindly Jews, who hovered about him, eager to explain the mysteries of God's Word. Those Jews, we may be sure, knew what Christianity was doing for them.

In 313, Constantine and his colleague, Licinius, who were jointly fighting civil wars against rival emperors, issued the so-called Edict of Milan, which proclaimed universal toleration for all religious cults and specifically named the Christians as cults to be tolerated. The two emperors undoubtedly felt that the support of the Christian organizations would be an asset in the civil wars, and Constantine may have foreseen that they could be especially useful to him when the time came for him to turn upon and destroy his ally and brother-in-law, Licinius. Of course, as soon as Constantine was safely dead, the Fathers of the Church concocted a story that he had been privately "converted" by a childishly-imagined miracle in 312, and had been actually baptized on his death bed, so that the soul of one of the most treacherous of rulers undoubtedly flitted right up to Jesus.

Christians still like to repeat the myth about the "conversion" of Constantine and the Triumph of the True Faith. All that really happened was that the Fathers of the Church, securely established by the edict of toleration, shrewdly used their bargaining power in intrigues with the various ambitious generals who were slugging it out for the grand prize. The real triumph of their Church came only with the final victory of Theodosius in 394, when the Fathers at last got the power to use the imperial police and army to begin persecuting in earnest. Their first concern, of course, was to exterminate their Christian competitors and destroy all their gospels. Some of those gospels, however, escaped them in one way or another. That is why we now know a good deal about the competing brands of Christianity.

We Aryans still have an instinctive respect for honesty and a peculiar respect for facts. We are shocked by the hypocrisy and mendacity of the Fathers, and Christians of our race cannot bring themselves to believe those ostentatiously pious individuals were what the record shows them to have been. In justice to them, however, we should remember that their deceptions were not un-Christian. They thought—or at least it was their business to teach—that Salvationdepended on belief in certain inherently implausible tales and on conduct they approved. From that premise, it followed that any lie or trick that would induce the desired faith in the yokels was not only justified, but meritorious. As a recent writer has said, "Lying for the Lord is a normal exercise of piety."

GOD'S RACE

The Fathers of the Church got down to work near the end of

the second century, when, incidentally, the Emperor in Rome, although he bore a Roman name, was a man from northern Africa, probably of mixed Semitic and Berber ancestry, whose native language was Punic, a Semitic dialect. Their overriding purpose, to judge from the results, was to preserve and protect the Jewish connection, which the Marcionites and other "heretics" had threatened.

When the Christians started scribbling gospels around the middle of the second century, they produced a very large number, and the composition of gospels to suit the whims or ambitions of would-be holy men went on through most of the next two centuries.

From such compositions, the Fathers of the Church collected and selected their favorites, making such revisions as they deemed expedient and probably composing supplements. These they eventually put together into a small anthology, which they called a "New Testament" and thus indissolubly joined to the Jews' story book, which they called an "Old Testament." The final selection of pieces for the anthology is said to have been made in 367 by Athanasius, a particularly bull-headed holy man, who is still revered for his services in establishing the incomprehensible doctrine of a three-in-one god, of which Jesus was 33 1/3%. His authority made it thenceforth impossible to compose new gospels with any chance of implanting them in the canon he had established. Thereafter, revision of the stories about Jesus was limited to short interpolations and verbal substitutions.

The effect of this combination of "Testaments" was to impose on Christians, under pain of eternal damnation, the odd belief that, throughout the greater part of human history, the Jews were the Chosen People of a terrible and truculent god, who savagely and often capriciously afflicted the lower races when they did not cravenly submit to his Master Race. To be sure, the Jews temporarily alienated his affections when they crucified one-third of him, but Christian doctrine assures us that God will eventually "change their hearts" and they will come flocking back to Jesus.

(No one seems to worry about the morality of changing a man's mind by a psychological process that must resemble hypnosis.) In the meantime, God still loves his erring children, even though they worship only a third of him, and they must be preserved for the coming miracle of their reconciliation with daddy.

Another consequence of the Fathers' convenient doctrine is that the Jews were God's Race until a date that Christians now set at sometime between A.D. 29 and 34; thereafter, they became a religion, since Jews who have been laundered in holy water miraculously cease to be Jews.

The effect of this paradox was to make Christianity seem anti-Jewish and therefore attractive to all the goyim who resented their exploiters, while preserving for the Jews their prestige as a wonderfully "righteous" and "god-fearing" people, who had long been the intimates of the Christians' own god.

Of the many advantages that Christianity conferred on the Jews, none was greater than the privilege of masquerading as a religion and thus concealing their race. It ensured them the protection of both church and state as they rapaciously amassed wealth in mediæval Europe. One has only to ask himself what would have happened, had Chinese or Malays swarmed into the cities to set up their enclaves (ghettos) to monopolize commerce, practice usury, and control finance. Even more important, it gave them perpetual access to the seats of power.

We are told that Ferdinand and Isabella expelled the Jews from Spain in 1492. Nonsense! By that time, Jews were safely and immovably ensconced in every important segment of Spanish society as "converts." A century later, one-third of the archbishops in Spain and of the higher clergy was composed of Jews who practiced Christian rites in public and privately snickered at the stupidity of the *goyim*. Toynbee estimates that Jews formed about the same proportion of the nobility. And no one need be told that a tightly cohesive third of any organization has effective control of it. The Inquisition, to be sure, caught a few of the *marranos* who were careless or inept in their dissembling, but that served to reassure and pacify the populace.

Edward I banished the Jews from England in 1290, and we are told that England was *judenfrei* until they swarmed in (with their money-bags) under Cromwell. No one, I believe, has tried to compute how many Jews, in keeping with the immemorial tactic of their race, had themselves sprinkled with the Christians' magic water, took English names, and tried not to laugh at the British in public. And one can only guess how much the masqueraders had to do with the rise of Puritanism, a brand of Christianity that was primarily based on the "Old Testament," and the revolution that placed in power fanatics who, for example, made the observation of Christmas illegal.

Christians today wax irate when they are shown translations of certain passages in the Jewish *Talmuds*, which are said to prove how much the Jews hate Christianity. It is true that there are pejorative references to Jesus of Nazareth, who was certainly one of the christs who contributed to the composite figure in the "New Testament." No one seems to notice that the *Talmuds* speak as pejoratively of the last of the important christs in antiquity, of whose Jewish orthodoxy there can be no question. Assuming the name Bar-Kokhba, he caught thousands of the Greeks and Romans off guard and butchered them, and he carried on a guerrilla war of terrorism for almost three years until the Roman legions gave proof that Yahweh had again forgotten to send celestial re-enforcements to help His People exterminate the *goyim.* Nevertheless, the Talmudists denounce him bitterly, even changing his assumed name from Bar-Kokhba ("the son of the star") to Bar-Koziba ("the son of the liar"). The Jews hate him and asperse his memory *because he failed.*

Theologians who are concerned to show Christians how much the Jews hate their religion translate as "Christians" or "Christianity" some or all of a dozen words and phrases in Rabbinic, of no one of which is the meaning so indubitable that the Jews cannot quibble about it. It would be a waste of time to quibble with them. The Jews do feel contempt for persons who believe the

Christian tales, and they do hate our race, which is probably meant by those words and phrases which are not merely synonyms of *goyim*, their general term for races and peoples who perversely refuse to recognize the vast superiority of the Jews.

THE DOCTRINE

It remains for us to consider the consequences of Christianity, now restricting that term to the religion established by the Fathers of the Church. It has dominated and distorted the mind of our race for fifteen centuries—and it continues to do so.

We must first eliminate a potential ambiguity. Various investigations and estimates made a decade or more ago agree that about 10% to 15% of the members of our race (including about 90% of our "right wing"!) are Christians in the sense that they believe the tales in the "New Testament" to be historically true or at least accept as true the dogmas about the divinity of Jesus, etc. Although the percentages have probably been increased by the intensive promotion of Christianity in very recent years, the religion by this estimate controls only a minority of our race. When we estimate the influence of the religion in our world, however, we must not overlook *Ersatz*-Christianity. As a recent writer has pointed out, a very large number of our contemporaries, who call themselves "Liberals," "Progressives," and the like, pride themselves on having rejected the incredible tales about supernatural beings and the other trappings of Christian mythology, but retain an abiding faith in its social superstitions. As Nietzsche keenly observed, almost all of the persons who think they have freed themselves from Christianity disdain its creed but love its poison. If we include this *Ersatz*-Christianity, the Fathers of the Church established an enduring dominion over our race, to which at least 95% of our contemporaries are now subject. That is a datum to be remembered when you read the following outline.

It is obvious—obvious at least to everyone who has made even a cursory study of religion as an historical phenomenon—that Christian doctrine is a forced combination of three incompatible constituents: Zoroastrianism, Buddhism, and Judaism.

I. The first of these, which is probably the most important, is appropriately symbolized in the well-known myth that Zoroastrian priests (Magi) came to attend the nativity of Jesus. This component did come directly from Persia.

If one compares the Zoroastrian cult to the more healthy polytheisms of antiquity, one sees how bizarre and irrational it is, although Christianity has so accustomed us to it that few reflect on how pernicious is a belief in an evil god. No mental poison has been more deadly than the Zoroastrians' great innovation, the basic tenet that the world is a battlefield on which two gods contend for mastery: a good god and an evil god, each of whom would be omnipotent, were it not for the other. For no intelligible reason, these two mighty supernatural beings, one of whom had the power to create the entire universe, have to recruit puny mortals for a war that is absurd anyway, since everyone knows that in the end the good god will overcome the evil god, take him captive, and settle down to torturing him for all eternity. In the meantime, however, all men must join one or the other army and fight desperately to destroy their enemies.

This fantastic notion has given rise to what may be the most pernicious idea in human history: a holy war, fought to destroy evil. Rational men go to war to extend their own dominion over other people or sometimes to maintain it against other nations that are trying to extend their own power, in conformity with what is the fixed and unalterable condition of human life. Under the Zoroastrian-Christian system, however, whole nations are subject to periodic fits of insanity. Crazed hordes imagine themselves chosen by the good god (Yahweh & Son, Inc.) to butcher and annihilate the diabolic minions of the evil god (Satan, alias the Antichrist). Our civilization has been repeatedly brought to the verge of destruction, and some of our greatest nations have in fact doomed themselves in such self-righteous paroxysms of homicidal mania, while the Jews watched happily, reaping both enormous

profits and spiritual satisfaction from the disasters the maddened
Aryans brought on themselves in their eagerness to slaughter one another to please the god whom the Jews foisted on the Christians. A
few examples will suffice.

The Protestant Reformation (which, incidentally, was sparked
and abetted by the Jews) precipitated the Wars of Religion, in just
one of which *two-thirds* of the population of Germany perished.
The crazed Aryans, highly resolved to extirpate the devil-possessed
legions of the Antichrist in Rome or the devil-possessed legions of
the Antichrist who had revolted from Rome, irreparably impoverished our race's genetic heritage while they made wastelands of
many of the most civilized and prosperous parts of Europe and
blighted their own culture for almost two centuries. They fought
valiantly on both sides, it is true, and equally mortgaged their
lands to the Jews.

In America, the northern states effectively destroyed the
American Constitution when they invaded the southern states in
1860 to deny them the rights the colonies had jointly won in
1781. Historians, to be sure, have identified economic causes, especially the greed of northern industrialists, but the crusade
against the South was essentially a holy war to liberate savages
from slavery, although the Christians' holy book expressly sanctioned and authorized slavery (even of higher races) in passages
that the howling dervishes in the pulpits conveniently forget. The
genetic heritage of the Americans was impoverished, while Jews
naturally cheered on both sides and, after the war, flocked into the
South to batten on the devastated land and its ruined people, and
in the North consolidated political corruption.

In 1917, a sleazy shyster, whom the Jews had cleverly installed
in the White House, proclaimed a holy "war to end wars." The
witless Americans, maddened as their holy men howled for blood,
as usual, stampeded into Europe, believing in their frenzy that the
Antichrist had become incarnate in the German Kaiser and his nation. No one needs to be reminded what profits that jihad
brought to the Jews.

Again, in our own time, when the Germans tried to make themselves independent of their Jewish parasites, the Jews proclaimed a holy war for the stupid Aryans in the rest of the world and incited them to a blind rage against the satanic nation that dared not to venerate God's Holy Race. In their fratricidal delirium, the crazed Aryans not only fought with the mindless fury of a holy war, but repudiated all their own racial sense of fairness and honor, degrading themselves to the level of the Huns and the Mongols, whose perfidious savagery they had once condemned. Thus did the frenzied Aryans consummate what is likely to have been the Suicide of the West and the irreversible doom of our race. Now, after that appalling outbreak of suicidal madness, the Jews happily suck out the economic blood of the stultified Aryans everywhere, demand that the cowering white men believe even such obscene fictions as the "Holocaust," and ever more openly display their just contempt for brutes who can so easily be stampeded to their own destruction.

The Zoroastrian idea of a holy war is, of course, but one component of the poison that has made our race schizophrenic. In the intervals between the attacks of self-righteous insanity that makes them run amuck in holy wars, they do not become rational, even momentarily, but instead babble in the throes of another hallucination. They jabber about pacifism and, in a kind of *delirium tremens,* imagine they see such impossible things as "world [!] peace" cavorting just beyond their reach. So the lunatics try to run hard enough to overtake the ever-retreating phantom.

II. The Buddhist component of Christianity reached it indirectly, perhaps largely through the Essenes, and was considerably adulterated on the way.

The essential element is the gloomy and cowardly doctrine that human life is not worthwhile—that all the things dear to healthy men, such as health, strength, sexual love, beauty, culture, learning, intelligence, wealth, and even individuality, are merely "vanity of vanities," empty illusions. (Christianity, of course, makes them *evil* illusions.) The proper attitude is that of a man hopelessly diseased and in pain: he longs for death. The cult, however, denies us a rational release from our misery in suicide, which it says is impossible, since some kind of ghost will survive the death of the body. What we can and should do, however, is to refrain absolutely from sexual intercourse, so that we will not engender fresh links in the chain of misery that is life on earth. Furthermore, some mysterious supernatural power has ordained that we can aquire postmortem benefits for our souls by frustrating all the desires that healthy men feel, and even greater rewards by inflicting physical pain on ourselves. There is a heavenly bookkeeping machine which makes entries to our credit whenever we make ourselves suffer pain and enters debits against us whenever we yield to temptation and enjoy something, whether it be a woman's love, the beauty of great art, the intellectual exhilaration of discovering a fact of nature, or any other pleasure, The balance of our account when we die determines the future of the soul. (Buddhism assumes that that future is reincarnation, but Christianity perverts and degrades that not implausible myth by adding the Zoroastrian notion of a final judgement: after our only life on earth, an angel will read the computer's print-out and, if the amount of our debts has made us insolvent, will pitchfork us into Hell, where our impalpable and intangible souls will be roasted on hot coals and suffer all other imaginable.bodily torments for all eternity—not a year or a century or a millenium or a billion years, but all the eternity of *infinite* time!)

From this notion, corrupted by the addition of some of the sexual obsessions that seem to be an innate part of the Jews' racial mentality, Christianity proclaimed the doctrine of race suicide for our people. Allowance was made, of course, for the men who did not have the fortitude to castrate themselves or otherwise frustrate the instincts of healthy men, but by a monstrously obscene transvaluation of rational values, disease was called "health" and strength was called "weakness." Men too "weak" to be eunuchs were permitted the "sin" of having offspring to provide customers for the next generation of shamans, but it was the will of Christianity's fearful god that our race be as celibate as possible. For fifteen centuries, enormous numbers of male Aryans were herded into the church, both as priests and as monastics, to blight their masculinity with homosexuality and perversion, mitigated only by the chance of furtive adulteries. And enormous numbers of our women were imprisoned in convents to become psychopathic or practice secret abortions.

It may seem to us now that the institutions for race suicide attracted, as today, only the misfits, the physically or psychically defective, who should always be prevented, so far as possible, from reproducing themselves. To some extent that was true, but for reasons which are historically obvious, some of the best blood of our race was irretrievably lost in mad efforts to curry favor with the god the Jews had exported to us. For century after century, the sexual superstitions of Christianity systematically weakened and impoverished our race. The Jews could have invented nothing better for their purposes.

The Jews despise our race for its gullibility, venality, and the debility of its racial instincts, but they also hate us, fearing that we may never become perfectly docile livestock on their world-wide plantation. The Jewish attitude toward us was somewhat indiscreetly revealed in English by Theodore Kaufmann in his *Germany Must Perish!* (Newark, 1941; recently reprinted by Liberty Bell Publications). Kaufmann demanded that every man, woman, and child in Germany be surgically sterilized to exterminate a people that had been guilty of insubordination to God's Race. The rabid Jew realized that it would be premature to urge similar treatment of the Aryans in other nations, and, as things turned out, it proved not to be feasible to carry out the Jewish plan even in Germany at that time. In the United States and other countries once ruled by our race, the same end is to be achieved more gradually by mongrelization and the incitation of a sexual mania, which, incidentally, is a revival of the early Christian sects that taught that Jesus had revealed that the only road to Salvation lay in male homosexuality or, conversely, in unlimited promiscuity and the abolition of families to liberate females for intense and indiscriminate copulation *ad libitum*.

Another derivative of the Buddhistic negation of the values of human life was also distorted and polluted in transmission. It is the mawkish sentimentality, the fatuous self-abasement, and the total repudiation of reason that appears in the so-called Sermon on the Mount, a concentrated poison for which Christians still have a morbid appetite. It is the essence of what Nietzsche called the "slave morality"—the morality of persons so degenerate or diseased that they are fit only for slavery. It is the negation of life itself. Glory is reserved for the meek and humble who take a masochistic delight in being trampled upon. They must be so abject and feeble-minded that they love their enemies. The dregs of human society are the "salt of the earth," and they are promised the joy of seeing their betters suffer, when "the last shall be made first." Nothing that makes life worth living is not evil, and the idiots are exhorted, "take no thought for your life"—indeed, to abstain totally from rational thought. The ideal mentality for Christians is that of vegetables, but since it is not quite feasible to attain that blessed state, Christians take pride in proclaiming they are sheep, the most stupid of all mammals, incapable of defending themselves, living only to feed, multiply, and be fleeced periodically. Christians even like to depict themselves as lambs that stare uncomprehendingly at the world about them. They recite with unction psalms that aver that they are mindless and will-less sheep, confident that the Jews' god will herd them to "green pastures beside still waters," where they may lie down to chew their cud in uninterrupted bliss.

Commanded to "take no thought for the morrow," but to have bird-brains and be "like the fowls of the air" that "sow not, neither do they reap," relying on their "heavenly Father" to feed them, Christians who actually believed the Drivel on the Mount would, if sufficiently numerous, simply precipitate the total breakdown of any civilized or even barbarous society—and would not even grow pelts for the Jews to fleece. Perhaps it is fortunate that Christians like to befuddle themselves with sentimental verbiage they do not understand and holy "mysteries" which they can contemplate with ovine incomprehension.

Christianity, indeed, enjoins pride in imbecility. Its god became incarnate to "make folly of the wisdom of this world." Its votaries must have an unthinking faith in an incomprehensible farrago of patently false statements. To abjure the use of reason is the only path to Salvation and the animal-like joys of eternal idleness in Heaven. Learning and wisdom must be despised. Every effort of human reason to understand the world in which we live is a sin, an affront to a god who has given us the perfect model of righteous wisdom in an oyster.

The repudiation of reason and sanity was a particularly deadly poison to our race, which, as several writers on ethnology have recently pointed out, has in some of its members, at least, an innate capacity for the objective and philosophical thought by which alone our race attained a partial control over the forces of nature and the power to defend itself by imposing its will on other races.

This power, which we have now fatuously surrendered, was won for us slowly and painfully by the often heroic efforts of a few men and only over the frantic opposition of the Christian witch doctors. The debased superstition that insanely exalts ignorance over knowledge and faith over reason repressed and deformed for many centuries our race's unique capacity for a rational and mighty civilization.

III. Students of religion commonly deny originality to the Jews, because all of the cosmogonic tales in the "Old Testament" were lifted from the mythologies of more civilized peoples, especially the Babylonians, and only superficially Judaized. They thus overlook or ignore what is unique in the religion professed by the Jews, especially after they had the brilliant idea of converting their religion from a henotheism to a monotheism to imitate and appropriate the monotheism of Greek Stoicism.

It is true that the peculiarities of Jewish religion are not mere superstitions, such as other races may ignorantly accept, but spring from their innate certainty that their race is immeasurably and categorically superior to all others, an absolute certainty that is independent of any mythological explanation of it they may give to others or even to themselves. That poses a biological problem which we cannot consider here but we must notice the specifically Jewish element that went into the Christian amalgam.

The Jews are, by nature, a proletarian people. It is a matter of common observation that when they invade a country, they infiltrate every prosperous city and set up their ghettos, in which they huddle together, like ants in their anthill, bees in the hive, or termites in their nest. Everyone has noticed that when a Jew or a few Jews associate with *goyim*, they successfully simulate the manners and culture of the people among whom they have planted themselves; but when Jews become a majority in any place, from a single room to a city, they become a swarm, a buzzing synagogue, an unmistakable alien species.

Some Jews, of course, become immensely wealthy, but they remain parts of the international swarm. According to a despatch in *Sunday Chronicle* (the official Jewish newspaper in London), January 2, 1938, the Jews, incensed that the Germans should dare to be disrespectful to God's Master Race, held a meeting near Geneva at which Jewish financiers promptly contributed 500,000,000 pounds to a fund to put the German *goyim* back in their place. I invite the reader, particularly if he has had some experience of "right-wing" activities in Europe, the United States, or other white nations, to estimate the chances that Aryan financiers would have contributed in 1938 a fund of $2,433,250,000 for the preservation *of* their race or would today contribute a proportionally larger sum of dollars—say one hundred billion dollars, to keep the estimate modest. If the reader thinks such a contribution unlikely, he has a measure of the difference between the Jewish race and our own. The wealthy Jew remains a part of his anthill, hive, or nest. He remains, in effect, merely a detached limb of his species.

This may explain what would otherwise seem unbelievable. The Jews, from the wealthiest to the poorest, seem instinctively to feel the envy and malice, the festering hatred, that we associate with the multi-racial dregs of the populace in large cities. This naturally leads to a lust for destruction, a psychopathic urge to defile and obliterate the objects of its malignant envy. And when the urge is no longer restrained by prudence, it becomes sheer insanity. The nihilism of the race was clearly shown, for example, in the Jewish outbreak in Cyrenaica in 117. In the capital city of that prosperous province of the Roman Empire, the Jews, naturally, had planted a huge ghetto and they undoubtedly controlled a large part of the trade on which the province's prosperity depended. Many Jews must have been among the wealthiest inhabitants. But nevertheless, the race's innate nihilism was excited by a christ, who announced the glad tidings that Yahweh had said that the time had come to put the *goyim* in their place. Filled with a zeal for righteousness, the Jewish swarm caught the stupidly complacent Greeks and Romans off their guard and slaughtered more than 200,000 men and women in various ingenious ways, such as sawing off their hands and feet and ripping out their intestines while they were still alive. God's People then destroyed all the property in the city (including their own!), apparently by burning the city and then leveling to the ground such walls are remained standing. They then rushed out into the countryside to destroy the villages and uproot the crops. That done, the demented horde descended on Egypt, leaving behind them only a scorched desert and dismembered corpses.

This nihilism was vividly expressed in the Christians' favorite horror story, the Jewish apocalypse that the Fathers of the Church selected for inclusion in their appendix to the "Old Testament." The wild phantasmagoria describes in loving detail all the disasters and torments with which Jesus will afflict and destroy the civilized peoples of the earth when he returns in glory from the clouds with a squad of sadistic angels. One should note the characteristic provision that *goyim* are not to be merely killed outright: they are to be made to suffer exquisite agonies for five months first. But what Lloyd Graham has properly called the "diabolical savagery" of the Jew god is not satisfied with exterminating all the *goyim* with every kind of torture a lurid imagination could invent. He destroys the land, the mountains, the sea, the whole earth; he destroys the sun and the moon; and he rolls up the heavens like a scroll, presumably including even the most remote galaxies. Everything is annihilated. And all this for the sake of Jesus's pets, an elite of 144,000 male Jews who despise women. For these, to be sure, he creates a New Jerusalem, in which they will loaf happily for a thousand years.

The Jews spiced Christianity with their rancor and nihilism. As Maurice Samuels said, with laudable candor, "*We, the Jews, we, the destroyers, will remain the destroyers for ever.... We will forever destroy because we need a world of our own, a God-world.*" And by inventing Christianity, they estopped credulous *goyim* from inquiring what kind of god their race created for itself.

ALL THIS, AND HELL TOO!

Christians like to prate about how much their bundle of irreconcilable superstitions has done for us. Well, it first gave our race schizophrenia and has now given it a suicidal mania.

It was bad enough when the Christians were under the spell of the Zoroastrian notion that the biological reality of race can be charmed away by a kind of magic called "conversion." They hired missionaries to pester everyone else in the world, from the highly civilized Chinese to the uncivilizable anthropoids in Africa. They believed that the aliens could be transformed into the equivalent of white Europeans, if they were dunked in holy water by a licensed practitioner. For the dunking, the *Ersatz*-Christians substitute "education," which they think a much more powerful kind of magic. But from this silly idea we have now progressed to a more baneful kind of unreason.

The Buddhist notion of equality, perverted by the proletarian malice of the Jews, has become the fanatical faith of 95% of our race today. In a recent article, Revilo P. Oliver observed that our "intellectuals," who disdain the Christian fairy tales about Jesus and preen themselves on being atheists or, at least, agnostics, nevertheless "cling to the morbid hatred of superiority that makes Christians dote on whatever is lowly, inferior, irrational, debased, deformed, and degenerate." Both groups hold frantically to the dogma of the "equality of all races" (except, of course, the vastly superior race of the "Old Testament"), and equally believe that moral excellence is evinced by faith in what daily experience shows to be patently preposterous. And when they can no longer close their eyes to shut out the real world, they have a solution. The various races (except God's People) must be *made* equal, must be reduced to the lowest common denominator of anthropoids. And so we come to the breathtaking transvaluation that is the dominant creed of our time: the Aryans, by virtue of the superiority they have shown in the past, are a vastly inferior race. They are burdened by the horrible guilt of not having committed suicide, a guilt they can expiate only by taxing themselves to hire their enemies to destroy them. They must love their enemies, but hate their own children. Especially in once-great Britain and the United States, the crazed whites are not only subsidizing the proliferation of their vermin and legislating to inhibit the reproduction of their own kind, but are importing from all the world hordes of their biological enemies to destroy their posterity. Especially in the United States, they condemn their own children to the most degrading association with savages in their "integrated" schools. American parents evidently feel a "spiritual" satisfaction when their own children—or, at least, their neighbors' children—are beaten, raped, and mutilated by the sub-humans. And British parents, who, if still prosperous, can protect their children from physical, though not from mental, squalor, abhor as wicked "racists" the few individuals who think their race is fit to survive. An honest psychiatrist (there are a few) could perhaps determine what weird mixture of sadism and masochism has been inculcated into the minds of our people.

Everywhere, the Christianized Aryans (including those who imagine they are not Christians) evidently agree that their race must be stamped out for the comfort of niggers and the joy of Jews.

What more could the Jews want?

HOW THE JEWS HATE CHRISTIANITY!

The Jews no longer make a serious effort to maintain the pretense of an antipathy to Christianity. It is true that once in a while they protest the public display of Christian symbols, such as the cross. But that merely spices their joke. When they erect a thirty-foot "menorah" in front of the White House to remind their tenant who owns the place, the cowed Christians never think of protesting.

Oliver, in his fairly well-known book, *Christianity and the Survival of the West*, claimed that it was a "Western" religion, but he had to base his argument on what had to be added to the doctrine to make it acceptable to the Nordic peoples after the collapse of the rotted Empire that had once been Roman. And in the postscript to his second edition, he admitted that the religion had been stripped of those additions and was being reduced to the superstition of the early Christian sects that either excluded non-Jews or admitted them only to the status of "whining dogs," which they could attain by having themselves mutilated sexually, observing the Jewish taboos, and obeying their God-like masters.

The holiness of the Jews is now an established dogma, especially among the *Ersatz*-Christians. A friend of mine, who is now in the United States, wrote to presidents of various colleges and universities that were trying to make a few extra bucks by offering courses to prove the "truth" of the Jews' hoax about the "six million" of God's People that the Germans are supposed to have "exterminated" by a procedure that is physically impossible. He had several very nasty replies from chief diploma-salesmen who intimated that he, who holds a Ph.D. in modern history, should be locked up for his "ignorance." I have seen copies of some of those letters. The irate prexies were clearly endorsing their own faith. They knew that Jews could not lie, just as their grandfathers had *known* that Jesus walked on water and held a picnic that was the least expensive fish-fry in history. It boots not to inquire how much of their grandfathers' faith or their own was founded on actual belief in what "everybody believes" and how much was based on a calculation that it would not be remunerative to doubt what "everybody knows." The results are the same. Woe to him who questions any tale told by the "righteous" race.

By this time, everyone must know that the Jews have acquired a working control of all the media of communication: the press, the radio, the boob-tube, and the publication of widely-distributed books. If the Jews had the slightest animus against the Christian religion, they would use these powerful weapons to destroy it. Instead, the real opponents of Christianity, the rational atheists, are systematically and totally excluded from the "media." No newspaper, no widely distributed periodical, dares print one of their articles or even to mention them without derision. No radio or television station will admit they exist, and even if they telephone on "call in" programs, they are shut off before their first significant word reaches the antenna. To get into print, they must organize their own starveling publishing companies to issue books or periodicals that are very expensive because only a few copies can be printed for a tiny audience that cannot be increased because no newspaper or radio could be hired to advertise such publications at any price. The managers, even if not Jews, prudently assume that atheists, who would substitute facts and reason for fairy tales and blind faith in "spiritual values," are very wicked, and they regret that it is not currently feasible to burn them at the stake. If the Jews had an antipathy to Christianity, they could change that attitude overnight with a few directives to their hirelings, and they could make the religion ludicrous in the eyes of the majority within a year or two. The boobs simply absorb what they are told.

The Jew-controlled "media" constantly and systematically lavish free publicity on the Christian churches and especially on the salvation-hucksters. The æther is clamorous with the bellowing and wheedling of "evangelists," who are plying their trade and raking in money

from everyone whose emotions can be stirred by their crude rheto-
ric. Even the richest of the gospel-businesses receive much of their
advertising free; when they do have to pay, they are given much
reduced rates. The "media" religiously report miracles that could
have happened only East of the Sun and West of the Moon. And
they religiously assume that the Christian shamans are so holy they
must "mean well," even when they are caught in embezzlement or
fraud.

I hear that about half a dozen white preachers, more or less
subtly "racist" or even anti-Jewish, are allowed to speak (for a fee) over
some of the smaller radio stations in the United States, provided, of
course, that they do no more than furtively intimate what they mean
on racial subjects. If they really annoyed the Jews, they would be shut up
on some pretext or other. The "evangelists" who make it to the big time
(an annual take of ten million dollars or more) all make it clear that a
Christian's first obligation is to adore God's People.

Furthermore, although the Christians and some sociologists
miss the point, the "media" are industriously creating the atmosphere most propitious to a recrudescence of Christianity. The religion
grew in the decaying Roman Empire with the growth of universal unreason: it had to compete only with other superstitions so gross that
historians are perplexed when asked to decide which was the most
grotesque. The "media" are today stridently promoting every kind of
hokum that encourages belief in the supernatural. They not only advertise, but even hire "psychics," "seers," astrologers, and mystery
mongers who spin tall tales about haunted houses, weekends on "flying saucers," "Bermuda Triangles," and similar boob-bait. All the ad-
epts of such cults are potential customers for the Christian fakirs.
When, for example, a man begins to practice the self-hypnosis called
"transcendental meditation," he will soon ripen himself for an access
of Faith. When he has so blunted his intelligence that he can believe
that the planets, while obeying the law of gravitation with mathematical precision, took the trouble to portend his future, he can
soon believe in the Second Coming and the End of Time.

I have seen no statistics that indicate how greatly the percentage of belief in the theological myths of Christianity has been increased by the Jews' strenuous promotion of it, but observe that in the United States clowns who are competing for the job of doing the Jews' work in the White House now think it good advertising to call for a "spiritual rebirth" and to claim that they have been laundered in "the blood of the Lamb" and have got themselves "born again." A candidate's chances of winning the popularity-contest now seem to be increased by evidence that he either is a liar or has hallucinations.

The Jews love Christianity. Why shouldn't they? The most stupendous of their hoaxes has become their most deadly weapon against us.

THE OLD ACTOR
AND THE JEWS

'I swear by Almighty God to uphold the right of the Bandit State of Israel to raid the American Treasury!'

THE OLD ACTOR AND THE JEWS

In the July issue of *Liberty Bell,* there appeared a letter from a gentleman from Michigan who identified himself as a conservative and a racialist, and, to the dismay of this observer, put forth the same, tired old Birch Society slogans about electing a "conservative" Congress and how Ronald Reagan would be "the best bet".

The Old Actor and the Jews was (under the by-line "By an Observer in Hollywood") Dr. Oliver's contribution to, and was first published in, *Liberty Bell* for September 1980. The 'letter from a gentleman in Michigan' Dr. Oliver refers to on this page is reproduced at the end of this article.

He capped his comments with the incredible statement that Reagan, though pro-Israel now, would somehow switch after the election! I had thought that no one who referred to himself as a "racialist" would have any illusions about this dyed-in-the-wool Hollywood phoney, but it seems that here and there, are a few who are still not immune from the potentially fatal disease of wishful thinking. Therefore, I would like to enlighten them regarding this packaged product of Hollywood's Jewish movie moguls.

It is utterly baffling to comprehend how any intellectually honest person could entertain any illusions whatsoever after viewing on television the kosher horror show called the Republican National Convention. The first night's agenda was given to "entertainment" by a number of Hollywood "celebrities" provided by a close Reagan friend, California Lt. Governor Mike Curb, who, up until two years ago, was a Hollywood record executive producing strident rock'n'roll records to destroy the minds and morals of America's youth with its jungle beat. Curb also managed several drug-soaked rock groups, one of which was "The Eagles", whose lead singer openly lived with Ronald Reagan's youngest daughter for a number of years.

No patriot viewing this show could have suppressed feelings of loathing and revulsion as a nearly all-White crowd of conventioneers, mostly middle-aged American, enthusiastically clapped along to the rhythm as six negroes and negresses howled out African blues at them from the podium. A few in the crowd did not clap but instead looked at each other and grinned weakly. The following night, this same mob of hat-wearing, horn-blowing hypocrites gave a STANDING OVATION, first to mulatto Benjamin Hooks of the NAACP, who harangued them to integrate faster, and then to the Arch-Jew Henry Kissinger! All of the above speakers and "entertainers" had been hand-picked by the Reagan staff. Doubtless the thousands of perspiring poltroons would have cheered Idi Amin and Meyer Lansky had Ronnie said it was ok!

A look at Ronald Reagan's roots is required to get a better picture of the real man behind the grin and the greasepaint. In his autobiography titled "Where's The Rest Of Me?", Reagan's description of his father proves most illuminating. When D.W. Griffith's great epic "Birth Of A Nation" came to the Reagans' home town, old Jack Reagan refused to let any member of his family see it! "It deals with the Ku Klux Klan against the colored folks and I'm damned if anyone in this family is goin' to see it!" he exclaimed. Ronnie writes that his was the only family in town who did not view the film. On another occasion, when the elder Reagan checked into a hotel, the clerk informed him that he would enjoy his stay because the hotel didn't allow Jews to stay there. "Well, I'm a Catholic, and if you won't take Jews you won't take me either!", thundered the old radical, who thereupon stalked out and spent the rest of that snowy winter's night in his car! Is it any wonder that Ronnie is what he is, with a masochistic lunatic like that for a father?

Ronald Reagan came to Hollywood in 1936 and began a forgettable film career in the stables of the Jewish Warner Brothers. His hereditary radical bent soon manifested itself and he became enmeshed in Red and Pink Hollywood front groups that the Jews were then setting up. The story of these front groups and how the Jewish movie moguls Louis B. Mayer, Barney Balaban, Darryl Zanuck, Herry Cohn, Adolph Zuckor, and Jack Warner controlled them as well as setting up the kosher-conservative *opposition* to the Reds is extensively documented by the late, great investigative researcher *Myron C. Fagan in his reports titled Moscow Over Hollywood* (1948), *Documentation Of The Red Stars Over Hollywood* (1961), and *Red Stars Over Broadway* (1954), as well as the monthly bulletins of his Cinema Educational Guild.

Ronald Reagan boasts in his autobiography that as president of the Screen Actors Guild, both in his days as Red-fronter and a kosher conservative, he worked closely with the Jewish moguls, especially with Dore Shary, the late unlamented head of the Anti-Defamation League of B'nai B'rith. He also supported the candidacy of James Roosevelt for Governor of California in 1950. Reagan was a member of United World Federalists from 1946 to AT LEAST 1959, and considering that he boasts in his book that he had been an "anti-communist" since 1950, that is quite a feat! He was also, as of 1962, on the advisory council of the American

Veterans Committee, which was exposed in 1958 as a communist front by the California Senate Un-American Activities Committee.

Reagan's first wife, Jane Wyman, divorced him in 1948 because his Red activities became too much for her. Reagan's present wife, Nancy Davis, is more compatible, her mother being the late Edith Luckett, a personal friend of Eleanor Roosevelt. Nancy shares her mother's taste for radicalism, though she prefers to stay in the background.

When Reagan first ran for Governor of California in 1966, his most enthusiastic backers included the following big-money Jews: mogul Jack Warner, industrialist Taft Schreiber, and shady millionaire Marco Hellman. In 1967, just after the so-called "Six Day War," Reagan was one of the featured speakers at a gala, star-studded "Israel Victory Rally" at the Hollywood Bowl. This observer recalls watching a news conference held at the time wherein Reagan was asked if his attendance at the rally would have a negative impression with the Arab states. Reagan replied with a smirk, "If there is, it'll be too bad." I would ask the gentleman who wrote the recent pro-Reagan letter to *Liberty Bell* what sentiments like these (which Reagan has never deviated from) bode for the peace of the Near East in a Reagan presidency?

A very revealing article appeared in the August 1st, 1980, issue of the *Wall Street Journal* about a very lucrative land deal made by Reagan in 1968 concerning the sale and subsequent resale of a parcel of land in Malibu, California, which was handled for Reagan by his wealthy Jewish trustee Jules Stein and which netted Reagan a substantial profit under questionable circumstances. It was Stein who introduced Reagan to Oppenheimer Associates of Kansas City, relatives of Stein's, who were able to get Reagan a generous tax shelter. The *Journal* article was subsequently picked up and amplified upon by the Los Angeles *Herald Examiner* for August 2nd.

In 1973 Reagan was the recipient of an award from the "Bonds for Israel Drive" in Los Angeles. The award was personally presented to him by Jew Eugene Wyman, then a top official in the Democratic Party! Reagan appointed Rockefeller Jew Caspar Weinberger to be California finance director, and has indicated that Weinberger will be Treasury Secretary in a Reagan presidency, with Jew Milton Friedman of Chicago to be his Chairman of Economic Advisers. And let no one be surprised if Henry Kissinger, whom Reagan lavishly praised as Secretary of State, ends up back in Washington under the old actor, probably as U.N. Ambassador. And the real Reagan is also known to another influential Jew, labor columnist Victor Riesel, who wrote of Reagan, "He's basically a liberal". Quite an understatement.

The above has been merely a capsule review of Ronald Reagan the man, as opposed to Ronald Reagan, the product of the Hollywood myth-making factory and the Zionist media. But to this observer, Reagan's whole career is summed up in the televised events on the night of his recent presidential nomination. Nancy Reagan entered the front row waving and smiling. Applauding her there were a negress and that sleazy, fat "Jewish" "lady"—Elizabeth Taylor. Nancy enthusiastically kissed both the negress and Liz Taylor and seated herself between them. The camera then focused on Ronnie accepting the cheers of the throng. Briefly, the camera cut away to show Henry Kissinger smiling and applauding. Reagan than gives his acceptance speech, mentioning our "gallant little ally, Israel" (to thunderous applause from the crazy *Goyim*), then, at the finale of the speech he speaks glowingly about how America is a "magnet of freedom" for the Asian boat people, the Cubans, and the Haitians. At this point, he chokes with emotion and cannot continue. The crowd roars, and one can almost see the ghosts of Jack Warner, Louis B. Mayer, and that black Irishman Jack Reagan chortling with glee.

I believe that all those film critics who panned Ronald Reagan's performances in epics such as "Bedtime for Bonzo" and "Hellcats of the Navy" have erred grievously. For the past twenty years he has been putting on an academy-award winning performance that would put Sir Laurence Olivier to shame!

Let the alarm sound! In this sly old actor, the Elders of Zion have a Trojan Horse who (while mouthing patriotic clichés) will finish off what remains of our freedoms and will quite probably take us into a nuclear Armageddon on behalf of the bastard state to which his masters owe their allegiance !

* * * * *

Dear Mr. Dietz   5 May 1980

This election year affords conservatives and racialists an opportunity unlike any other, even '76. In '76 we were not so close to utter catastrophe as we are now. Which is why I am actively working in the Reagan campaign. I realize Reagan is far from perfect, yet there is no other choice. Even Nixon, crook that he was, was no match for Carter and his ineptness. At the height of "Watergate," things had not eroded to the point they are at now. I am also working to elect good men to Congress, because Congress is the key to winning back lost and threatened freedoms. It would be nice to have a right wing President and Congress for a change! In a recent appearance, Reagan was jeered by a mostly black audience, when he exclaimed, "If I were in favor of war, I'd declare one on you jokers." RONALD REAGAN IS OUR BEST BET. I am aware that Reagan is pro-Israel, but I am betting he'll reverse his stand after election.

Sincerely, R.G.B., Michigan.

(Ed. Comment: Sorry, R.G.B., but we simply cannot share your enthusiasm for either Reagan or for conservative congressmen. Once elected, they'll soon find out from which direction the wind is blowing and will follow the party line as prescribed by the Jew manipulators behind the scene, or else. Yes, "conservative" and "democratic" talk is music to the ears of the "masses of asses", but, have you asked "conservative" Reagan or your "conservative" would-be Congressmen what they intend to do about the Federal Reserve Act—the main tool of enslavement to the international Jew bankers—about Jew catch-as-catch-can capitalism and support for the bandit state Israel? Our suggestion: save your breath and your efforts. Neither of these "institutions" is likely to be attacked by either "conservative" Reagan or "conservative" Congressmen. Once in office, they'll go right on playing the "left-wing right-wing", "democratic republican", "two-party system" of deception.)

A
Book
Review

by

Revilo P. Oliver

Western Man Must
Assert Himself or Perish

To answer the question posed in the title of his book, William Gayley Simpson has condensed into 762 closely-printed pages the experience, the research, and the philosophical thought of a lifetime. He is now 87, and he began to write the present book 35 years ago. It is a veritable encyclopedia of everything that is directly pertinent to our race's position in the world today and our problematic future.

The book is unique. What makes it so cogent is that it is both an intellectual autobiography and a synoptic treatise. The reader, even if he begins with conditioned reflexes that make him hostile to his own race, can follow, step by step, the process by which reason and intellectual honesty forced Mr. Simpson to his conclusions.

His work may also be taken symbolically as an epitome or recapitulation of the course of Western civilization, which likewise began with the Christian faith of the Dark Ages and has now brought us to the point where we can no longer refuse to face the grim realities of the world in which we must either live or perish.

Born in 1892 in an educated but sternly Christian family, Mr. Simpson was graduated, *magna cum laude*, from a highly reputed theological seminary. He became a minister, and, unlike most clergymen, had a religious faith so ardent that, instead of regarding some of the most striking parts of Christian doctrine as convenient

This review of *Which Way, Western Man?* was Dr. Oliver's contribution to, and was published with the author's permission in, Liberty Bell for September 1980. It was first written for, and published in, *National Vanguard*, October 1979.

subjects for professional oratory, he, like St. Francis, tried to live in logical conformity with them.

Our race, like some others, has a strain of sentiment that can be excited by the idea of *tapas*, the mirific virtue and spiritual power produced by austerity, self-sacrifice, and self-mortification. The notion of *tapas* was a fundamental part of Aryan religions from India to Scandinavia, and it was not remarkable that our ancestors, accustomed to venerate Odin, a god who, by an act of supreme self-sacrifice, hanged himself on the great world-tree so that he might arise from the dead, should have accepted the cult of a god who had himself crucified and likewise rose from the dead; nor that, so long as they believed in their new religion, they held to the faith that spiritual excellence could be attained by inflicting degradation and pain on oneself. St. Francis was merely one of the many who had the fortitude to live up to that faith.

Mr. Simpson, too, tried to carry the religion to its practical consequences, but, unlike St. Francis, he did not lapse into a kind of amiable insanity. He learned from his dolorous experience that reality is not to be denied and that magic is either clever trickery or an hallucination. He realized that there was no way in which he "could be an honest man and remain a minister."

Innumerable clerics, even in the darkest ages of Faith, found their creed unbelievable, but either took refuge in the Medæval aphorism, *"populus vult decipi, ergo decipiatur"* ["the people want to be deceived, therefore let them be deceived" —Ed.], or, if not without honesty, accepted Cardinal Dubois's celebrated dictum that God is a bogey that must be brandished in order to scare the masses into some semblance of civilized behavior. But since the forced unity of Christendom was effectively broken in the sixteenth century, not a few clergymen have publicly denounced the religion to which they gave assent in their youth.

One of them, the first great apostate of the nineteenth century, the Reverend Mr. Robert Taylor, disregarded the pleas of his ecclesiastical superiors and friends, who urged him not to ruin a promising career in the Church, in which his talents destined him for high office, by publishing facts that could only disturb the placid credulity or proletarian fanaticism of the lower classes. His *Diegesis* (1829), an historical investigation of Christianity and its relation to earlier religions, is a work of great learning and incisive scholarship, the more impressive today since many of the Christian gospels were still unknown when he wrote and he had at his disposal only a small fraction of the copious information about other early religions that subsequent discovery and research have now made available.

Taylor perceived that the early Jews, with the duplicity that is their outstanding racial characteristic, "plagiarized the religious legends of the nations among whom their characteristic idleness and inferiority of understanding caused them to be vagabonds; and pretended that the furtive patchwork was a system of theology intended by heaven for their exclusive benefit." Under the cover of that brazen pretense, the Jews insinuated themselves into every nation whose prosperity they wished to exploit. Their migratory bands of "commercial, speculating thieves" were ever "ready to play into and keep up any religious farce that might serve to invest them with an imaginary sanctity of character and increase their influence over the minds of the majority, whose good nature and ignorance in all ages and countries is but ever too ready to subscribe the claims thus made upon it."

Taylor was not really a precursor of Nietzsche, but he did identify the greatest of the innumerable hoaxes by which the Self-Chosen People have throughout history imposed on the gullible *goyim* and thus raised themselves from a miserable tribe of despicable barbarians, practicing primitive taboos and grotesque sexual mutilations, to the most formidable power in the world today.

Taylor differs from other prominent apostates and most of their contemporary deists and atheists, who inclined to esteem the Jews as enemies of Christianity. The others were taken in by another great hoax, the endless whining by the Jews that they were "persecuted" during the Middle Ages, when the Church gave them a virtual monopoly of usury, sorcery, and international trade; when they spun financial webs about kings and noblemen and most rulers were attended by skilled Jewish physicians, always spies and potentially executioners; when the Jews exercised such political, intellectual, and economic power that, as Bernard S. Bachrach has shown in his *Early Medieval Jewish Policy in Western Europe* (University of Minnesota, 1977), out of the 98 rulers whose policies he examines in detail, 88 (including Charlemagne) had to pursue pro-Jewish policies, while the ten who attempted to oppose the aliens in their domains went down to failure in one way or another; when the Jews could usually count on royal or ecclesiastical protection whenever their depredations excited local resentment so strong that it became violent; when even the famous and belated expulsion of Jews from England and Spain overlooked those who thought it worth while to have themselves sprinkled with holy water; and when the Church itself was a great ladder by which marranos climbed to power and wealth, laughing among themselves at the stupidity of the *goyim* who imagined that a Jew could be transmuted by a few drops of magic fluid.

I therefore exempt Taylor from the generalizations about apostates I shall make below. His was a vigorous and incisive mind, and I am unwilling to guess how much of Christian doctrine he unwittingly retained.

Almost all of the apostates and anti-Christians of recent centuries exemplify the operation of what may be called the law of cultural residues. In all civilized societies, when a long-established and generally accepted belief is found to be incredible, good minds abandon it, but they commonly retain derivative beliefs that were originally deduced from the creed they have rejected and logically must depend on it. Thus it happened that modern enemies of Christianity rejected the mythology, but uncritically retained faith in the social superstitions derived from it—a faith which they oddly call rational but hold with a religious fervor.

They laugh at the silly story about Adam and his spare rib, but they continue to believe in a "human race" descended from a single pair of ancestors and hence in a "brotherhood of man." They speak of "all mankind," giving to the term an unctuous and mystic meaning with which they do not invest corresponding terms, such as "all marsupials" or "all ungulates." They prate about the "rights of man," although a moment's thought should suffice to show that, in the absence of a decree from a supernatural monarch, there can be no rights other than those which the citizens of a stable and homogeneous society have, by covenant or established custom, bestowed on themselves; and that while the citizens may show kindness to aliens, slaves, and dogs, such beings obviously can have no rights.

They do not believe that one-third of a god became incarnate in the most squalid region on earth to associate with illiterate peasants, harangue the rabble of a barbarian race, and magically exalt the ignorant and uncouth to "make folly of the wisdom of this world," so that "the last shall be first"—that they do not believe, but they cling to the morbid hatred of superiority that makes Christians dote on whatever is lowly, inferior, irrational, debased, deformed, and degenerate.

They gabble about the "sanctity of human life"—especially the vilest forms of it—without reflecting that it takes a god to make something sacred. And they frantically agitate for a universal "equality" that can be attained only by reducing all human beings to the level of the lowest, evidently unaware that they are merely echoing the Christians' oft-expressed yearning to become sheep (the most stupid of all mammals) herded by a good shepherd, which is implicit in all the tales of the New Testament.

Although the "Liberal" and Marxist cults have doctrinal differences as great as those that separate Lutherans from Baptists, they are basically the same superstition, and whether or not we should call them religions depends on whether we restrict the word to belief in supernatural persons or extend it to include all forms of blind faith based on emotional excitement instead of observed facts and reason.

When those "atheistic" cults scream out their hatred of "Fascists" and "Nazis," they obviously must believe that those wicked persons are possessed of the Devil and should therefore be exterminated to promote holiness and love. And when they see "racists," who impiously substitute fact and reason for unthinking faith in approved fairy stories, their lust to extirpate evil is as great as that of the Christian mob that dragged the fair and too intelligent Hypatia from her carriage and lovingly used oyster shells to scrape the flesh from her bones while she was still alive. [Hypatia was a Neoplatonic philosopher, renowned for her beauty, who taught at Alexandria and was murdered by a Christian mob in the year 415 at the incitement of Cyril, archbishop of Alexandria.— Ed.]

With very few exceptions, the anti-Christians, no doubt unwittingly, retained in their minds a large part of Christian doctrine, and they even revived the most poisonous elements of the primitive Bolshevism, which had been attenuated or held in abeyance by the established churches in the great days of Christendom. And today professed atheists do not think it odd that, on all social questions, they are in substantial agreement with the howling dervishes and evangelical shamans who, subsidized with lavish publicity by the Jews who control the boob-tubes and other means of communication, greedily participate in the current drive to reduce Americans to total imbecility with every kind of irrational hoax, from astrology to "pyramid power."

It is to the great honor of Mr. Simpson that, as he says somewhere in his book, he is not a man "to do things by halves." When he ascertained that the Biblical fictions were unbelievable, he logically perceived that the residue of derivative superstitions was equally mythical. He had the intellectual vigor and integrity to begin a search for truth, i.e., ascertained facts about the real world—a search that is an intellectual drama narrated in his candid pages. His studies of all subjects relating to the social realities of our time were thorough and almost exhaustive, and his citations from writers of recognized scientific and scholarly competence form a bibliography of almost encyclopedic scope.

Mr. Simpson resolutely examines the psychological and social consequences of our great industrial technology, which made us masters of the whole earth until Jewish superstitions paralyzed our vital instincts as well as our rationality, so that now our own technology is being used by our enemies "with deadly effectiveness to produce a herd of fellaheen, bemused, stupefied, tamed cattle, whom it will be easy for them to milk in the world-state corral they now have nearly ready to receive them." That is a fact that no candid observer of the present will doubt, but Mr. Simpson goes on to consider the effects of industrial organization, which is necessarily inhuman, on the biological entity that is man.

Needless to say, there can be no question of abandoning the technological power on which alone depends our only chance to survive in the world we lost, but it is well that we understand the price that we must pay for power.

One chapter in this book ruthlessly demolishes a prejudice that has been inculcated into all of us by the dominant mythology. Sixty-five years ago, when the great American student of historical causality, Correa Moylan Walsh (who would be ranked with Spengler, had he been born in Europe), identified the causes of the catastrophic decline that was then already imminent, he noted the perverse "effeminization of men, for which the masculinization of women will be no compensation," and he devoted the third volume of his *Climax of Civilization* to the systematic illusion called Feminism.

Limiting himself to essentials, Mr. Simpson has more concisely shown that, as should be obvious to anyone who looks about him, "men and women are *fundamentally* different creatures," both physiologically and, what is even more important, psychologically. It is, of course, irrelevant that a dream of sexual equality may, like a dream of immortality, fascinate tender minds that need hallucinations to shield them from reality; and a calm consideration of the facts is particularly timely now, when screeching Jewesses are whipping the disinherited and bewildered females of our race into epidemic hysteria, thus applying the immemorial technique of their race, which, as some of its leading agitators have

frankly stated, consists in creating dissension, antagonisms, and social disruption by finding groups of individuals who can be isolated on the basis of some supposed common interest and
persuaded by artful sophistries that they are the victims of "social
injustice" and "oppression."

It is a grim fact that our people today is as hag-ridden with superstitions as were our ancestors in the Middle Ages. We have vol-
untarily shut our eyes to reality as though life were a child's game
to be played by capering blindfolded, until now we stand, as A. K.
Chesterton says in his posthumous book of that title, facing the
abyss. Our recent history reminds one of the old Mexican myth of
Toveyo, the cunning sorcerer, who exterminated the Toltecs by
beating faster and faster on a magic drum that made the hypno-
tized people dance ever more furiously until they, exhausted, made
a final leap into the abyss of eternal night.

If we are not to follow the Toltecs, we must at last use the cogni-
tive and objectively rational powers that are peculiar to our racial mentality. Whether our decaying race still has the will or even the capacity
to make that effort is the only question, and it must be answered soon.

Mr. Simpson is too honest to palliate our peril with illusory
hopes or tranquilizing verbiage. His book, I warn you, is only for
those who dare look upon the stark realities of a terrible universe.
The sun is but a lonely spark amid billions of suns that are themselves lost in endless night, and in all of infinity our planet may be
the only lump of rock infected with sentient life, of which men are
merely a peculiar and ephemeral variety.

Among the mammalian bipeds, our race is a small and hated
minority. For us there is no help from the infinite void that en-
compasses us, and no help beneath the clouds, except in ourselves.
Like all living organisms, we must fight to survive in the unceasing
struggle for life. But, as Mr. Simpson reminds us, seeking mere
survival is not enough: a race can survive *only* by aggression.

At their origin through some biological mutation or phenomenal hybridism, the Jews can have been no more than a band
of squalid savages, less numerous and less important than the Mo-

hicans or the Algonquins on this continent. Had their ambition been only to survive as a tribe, they would soon have disappeared, absorbed into the teeming populations of the Near East. But that minuscule race, inspired by implacable hatred, perfected through ruthlessly selective breeding a very high degree of predatory intelligence and a genius for dissimulation and deceit. Endowed with a loyalty to their own race that maintained their unity in dispersion, they infiltrated more civilized nations to exploit the superstitions and appetites, the gullibility and venality, of the masses. Thus, in only 25 centuries, they became the arbiters and virtually the masters of the world today.

If our race has been so debilitated by menticidal illusions that it no longer has the will to subjugate and dominate other races, then, by the irrevocable law of all life, it has become unfit to survive. If that is so, the superiority that we won by our courage and technological power and have now lost by our fatuity is lost forever, and despite what you and I may wish or hope, we are, in the grim balance of nature, what the Jews believe us to be, an irredeemably inferior species, fit only for brutish servitude or, at best, extinction.

Race And
History Distortion

Revilo P. Oliver

Race And
History Distortion

IN THE DECADE before us, the methods of historiography will undergo a very considerable modification.

History depends primarily on written documents, from the clay tables of ancient Sumeria and the earliest Egyptian hieroglyphs to the archives of modern states. In the absence of documents, the historian can only elicit tentative conclusions from artifacts disinterred by archaeologists or surmise what actual events gave rise to folktales and legends, such as the myths about Hercules or the story of Heimdall in the *Rigsthula*.

It is the function of the historian to submit all documents, whether purported originals or copies of lost originals, to the most rigorous critical analysis to determine their authenticity and their veracity. Wherever there is an apparent motive for forgery or mendacity, the document and its contents must be tested by every available criterion and technique, and only rarely are these sufficient to give results that have so high a degree of probability as to be virtually certain.

Inevitably of course, there are a few documents of great historical import about which doubt subsists. The famous letter of the younger Pliny, evidently written in A.D. 112, which is the earliest evidence for the existence of a sect with which modern Christians would admit an affinity, is now accepted as genuine by the majority of scholars, chiefly on the grounds that if it were a forgery concocted by the Christians and inserted in the corpus of Pliny's letters that came down to us in only one manuscript, now lost, it

Race and History Distortion, by Professor Revilo P. Oliver, was first published in *New Nation,* Nr. 1 – Summer 1980, and was reprinted with the author's permission in *Liberty Bell* for October 1980.

would presuppose in the forger a degree of learning, skill, and care much greater than is found in other Christian compositions. But we cannot be quite certain. The letter was quoted, with some odd variations, by Tertullian in the very *Apologeticum*, written around 200, in which that Father of the Church and shyster lawyer cites one of the most audacious of Christian forgeries, a purported letter from Pontius Pilate to Tiberius; recent studies have disclosed two odd anomalies; and it is not *impossible* that Tertullian or an accomplice had the requisite skill and diligence: so doubt remains.

The famous Kensington Rune Stone, which purportedly attests the presence of Norse explorers in what is now Minnesota in 1362, has long been regarded as a forgery perpetrated by a local resident for the glory of Scandinavia, but a recent linguistic analysis makes it seem unlikely that the supposed forger could have introduced subtle dialectical variations of Old Norse unrecorded in his time; so doubt remains.

These examples suffice to show the underlying assumption in all historical criticism: forgeries or impostures are always the work of an individual or a small group of individuals for profit, piety, or political ends. The most recent Christian gospels are good examples. When Joseph Smith found that swindling farmers with tales of buried treasure entailed legal hazards, he manufactured the *Book of Mormon*, possibly with one assistant author, and enlisted eleven perjurers to attest to its authenticity. In 1879 and 1883, the Reverend Mr. William Dennis Mahan produced a whole sheaf of forgeries to prove the historical truth of a religion to which he had a deep emotional attachment, and it seems that only his wife was a party to his pious hoax, although other clergymen soon tried to muscle in on what had become a lucrative imposture by producing supplemental forgeries. Smith founded what became the staunchest, most stable, and most cohesive church in the United States, exciting the emotional faith of millions who never suspected that the "Newest Testament" was a fraud. Poor Mahan undertook a more difficult task, for which he had neither the education nor the financial resources, but he stimulated the glands of many thousands of yearning Christians, and many enterprising publishers since his time have found it highly profitable to reprint, *ad maiorem gloriam Dei*, what some of them call "the Archko Volume."

Forged letters

Some political hoaxes are comparable. The forged letters of Winston Churchill, which aroused considerable excitement in Italy in 1954, were plausible in content and deceived many well-educated Italians, for whom English was a foreign language and who had never noted the minute characteristics that distinguish the work of the various brands of typewriters. It is uncertain whether the forgers were interested only in collecting the large sums of money they obtained from Italian conservatives for the precious historical documents, or had been inspired by the Italian Premier, De Gaspari, who used the hoax to prosecute and discredit the conservatives who had earlier obtained possession of possibly genuine letters that he wrote while hiding out in the Vatican in 1940-43.

In the absence of documents, the historian's task is more difficult, and where there is no trustworthy evidence and the doctrine of "cui bono?" does not yield conclusive results, we naturally have one of the innumerable mysteries or ambiguities that season the pages of history. The facts concerning the death of the Austrian Crown Prince at Mayerling were so successfully covered up that, while we may have strong suspicions, we do not know whether or not Rudolph murdered his mistress and committed suicide. We shall probably never know why the Great Fire of London in September 1666 "happened" to begin on the eve of the very day for which it had been scheduled by a conspiracy, directed by unidentified persons residing in Holland, some of whose agents were arrested, confessed, and were executed in the preceding April. Nor shall we know why so remarkable a "coincidence" excited no official investigation after the event.

Evidence destroyed thoroughly

When conspiracies have governmental powers, they can usually cover up their guilt at the time and they often destroy evidence so thoroughly that later generations are left with a puzzle they can solve only partially or tentatively. We now know only that the assassination of Abraham Lincoln was arranged by a conspiracy for the dual purpose of eliminating a political figure who was no longer useful and of exciting fresh animosity against the Southerners who had been conquered, and whose country had been destroyed, in the unconscionable war of aggression of which he had been the ostensible leader; but, aside from a few hirelings, the only person who we can positively identify as a member of the conspiracy is Stanton, who was the Secretary of War in Lincoln's cabinet, arranged many of the practical details, and was able, after the event, to silence key witnesses, although we can only guess what it was they knew that made it necessary to have them judicially murdered. And Stanton seems to have been only a local manager for principals whose identity we can only surmise.

The second-class battleship *Maine*, significantly the least useful ship in the comparatively small American navy, was sent to Havana to overawe the legitimate government of Cuba, and was there destroyed, with great loss of life, by an internal explosion. The American government, however, was able to cover up that fact and to claim that a Spanish mine or torpedo was responsible, thus preparing the excitable American populace for the desired war of aggression against Spain. So far as I know, no one has thus far found evidence to fix the responsibility for what is likely to have been more than a happy "accident" at just the right time.

It frequently happens, of course, that all the evidence is not thoroughly destroyed. The work of Mr. Colin Simpson, published in 1972, amply documents the facts concerning the sinking of the British cruiser and munitions ship, *Lusitania*, which had been disguised as a passenger liner to attract a large number of American passengers in the hope that a German submarine would take the "livebait" dangled before it.

It is now clear that the atrocious gambit, which would certainly have offended the sensibilities of the English public in 1915, was contrived by Winston Churchill with only a few accomplices. After the event, there were in Britain a considerable number of persons who knew that the official tale was false and had solid grounds for suspecting the truth, but gentlemen (e.g. Lord Mersey, who retired from the bench after his part in what he termed "a damned dirty business") were silenced by appeals to patriotism and the *raison d'état*, while lesser men were intimidated. In the United States, the great deception was assiduously promoted by the cynical gang that surrounded Woodrow Wilson, a muzzy-headed shyster whom the Jews had trained for the Presidency into which they boosted him by the simple expedient of playing on the vanity and gullibility of Theodore Roosevelt. Their efforts were, of course, abetted by the large corps of journalistic hirelings, who probably disseminated sensational lies with the efficiency and in the spirit with which they would have waited on tables or operated taxicabs.

Many millions of citizens of both Great Britain and the United States were successfully duped, while the facts were known to only comparatively few persons and, in all probability, the ultimate purpose of the operation was known to yet fewer.

Mental logistics

Experience has shown that the mass-armies of "democratic" states fight with greater zeal when they are animated by hatred and supported by a hate-crazed populace that fancies it is fighting a holy war. Lies have therefore become military equipment, a kind of mental logistics; but it is the essence of such propaganda that its spuriousness is known only to the persons who manufacture it. The model of such operations is the famous lie-factory managed by Lord Bryce during the First World War, in which a corps of expert technicians forged photographs, while expert liars, including Arnold Toynbee, concocted stories, of "atrocities", to inspire the emotionally overwrought British with a fanatical hatred of the incredibly bestial Germans and with a noble Christian ardor to kill them.

Lord Bryce's superiors in the government undoubtedly knew what his merry knaves were doing, and a small number of educated and judicious men must at least have had suspicions which they concealed from fear or unwillingness to impair the "war effort," but the number of persons who knew or suspected the truth was very small in comparison with the vast majority that was successfully deceived during the war. And after the war, the secret could no longer be kept.

It is a truism, of course, that in "democratic" states the populace must be encouraged to imagine that it makes important decisions by voting, and must therefore be controlled by suitable propaganda, which implants ideas to which the voters respond automatically as trained animals respond to words of command in a circus, thus leaving to the masses only a facetious choice between Tweedledum and Tweedledee on the basis of their preference for a certain kind of oratory, a hair-style, or a particular facial expression.

The production of such propaganda requires a very high degree of technical skill, as may be learned from the most complete treatise on the subject, Jacques Ellul's *Les Propagandes* (Paris, 1962), which is also available in an excellent English translation. The conditioning of the populace must be directed by a small corps of expert technicians in the employ of an oligarchy, with only a limited number of assistants who are fully aware of their task. When we consider the British and Americans (as distinct from resident aliens), we may be certain that most of the teachers who inject illusions into the minds of the young, many of the journalists who manufacture tripe for the press and radio, and even quite a few of the "social scientists" who concoct sophistries for the half-educated, are not conscious of what they are doing, being themselves deceived. And the individuals who suspect that they are deluding their victims probably soothe their consciences with assurances that they are engaged in noble work for "democracy" and their salaries.

Thus, although it is true that the manufacture of propaganda, like the manufacture of shoes or stoves, requires today a larger number of technicians and other employees than were needed even a few decades ago, the number concerned in its production is relatively small and the employees even fewer, so that historians still think in terms of a small group engaged in conscious and calculated deception of a great majority.

To take a specific example, *adhuc sub iudice*, a photograph with some collateral evidence has recently been published to show that the holy man who has been raising Hell in Persia is not Khomeini who appeared in France as a refugee some years ago. We automatically assume that if the evidence is spurious, it was fabricated by a few men, no more, perhaps, than half a dozen. If it is genuine, then the impersonation was arranged by the secret service of some major nation or international state, requiring the complicity of no more than a dozen men, including the director who gave the orders. We should think it fantastic to suppose that there are as many as four hundred persons, now in Europe and able to tell the truth, who are party to the hoax, whichever it is.

Historians have never thought of calculated deception as the work of any large number of persons. It is true, of course, that some minority groups, religious or conspiratorial, have tried to disguise their beliefs. The Mandaeans are reputed to have lied about their faith to strangers, but if their religion is fairly represented by the scriptures that have been recently obtained and published (e.g., their Canonical Prayer Book, edited and translated by Professor E.S. Drower in 1939), one wonders why they took the trouble. In past centuries, Persian Shi'ites, when they made a pilgrimage to Mecca, understandably practised *takiyah*, concealing their heresy from the more orthodox Moslems among whom they had to travel at the risk of their lives.

In the United States, the American Republican Party, which limited its membership to American-born white men, excluding

Jews and other unassimilated aliens, earned the sobriquet by which it is now commonly known by urging its members to avoid futile debate with their adversaries by saying, "I Know Nothing about it." But their aim was not to keep secret purposes which, indeed, were so well known that, despite the furious opposition of professional politicians, they might well have achieved control of the Federal government, had they not been disrupted and dispersed by agitation about slavery in the South. One could cite other instances of evasion to avoid inconvenience or harassment, but such expedients differ totally from the perpetuation of hoaxes and do not impugn the historian's premise that forgeries and impostures are secretly contrived by a few individuals.

Historians must now drastically revise that premise. No matter how timorous they may be, they cannot, if honest, close their eyes to proof that massive deceptions can be carried out by thousands, even millions, of individuals who act unanimously with a common purpose.

40 million too preposterous

The great Jewish hoax about millions of God's Chosen People whom the Germans supposedly exterminated seems to have been devised late in 1942, when it was claimed that in the autumn of that year the Germans had murdered two millions of the Holy Race in various ways. By 1943, the number had been increased to six million, and to keep up the progression, it was later increased to 40,000,000. which was seen to be so preposterous that it was reduced to 12,000,000, and at the end of the Crusade to Save the Soviet, the figure of six million was taken as the largest that could impose on the gullible goyim.

The obvious original motive, common to all war propaganda, was to pep up the cattle that were being stampeded against Germany, but there may have been a further purpose in a hope that after the war it would be possible to carry out the Jewish plan, formulated and published by Theodore Kaufman in 1941, to exterminate the entire population of Germany as an object lesson to lower races that might want to have a country of their own, not under the management of God's Chosen People.

Since that proved not to be feasible, the hoax was used as a pretext for the obscene murders perpetrated at Nuremberg by the American, Soviet, British and French victors, for their repudiation of the conventions, called international law, that had been observed by all civilized nations, and for the innumerable and ghastly atrocities by which all the victors, guided by their Jewish supervisors, equally and forever forfeited their claim to be morally superior to Atilla's Huns or Hulagu's Mongols. And the hoax is still being used to loot Germany and, indirectly, all the nations of the West to subsidize the Jewish seizure of Palestine and adjacent lands.

It is no longer possible to think of a deception of many by a few. The utter falsity of this hoax, which was made the more preposterous when the physically impossible gas chambers were invented to dress it up, was necessarily known to hundreds of thousands of Jews who remained on German territory during the insane war, many of whom—probably 250,000—the Germans naturally interned as domestic enemies, although not with the thoroughness with which the Americans put resident Japanese in concentration camps during 1942-45. The Jews who remained in Germany, both those who were foolishly trusted and held governmental positions and those who were confined to the various camps, necessarily knew that there were no "gas chambers" and there was no "extermination" (although, of course, many individuals died from disease, old age, and Anglo-American bombing raids on the various camps, and, no doubt, some were slain by individual Germans when they foresaw the defeat and ruin of their country by the maddened hordes that the international race had mobilized against them and by the Polish and Russian populations of occupied territories when the German armies failed to control their long-standing resentment of their parasites).

Furthermore, since the race has always been truly international, many hundreds of thousands, perhaps millions, of Jews throughout the world and especially in the United States must have known or suspected the truth when their supposedly exterminated relatives flocked into the country or corresponded with them. In addition, there must have been a considerable number of Jews who, even if without sources of direct information, were intelligent enough to see that the hoax was inherently incredible, psychologically improbable and physically impossible.

But nevertheless, so far as I know, only one Jew, Josef Ginsburg, who resided in German or Rumanian territory throughout the war, has borne witness that there was no German policy to "exterminate" his race; and although he published his books under the pseudonym of J.G. Burg, he only accidentally escaped death at the hands of Jewish terrorists in Munich.

The great Jewish hoax, which is currently imposed by the Jewish Terror on the population of Western nations, must be distinguished from the tall tales now told in Soviet territory, where the yowling about fictitious Jewish victims was long ago replaced by an official claim that the Germans deliberately exterminated six millions of high-minded Slavs. How much of this propaganda, much of which is so phrased that it could include casualties in battle, is believed by intelligent Russians, it is impossible to say, and no one will wonder at the lack of public protest from persons who know better but live in Soviet territory, under a supervision more strict than any that has thus far been imposed on any Western nation, although the Jews are naturally trying to approximate it for purposes of their own and have attained a very considerable success in Western Germany, where the corrupt government in Bonn has virtually made it illegal to disbelieve any Jewish imposture, and many books that the Jewish censorship has not approved for *goyim* can be circulated only clandestinely.

Although the hoax about the "six million" has always been inherently unbelievable in all of the various revisions that have been made from time to time, and although it has been definitively exposed and demolished by Professor Arthur A. Butz in his *Hoax of the Twentieth Century* (Historical Review Press, 1976), the entire race, numbering at least thirty millions throughout the world, is frantically insisting, with apparent unanimity, that the lower races must believe whatever they are told by God's Master Race, and what is most significant, Jewish professors ensconced in Western universities and necessarily knowing something of the methods of Western scholarship, automatically shrieked and spat at Professor Butz, although they had never seen his book and did not even know its correct title. One cannot avoid the conclusion that however well they had learned or simulated the methods of scholarship, all questions of fact were to be rigorously subordinated to the interests of their race.

Anne Frank's Diary

A second example is the astoundingly crude forgery called "Anne Frank's Diary," concocted so negligently and with such contempt for Aryan minds that its many internal contradictions proclaim its falsity. It can have imposed on no reader who had even a modicum of critical judgement and a memory sufficiently good to retain what he read on one page when he read a passage a few pages later. The blatant contradictions in the text of this fraud have now been listed by Swedish writer, Ditlieb Felderer, in *Anne Frank's Diary: a Hoax* (Institute for Historical Review, Torrance, California, 1980), but the mystery is why such a booklet was ever needed.

Many persons, it is true, read religious texts in an emotional trance that paralyses their reason, and one can only assume that sentimental persons who have been so prepared by preliminary propaganda that they blubber as they read the first page of the "Diary" can go on reading in a similar stupor. No critical reader can ever have been deceived, whatever his race. But here again, thirty to sixty million Jews, with apparent unanimity, are determined that the *goyim* shall believe, or profess to believe, that preposterous canard, if they are to escape punishment for being rational. And one hears that the courts in Western Germany have held that it is a criminal offense to express doubts about what no intelligent man can believe. One cannot predict when the same courts will hold that it is an "insult" to the "Jewish nation" to deny that the earth is flat, as was specifically stated by the God who covenanted to deliver the whole earth to His people.

[On May 28, 1979, the federal law enforcement agency of West Germany (Bundeskriminalamt - Case no. Az.: KT 41-2104/79) in Wiesbaden, rendered an opinion in regard to the veracity of "Anne Frank's Diary" which reads, in part, as follows: "A part of the entries attributed to Anne Frank were made subsequently with black, green and red ballpoint pen ink. Ballpoint ink, however, was not marketed until 1951." That leaves us with two alternatives: Either Anne Frank did not die in 1945 as claimed and edited the manuscript herself again, or Anne Frank did in fact die in 1945 and, consequently, can not have been the author of the "Diary"! - Ed. Liberty Bell]

Even more significant is the Jews' progressive abandonment of their usual measures for herding the *goyim*: bribery, open or surreptitious financial pressures, and the manipulation of venal politicians. Mobs of Jewish hoodlums now openly assault French professors who dare to doubt the incredible, wield iron clubs to crack the skulls of a few French writers who have met privately to discuss the forbidden topic, and openly boast they have murdered with a time bomb a French professor who dared to stand for election to the Chambre des Députés. And there is comparable violence by Jewish thugs, with or without an admixture of zombies from the lower races, in West Germany, England, and the United States, while thirty to sixty million Jews, without significant exceptions, applaud the good work and protect the criminals through their control of virtually all the means of communication and their control or intimidation of police forces and courts.

The drastic import of these facts for historiography is obvious. An entire race (or sub-race, if you prefer that classification) can show effective solidarity in the perpetration of outrageous hoaxes, while many thousands or even millions who cannot but know the truth, knowingly participate in the fraud, whether from fear of reprisals by their fellows, hatred of their victims, or a confidence in their biological superiority, such as we show when we imprison or kill wild animals and make cows, horses, sheep, and dogs our domestic servants or our food. The implication for historians in their consideration of all information, ancient or modern, that has come to us from or through Jewish sources is emphatically clear and imposes an inescapable obligation. And it remains to be ascertained whether there may be, or have been, comparable phenomena in seemingly unanimous asseverations by other races.

Religion and Race

Religion and Race

I have read with the most sympathetic interest the article by Donald Vincent Clerkin that appeared in the October issue of *The Liberty Bell* in rebuttal to my article, "The Jews Love Christianity" in the August issue. Mr. Clerkin ably presents a Christian point of view, and he and his comrades are obviously allies whom we must welcome. I wish I could leave his argument unanswered.

The question, stated bluntly, is a practical one. With all due respect to the Christian remnants, so capably represented by Mr. Clerkin, we must ask ourselves what policy will best serve our race, which is as dear to them as it is to us. If, out of courtesy to them, we refrain from criticizing their religion, will our cause gain more than it will lose because we will seem by silence to endorse Christianity?

As it happens, the answer is indicated by the September issue of *Liberty Bell*, which contains an excellent article, "A Summary of New Testament Studies," [reprinted in Appendix C of this volume] by Ronald S. Hand, an ordained Christian minister. An editorial note informs us that the Reverend Mr. Hand was expelled from his pulpit, and apparently unfrocked by his sect, because he was associated with a racialist organization. Some twenty years ago, there was in the United States a Christian group, Circuit Riders, based in Cincinnati, Ohio, which published lists of the names of clergymen who were active in Communist subversion—so ostentatiously active that they championed organizations that had

Religion and Race was (under the pseudonym of Ralph Perier) Dr. Oliver's contribution to, and was first published in, *Liberty Bell* for November 1980. This article was written partly in response to an article in *Liberty Bell* for October 1980, "A White Christian Racist Defends His Faith," by Major D.V. Clerkin, which is reprinted in APPENDIX A of this volume.

that had been officially pronounced subversive by investigatory committees of the American Congress. Between 1958 and 1962, Circuit Riders published five scrupulously documented books: *2709 Methodist Ministers; 7477 Protestant Episcopal Rectors; 614 Presbyterian Clergymen; 660 Baptist Clergymen;* and *42% of Unitarian Clergymen.* There were at least two similar compilations that did not reach me. So far as I have been able to learn, not one of those avowed enemies of our race was ever unfrocked by his sect or expelled from his pulpit for poisoning American minds with the Jews' vicious hoax about the equality of races. And I have not heard that even one member of their befuddled congregations objected to their efforts to destroy our race, although there were reports that a very few individuals, here and there, expressed some dissatisfaction with the Communist economics, which, in comparison with the racial poison, were utterly trivial.

Mr. Clerkin claims that he represents the true Christianity of the West. I believe that he does. But we cannot possibly impose that Christianity on 99.9% of the Christians today, no matter how adroitly we might present arguments which we ourselves do not believe. With the exception of small remnants here and there, the whole of Christianity today, including every organized sect of any size, is an instrumentality of our implacable enemies. It captivates the credulous with its theological myths, and it propagates, even among "Liberals" who imagine they are atheists, social superstitions that are simply deadly. And it rests on foundations of fraud and chicanery and on historical falsifications so patent that their absurdity is readily exposed by rational criticism. In the desperate plight of our race today, it is clearly to our advantage to overturn the whole edifice of pretense and imposture.

Mr. Clerkin, who is eminently right in much of what he says, asks why, if my view of Christianity as a Jewish hoax is correct, the religion did not abort European civilization or destroy it in its incunabular phase. That is indeed a crucial question, but he has himself answered it.

He rightly observes that "after the fall of Rome,... Christianity,

Magian-Semitic at its birth, took on a Gothic physiognomy," so that "Christianity underwent a profound metamorphosis during its European sojourn." The religion was adapted to what Spengler calls the Faustian soul. And that cannot be denied.

THE NORDIC ADAPTATION

In his *Christianity and the Survival of the West*, R.P. Oliver correctly says that the new religion was superimposed on the antecedent morality of the Aryan race when it was accepted by our ancestors after the collapse of the rotted Roman Empire. What he does not tell his readers is how little of what is now considered Christianity was accepted by the Nordic peoples who were "converted" to the cult that had been "Magian-Semitic" in its origin. A clear and cogent example of what Professor Oliver omitted may be found in England's native epic, *Beowulf.* Although literarily crude by Classical standards, it is a noble poem and deservedly well-known. It has been read by everyone who can read Old English, and most educated persons of English origin will at least have read one of the sixteen or more versions of the epic in modern English.

The extant text of *Beowulf* comes from a manuscript written in a British monastery at the very end of the tenth century A.D. and has a Christian coloring. Some scholars believe that the poem was composed as early as the seventh century, and that the superficial Christian coloring was added by some monastic who replaced *wyrd* ('Fate') and *Alfaeder* ('All-Father,'i.e., Odin) in the text with words meaning 'god' (really ambiguous, but taken as referring to the Christian deity when used in the singular), and interpolated a few lines containing allusions to the Christian's anti-god, the Devil, and to the myth of Cain and Abel. Other scholars as confidently maintain that the epic was composed at a somewhat later date by a poet who was a Christian and intended to write a Christian poem about traditional heroes. What is certain is that the epic was accepted as authentically Christian and copied in the monasteries of Christian England.

I have no wish to adjudicate the debate among scholars: the

I have no wish to adjudicate the debate among scholars: the important thing is that such a debate is possible—that *Beowulf,* whoever wrote it and whenever it was first composed, was accepted as consonant with Christianity around the year 1000. It was one of the great documents, the true scriptures, of Western Christianity, but if you said that it was such today, you would shock into conniption fits all the sentimental females who drool about their Jesus and Love; and all the pulpit-punks who prey on those females would declaim sophistries to prove it doesn't represent their up-to-date religion, as, of course, it doesn't.

Beowulf is a noble poem. It celebrates the achievements of a great warrior, in whom we may see the prototype of mediaeval knighthood, the high ideal that Mr. Clerkin prizes so highly and justly, but for which he could find no sanction in the Christian holy book. The Old English epic celebrates the virtues that our race instinctively venerates, although they seem contemptible to the minds of Jews and of other alien races. It is the code of personal honor, of unflinching loyalty to one's own people and nation, of unfaltering courage, of willingness to fight and, if need be, die for the glory of one's own nation or to defend one's kinsmen across the sea. The basic morality is that of men who tell the truth because they are too proud to lie. It is the morality of men who fear neither human enemies nor supernatural powers, but dread only a stain upon their own honor, of men who never even think of praying to unseen gods for a strength that is not in themselves, and who die, as they have lived, proudly.

In *Beowulf,* "the Almighty" has replaced Odin, but there is no hint of Jesus. There is no imbecile talk about loving one's enemies. There is nothing of the slavish masochism of the Jesus who wants us to turn the other cheek. There is nothing of the Yiddish sadism of the Jesus who wants to watch and gloat over the slaughter of all "who would not that I should reign over them."

When men die in the epic, they give up the ghost, and there is a hint that the ghost survives somehow, but there is no notion that its future state depends on its having been "saved" by some magic

rite or by professing belief in a Saviour who will take it to some
mansion in the sky where it can loaf forever. The only life we
know is the one on this earth, where men are born to toil and pain
and sorrow as surely as the sparks fly upward from a fire, and no
one imagines that we can talk some invisible being into delivering
us from reality. All men must dread their weird. And the noble
and realistic ethic the Norse proudly accepts the ineluctable trag-
edy of a world in which the hero always dies defeated because he
grows old.

Beowulf, to be sure, is an extreme example of what Western
Christianity could admire in its springtime, but it is also typical.
Almost all of the Icelandic sagas were certainly composed by men
who thought themselves Christians, and they all show how little
the new religion was thought relevant to men's conduct on earth.
(There are many sagas that are still untranslated, but for a convenient summary, see M.J. Steblin-Kamenskij's *The Saga Mind* in the
English version by Kenneth H. Ober, Odense University Press,
1973.) The famous Norse scholar, Snorri Sturlason, was a Christian and claimed to believe in the miraculous powers of the Christian's god, but he devoted a large part of his life to lovingly
collecting, in the prose *Edda,* the *Heimskringla,* and other works,
the traditions and myths of an heroic age and the memory of men
whose achievements were not even tinged with specifically Christian virtues.

The truth is that the Oriental religion only slowly and very
gradually affected the practical life of our race. That is why it did
not abort before birth the civilization that we call Faustian, which
significantly derives its name from a cultural hero who sought
knowledge and power in this world, not "salvation." It was not in
the ninth century, but in the nineteenth, that the superstition began to have an appreciable effect on the actual conduct of our
race, except in the one area where the religion imposed Semitic
notions of sexual magic on the Nordics' instinctive respect for
womanhood. And it is only today that the blight of Christianity
has become fully virulent: it has made us weak and foolish. It took

takes Spanish moss a comparatively long time to kill the tree on which it has fastened itself.

TOLERABLE DOSES

Today, if you listen to an evangelist when he peddles holiness, the chances are that when he makes his pitch he will tell you that "Christianity hasn't failed, because it has never been tried." There is a large measure of truth in that sales-talk. No human society thus far has been so insane as to take seriously the much-touted Drivel on the Mount, on which I commented in my article, but we are approaching that final stage of suicidal mania.

The reason why our civilization was able to grow in spite of Christianity is clear, and Mr. Clerkin has stated it concisely. Throughout the Middle Ages, the unity of Christendom was maintained by a disciplined organization, a vast international bureaucracy that was undoubtedly self-seeking and avaricious, but was also prudent and administered the religion to laymen in safe doses, such as society could tolerate, much as the human body can usually tolerate as much as a twentieth of a grain of strychnine and may even derive a temporary stimulus from it. Few men and women could read the Bible, and of the few who could, no one bothered to read it, if he was not a professional holy man; and even theologians read no more than they had to for business purposes, preferring to repeat or twist the quotations they found in the Latin "Fathers of the Church." During the Middle Ages the Church carried the Bible in its luggage, like a time bomb that was quietly ticking away, and everyone was taken by surprise when the bomb exploded.

During the Middle Ages, theologians jostled for promotion and power, much as members of the Communist hierarchy do today, but the Church successfully kept such competition under control, while the disciplined clergy throughout Europe preached the gospel that the Popes judged expedient. God's vicar could always be consulted about the wishes of his employer, and when one could ask him, why puzzle one's head over the contradictions in a mass of poorly edited scribblings?

During the Middle Ages, naturally, many men of learning had their doubts, but they prudently refrained from advertising their disbelief. Most of them were probably learned enough to have no wish to disturb the established order, and anyone who felt an itch for notoriety as a rationalist found himself deficient in philoparaptesism, i.e., the yearning to be roasted over a slow fire that is said to have inspired Christian martyrs. It is true that some unidentified man, probably in the thirteenth century, wrote and surreptitiously circulated the famous treatise *De tribus impostoribus,* identifying Moses, Jesus, and Mahomet as the three great con men who had exploited the credulity of mankind, but every copy of his work was destroyed. (The extant work of that title is an eighteenth-century forgery.)

There were heresies in the Middle Ages, of course. Some man, probably an intelligent priest, profiting to an uncertain extent from a tradition that may have survived underground from the second century, read his Bible and took it seriously. In his essay, *De duobus principiis,* he easily proved that the vicious god of the Old Testament, who so shamelessly helped the Jews swindle and steal, must be an evil and Satanic deity; having proved that, he went on to construct from snippets of the New Testament and his own imagination a Christianity for decent and honest men. One copy of that treatise was so cunningly hidden from the Church's inquisitors that it survived to be found in the present century and first published in its entirety in 1939.

While there was undoubtedly much of bureaucratic self-interest and perhaps some religious fanaticism in the Catholic Church's determination to extirpate heresies by fire and sword, the most intelligent members of the hierarchy must have perceived or sensed the need to preserve the unity of Christendom at all costs. The Church's vigilance was at fault only when it failed to suppress Francis of Assisi as soon as that young man, after an attack of some form of brain fever from which he never fully recovered, began to talk to the birds and recruit his twelve disciples. When Innocent III bestowed his blessings on the youthful halluciné in 1209, he did not foresee that he would eventually let loose on Europe swarms of preaching mendicants who would inevitably become rabble-rousers. There were many friars, members of the Franciscan order or its several imitations, who did make contributions to the civilization of Europe, but they did so as scholars and by using revenues for purposes Francis did not intend. But their work does not offset the harm done by the vagabond evangelists, who, to the disgust of the regular clergy, held "revival" meetings wherever they went and stirred up trouble with Franciscan notions. Francis of Assisi, after his brain was turned by disease or fantasies, tried to implement the peculiar teaching of Jesus: that was fatal. That was the first fissure in the monolithic structure of the Church that presaged its ultimate ruin.

THE TIME BOMB

The Biblical bomb was detonated early in the sixteenth century.

It is true that, as Mr. Clerkin says, the Protestant "reformation" was largely incited by Jews. They began by peddling to gullible *goyim* (at very high prices) their Kabbalah, which they guaranteed to be the "key to the Christian Mystery," and, strange as it seems now, that bundle of "theosophic" balderdash strongly influenced Protestant theologians for almost two centuries. When Luther appeared, the marranos ensconced in the Church and the bankers outside it helped foment the schism, and Luther promptly had Jewish friends, who gave him such generous help and counsel that they convinced him that God's Chosen People were being "persecuted," and he even went on record as claiming that the wicked Christians were "forcing" the poor dears to practice usury! (It was only late in his life that he perceived how he was being used by the alien race, and, four years before his death, he published *Von den Jueden und ihren Luegen,* * in which he urged that Germany, at least, be rid of her insatiably venomous parasites.) The Jews undoubtedly

* Both the German text and an English translation are available from *Liberty Bell.*

helped trigger the bomb they had planted centuries before.

The explosion came when men began to read the Bible to find out what God wanted. They tried to puzzle out for themselves what God's Word meant, instead of simply asking the Pontifex Maximus, who was presumably in constant telephonic communication with the author. The Renaissance had made it possible for any person of some education to consult God's slovenly Greek in the New Testament, and pious Jews were always eager to teach the *goyim* (for a fee) as much of God's native language as was good for them, so that they could read his Old Testament. And finally, what was most disastrous, heresiarchs began to translate the holy books into the various vernaculars of Europe, and enterprising printers marketed the "best sellers" to everyone who thought he could read the language he had lisped at his mother's knee.

No one has ever believed the Bible. Not all of it. No one could—except, perhaps, a polyphase schizophrenic. In addition to many statements that have irreconcilable implications, there are numerous passages which *explicitly* contradict each other.* No sane man could believe both. It appears, however, that Christians, when they have worked themselves into the emotional state called Faith, read their god's words in a kind of hypnotic trance in which the powers of reason are held in abeyance, as they are during sleep, when the dreaming mind accepts the wildest inconsistencies in, and transformation of, the images that drift or swirl through its umbratile consciousness. And if a Christian has doubts when he awakes, any moderately competent theologian can twist words and juggle concepts to convince him that God, instead of saying what he meant, devised a combination of a cryptogram with a jigsaw puzzle to exercise the Faithful in their Faith. And then there are the Sacred Mysteries, a kind of intelligence test to measure ability to believe the impossible.

Christians believe in the Virgin Birth of Jesus, although that is

* Compendiously presented in parallel columns by G.W. Foote and W.P. Ball in their *Bible Handbook* (London, 1888 *et saoepe;* available in the United States from the Truth Seeker, Box 2832, San Diego, California.)

only half as wonderful as the birth, some six hundred years earlier, of the Mahavira, which required the uterine coöperation of *two* virgins, thus providing a somewhat better test of Faith.* And then there is the Great Mystery of the Trinity. It would be comprehensible, if it were like the Hindu Trinity, an indissoluble partnership of three quite distinct gods to combine their respective talents for creation, preservation, and destruction. It would be comprehensible, if the Christian god were like Cerberus, one being with three heads, or like Brahman, who has only one head, but four faces. But we are to believe that one-third of a god impregnated a virgin so that she could give birth to another third of himself, which, however, turns out to be the son of the third that did not impregnate the virgin! And this son, when committing suicide by having himself crucified, then asks the paternal third of himself why that part af him has abandoned him! Such schizoid divinity would have strained the credulity of even the Egyptians who had enough Faith to believe in a goddess who was the mother of her own father.

Cogitation about the "truths" of the Bible is certain to have an effect comparable to that of three magnums of champagne taken on an empty stomach, and one can only sympathize with Christians who try to understand God's Word. It was only to be expected that brains, superheated by circular attempts to understand the unintelligible, would have inspirations and discover ways to square the circle. When Christians tried to make sense out of their Bible, the Protestant fragmentation of Christianity into hundreds

---

* The Christian Miracle, however, incidentally provides us with an instructive lesson. The Reverend Mr. Hand, in the article in *Liberty Bell* I cited above [reproduced in Appendix C of this volume], mentions the anxious efforts of the early Scholastics to determine the condition of Mary's hymenal membrane before, during, and after parturition, and he could have gone on to list their speculations about the organs through which the philoprogenitive Holy Ghost introduced his divine semen into the Virgin's womb. Such inquiries are, as Mr. Hand says, rather ludicrous, but we may also see in them a manifestation of the distinctively Aryan mentality, which, with its instinctive respect for facts, needed to know *how* such an unusual event was *physically* possible. The Oriental mind would not be troubled by such questions.

of exclusive sects was assured.

It was also inevitable that, sooner or later, minds worn out by efforts to comprehend a three-in-one god and to untangle and reconcile myths that were irredeemably tawdry and vulgar, would eventually excogitate a Christian heresy that would jettison the incredible miracles but preserve the social superstitions that had been based on them. Rousseau quite appropriately placed his gospel of revolutionary sentimentality in the mouth of a *vicaire savoyard*, a priest who professed a monotheistic deism that amounts to a Christianity stripped of the myths that had become unbelievable by that time. What was left was "the social gospel," the whole fetid mass of virulent superstitions that has infected the West ever since with the mortal disease from which we are dying today.

Had Rousseau wished to take the trouble, he could have cited a Biblical chapter and verse for every point in his grotesque doctrine, and from Rousseau to Marx the well-trodden path is unmistakable. If one considers the filiation of the social superstitions, it is quite reasonable to describe the Marxists as just another Christian sect, comparable to the Anabaptists, Sabbatarians, Unitarians, Quakers, Shakers, and hundreds of others. Such a classification of the Marxists, to be sure, will startle and incense many of our contemporaries, who, in their ire, refuse to perpend the highly significant fact that in the United States, for example, the Union Theological Seminary filled the Protestant churches with ministers who were covert or avowed Communists, while in South America (and elsewhere) the leading inciters of sedition are Catholic priests who declare that they are Marxists and act accordingly. Persons who are shocked by the undeniable facts often claim that the ordained Bolsheviks are hypocrites, and it is, of course, true that when one considers the howling dervishes of any religion, it is seldom possible to determine what a given salvation-huckster actually believes, as distinct from what he deems it expedient to profess *ad captandum vulgus*. But it is to the point that the peddlers of the "social gospel," who have now gained control of all the major Christian sects, do cite, *ad nauseam*, Scriptural authority for all

their propaganda, and they quote correctly from accepted translations (or, if extraordinarily well educated, from the original texts).
They may do so with tongue in cheek, of course: I do not know
and it would be a waste of time to guess about any of them. But
the fact remains that when one takes God's Word as a revelation
of truth, the first thing one has to do is decide which passages
must not be believed.

Many Christians accept the minimal definition of their religion that is given in Professor Oliver's *Christianity and the Survival
of the West*: belief in the divinity of Jesus. But that will not do. The
New Testament does aver that Jesus was begotten somehow by the
Holy Ghost, i.e., by another part of himself by what appears to be
a kind of divine masturbation. But, as everyone knows, there are
also passages in the same collection which state unequivocally that
Jesus was the son of a man named Joseph. So we have a conflict of
evidence. In most cases of disputed paternity, the only person who
can really know is the mother, provided that she has been relatively chaste. The Pope could presumably ascertain the facts by inquiring of Mary through the proper channels, but if we reject his
adjudication, we cannot prove from Holy Writ that the "social
gospel" boys are not right in claiming that Jesus was just a revolutionary agitator—and, what is worse, all the historical evidence is
in their favor.

The French Revolution was undoubtedly fomented and exacerbated by the Jews and their many subsidiaries, including such
foul conspiracies as that of Adam Weishaupt, who, whatever else
he was, was a highly talented confidence man, and who, be it
noted, had no difficulty in enlisting large numbers of the Christian clergy to help fill his money boxes. But in a larger sense, that
ghastly blot on European history was the homicidal insanity of a
society driven mad by the residue of Christianity in its collective
mind. Having lost faith in the Jesus whose kingdom "was not of
this world," the *sanglants abrutis* of the Revolution, many of
whom were men of our race, made an insane attempt to realize the
Heaven of perfect equality etc. on this earth, which the same Jesus,

according to Holy Writ, had promised to institute as soon as he returned from his home in the clouds with angelic reinforcements to destroy civilization and slaughter everyone except his righteous pets.

The bloody frenzy was finally stopped by Napoleon, who decided that the variety of organized Christianity represented by the Roman Catholic Church was an effective hellebore, which would quiet the convulsions and restore a modicum of sanity, sufficient at least to permit reconstruction of a stable society. His example did much to propagate the belief that was widely held in the nineteenth century and has persisted, though ever more feebly, to the present day: the belief that the religion was a potent tranquilizer, an antidote to revolutionary epilepsy.

This belief, it must be noted, was in the efficacy of tightly organized sects that kept the eyes of votaries firmly fixed on the putative joys of the Hereafter and their minds resigned to the normal condition of life on earth. In France, where the Roman Church was the dominant sect and talented literary men, such as Chateaubriand, undertook to celebrate in brilliant prose *le génie du christianisme,* the revival of Christianity as a stabilizing force attained its fullest development, and it rallied conservatives until it expired, with an ignominious whimper, in the final failure of *l'Action française* in 1944. In Germany, where the writers of the *Sturm und Drang* initiated the literature of romanticism, which, with its passionate adulation of the largely fictitious glories of the Ages of Faith, contributed more than is usually admitted to respect for the religion of the sentimental and miraculous, an uneasy truce between Catholics and Lutherans helped sustain the monarchy until it fell. In England, the Anglican Church offered hope to conservatives for a long time. In South Africa, the well-organized Dutch Reformed Church seemed a pillar of civilization until a few years ago, when the mouths of most of its holy men began to water as they smelled the appetizing aroma of Jewish gold. In the United States, afflicted with the widest and wildest variety of sects to be found anywhere in the world, belief in Christianity as a unifying force can never have been more than a dulcet hope or the sales-talk of evangelists after the failure of the Edwardian Conspiracy around 1800—and that was only a pip-squeak affair. But nevertheless the American conservatives, when they belatedly took alarm in the 1920s, espoused Jesus as their Lord and master and were left in ludicrous bewilderment when he eloped with their enemies.

WHICH JESUS?

Christians generally assume that the tales in their "New Testament" veraciously describe the activities of a man, who was also an incarnate god, named Jesus. If, starting with that faith, they then try to make sense out of that mass of inconsistent and contradictory stories, they must puzzle and fret themselves into a state of quasi-hypnotic befuddlement. I do not see how one could otherwise explain, for example, the willingness of Aryans to worship the Jesus who assures them (*Matth.* 15.22-27; cf. *Marc.* 7.26-28) that the Aryans and all other races except the Jews are dogs, curs that, at best, are fit only to lie under the table at the feet of God's People and lick up the scraps that fall from the hands of the feasting Jews.

People who retain their critical sense when they read the tales, but nevertheless want to worship a Jesus, naturally come to the conclusion that the stories are largely or entirely maladroit fictions. Thus the noted Catholic theologian, Father Alfred Loisy, was forced to the conclusion that there was no evidence whatsoever of what Jesus had actually said, since no one had thought to record his words when he was alive: his illiterate followers expected him to return from the clouds in a few years, and only after their generation had passed away did anyone try to compile collections of what he might have, or ought to have, said. An odd American sect, (if, indeed, it consists of more than one or two men and a post office box) proposes to reform Christianity on the basis that "virtually everything" that Jesus "said or did from the time he was 12 until he was 30 was censored out of the Bible by the Council of Nicea in 325 A.D." Granting that, how do they know that their Jesus did or said anything or, for that matter, that he ever existed? They do not appeal to the many gospels that Athanasius did not include in his "New Testament," but they *know* what Jesus *must* have said, because he was a reasonable man!

When one adds to Athanasius's anthology the very large number of other gospels that have survived, in whole or in part, it is only confusion worse confounded. There is no conceivable way of guessing which of the many gospels is more likely than others to contain the remnants of authentic information. There are so many gospels now known that it would take two pages even to list them compendiously, but I cannot refrain from noticing a "new" one, which may touch off a great revival of Christianity in the United States.

J. Edgar Bruns has pieced together from fragments of various early gospels a text to which he has given the rather sensational title of *The Forbidden Gospel* (New York, Harper & Row, 1976). It opens with the revelation that the Holy Ghost, in the plenitude of her wisdom, extruded from *her* tumid breasts the milk that *she* infused into the womb of the Virgin Mary to engender Jesus. The Jesus produced by this *really* virginal fecundation was a practicing homosexual who despised females, but taught that pious women will avoid becoming pregnant and that he would reward them by making men out of them. In the United States, where ordained homosexuals, reportedly male, are performing marriages between two persons who both claim to be male, and where screeching Jewesses are driving weak-minded Aryan females into hysterical tantrums because women are not men, Bruns' pithy synthesis of early Christian gospels (as "authentic" as any others) should become a phenomenal success, if it is taken up by some young evangelist, ambitious to reach the big time in holy vaudeville.

The example will suffice to show that, whatever you may want to promote, you can easily find a Jesus to fit the bill. But even if we limit ourselves to Athanasius's anthology, the most reasonable explanation of the Christians' Protean Jesus is that he is a composite figure, conflated by traditions about several of the Jewish agitators who bore the extremely common Jewish name that has become Jesus in English. It is likely, therefore, that all of the gospels preserve some recollection of what was done or claimed by one or another of those agitators or reported, with imaginative amplification, by his followers. There were many such agitators.

A writer in *Instauration* (Sept. 1979) listed eight Jesuses "whose careers could have contributed elements to the various Christian legends." And he did not include either Jesus ben Sirch ben Jesus (who wrote *Ecclesiasticus*) or Jesus ben Pandera! The latter deserves some notice, since he may be the prototype about whom the varied stories coalesced, perhaps including some about christs who bore less common Jewish names.

JESUS, SON OF 'PANTHERA'

Mr. Clerkin was misled by the Christian apologists who claim that the tradition about this Jesus comes from the *Talmud* and was invented by the Jews to traduce the founder of Christianity. That is impossible. One version of the tradition about this Jesus was known to Celsus around A.D. 180, at a time when there was no flagrant hostility between Jews and the various Christian sects, some of which were restricted to Jews, while some admitted *goyim* and others were anti-Jewish. The compilation of neither of the Talmuds was begun before some four centuries later.

A much fuller account of this Jesus is given in the *Toledoth Yeshu*, which, to be sure, is a Jewish work of uncertain date and extant in several versions, which, however, do not significantly differ from each other. The *Toledoth Yeshu* cannot be supposed to refer to the Christians' Jesus, because its Jesus is said to have flourished a full century earlier and in entirely different circumstances. Jesus ben Pandera/Pandara is said to have been born at a specific date, 90 B.C., during the reign of a Jewish High Priest and King who had assumed a Greek name, Alexander Jannaeus. The Christians' Jesus, according to the "New Testament," was born either c. 8 B.C. or c. A.D. 6, depending on which gospel catches your fancy. Jesus ben Pandera flourished when Judaea was an independent kingdom under Jewish rulers; the Christians' Jesus is said to have been active when Judaea was a Roman province. Jesus ben Pandera, after making himself obnoxious to his Jewish rulers, was hanged on the orders of Alexander's widow, a Jewess who had assumed the Greek name of Alexandra Helene, in 70 B.C.; the Christians' Jesus was *crucified* by a Roman governor to content the Jews' Sanhedrin at a date variously set between A.D. 29 and A.D. 33. No one would have wished to retroject the later story to an earlier century or, in all probability, have had the patience and knowledge to situate it in a precise historical setting, but the earlier account could well have been the nucleus about which accreted tales about later religio-political agitators who bore the same common name. It is likely, therefore, that the story in the *Toledoth Yeshu* has some historical basis.

The accounts of the paternity of the earlier Jesus are probably gossip or conjecture and are of no real importance, except to Christians. In the version known to Celsus, this Jesus was the son of a low-class Jewess by a soldier who bore a Greek name, properly Pantheras, which is a Doric personal name (meaning 'hunter') which might well have been borne by a common soldier in the Macedonian armies of the Seleucids. According to the *Toledoth Yeshu*, this Jesus was the son of a Jew named Joseph Pandera, and since the second name, which is certainly not Aramaic, must represent the name Panthera, that Joseph must have assumed a Gentile name for business purposes, as Jews have done throughout history and as Jews today masquerade under such names as Montagu, Stewart, Hunter, Miller, etc. Joseph, alias Pandera, under the cover of night, seduced the chaste Mary by impersonating her spouse, John, and the result was Jesus, whom the cuckolded husband carried off to Egypt together with his ravished wife to avoid scandal. This part of the story is, of course, trivial and irrelevant.

The significant part of the *Toledoth Yeshu* is its account of the career of this early Jesus. When adult, he returned from Egypt as a miracle-mongering evangelist, who actually convinced Alexandra Helene, the Jewish queen-regent, of his holiness, but without claiming divine parentage for himself. He enjoyed her favor and patronage for a time, but eventually lost it. After wandering off to Galilee to stir up the Jews there, he returned with some three hundred followers and, disguised and mounted on an ass, led them into Jerusalem on the eve of the Passover. He was betrayed, however, by a follower named Judah Iskariot, and the queen-regent had him hanged. There was hanky-panky when the corpse was taken down, and it disappeared for a time, thus enabling the holy man's disciples to claim that he had ascended to Heaven and would shortly return to raise Hell on earth in the manner of the Jesus in the Apocalypse included in the "New Testament."

That story could have a factual basis. Historians will be particularly impressed by the characteristic change of mind attributed to Alexandra Helene, who is known to have reversed herself suddenly in much more important matters. The story in the *Toledoth Yeshu*, from which I have extracted the summary above, is as full of magic and other absurdities as any gospel in the "New Testament." For a fuller summary in English, see the excellent study by the learned Dr. Martin A. Larson, *The Essene-Christian Faith* (New York, Philosophical Library, 1980).

As Dr. Larson shows, Jesus ben Pandera can almost certainly be identified with the "Teacher of Righteousness," the unnamed but martyred christ of the Essenes, a sect of Jewish communists, directed by a secret council of Elders, who flourished during the last two centuries B.C. and the first century A.D. The practices and exoteric doctrines of the Essenes have long been known from fairly reliable sources, and as early as our eighteenth century judicious students began to identify the Essenes as the original Christians—a conclusion which naturally aroused the fury of holy men who had a vested interest in making everything begin with the tales in the "New Testament." That conclusion was too sweeping, unless one allows for considerable modifications of the Essenes' propaganda to make it more palatable to the *goyim.* Dr. Larson shows that they probably were the principal channel through which "orthodox" Christianity derived the Zoroastrian and

Buddhistic elements (briefly described in my article in the August issue) that are its real framework. For the details, I must refer you to Dr. Larson, who, more clearly than any other writer known to me, identifies as Essene some gospels that were excluded from the "orthodox" anthology called the Bible when it was put together in 325, although they had been accepted as canonical by even the Fathers of the Church before that time and continued to be quoted by them until later. He also identifies as Essene most of the famous "Dead Sea Scrolls" that are religious in subject and have been thus far published.*

AT THE FEET OF THE MASTERS

For a description of the Essenes, I must refer the reader to Dr. Larson's lucid book. But there are problems. There always are problems in this field. A man who tries to find his way among the innumerable Jewish and Christian sects of this period and tries to understand their mad hariolations soon begins to feel vertigo and, if he persists in that vitiated atmosphere, to doubt his own sanity. But there are two questions that have some importance for us.

The Essenes are reported to have consisted of only four thou-

* In his preface, Dr. Larson, citing an article in *Harper's* magazine by the distinguished British scholar, John Allegro, that I have not seen, calls attention to the disquieting fact that so many of the scrolls found years ago remain unpublished and seem likely so to remain indefinitely, although a commission composed of Jews and Roman Catholics has supposedly been laboring strenuously ever since the first publications more than thirty years ago. Even more disturbing is the fact that Professor Allegro was not even permitted to see the unpublished documents, although he is certainly the most distinguished scholar in the field who has no axe to grind. The documents that were found in caves near the Dead Sea are of two major types: (1)gospels, and (2) letters and other records of the activities of the last Jewish christ, Bar-Kokhba (mentioned in my article). The apparent determination to publish no more of the religious works is ominous, and there is reason to apprehend a conspiracy between the Jews and Roman Catholics involved to suppress information that would be bad for their business. That will distress scholars, who naturally want to work out all the intricate problems to their last details, but we may comfort ourselves with the reflection that all the Judaeo-Christian religious gabble is mere trash anyway.

sand male Jews who had never polluted themselves by touching females and never would so defile themselves. One is reminded that
the homosexuals who have become so numerous in all Aryan
countries today fall into two clearly distinguishable groups: some
have a psychopathic abhorrence of females, while others follow the
liberal doctrine popularized by the daughter of a once-famous
American senator: "Male sex? Female sex? What do I care, so long
as it is sex?"

The Essenes maintained a kind of auxiliary organization for
men who weren't strong enough to spurn the nasty sex and actually consorted with women and begat children. The auxiliary
doubtless added to the revenues and may have been the means
by which the sectaries principally exercised an influence, much
as the Communist cells in the modern world operated largely
through "fellow travelers." The males of the core organization
owned no property, having everything in common, thus resem-
bling the Christian monastic orders and, like them, becoming
very wealthy. The Essenes professed a great concern and love
for the poor, and regarded the wealthy—even wealthy Jews—
with a hatred of Bolshevik intensity.

Now one cannot but wonder what relation the proletarian
doctrine of the Essenes, Christians, and Bolsheviks bears to the
standard technique that the Jews use whenever they swarm into
a nation to plunder it. One division of the invaders settles
down to battening on the poor as usurers, vendors of shoddy
merchandise, bankers, pawn brokers, saloon keepers, pornogra-
phers, brothel-keepers, showmen, and the like, and they soon
have the proletariat reduced to the serfdom of perpetual debt,
as they have done today in Aryan nations throughout the
world. Another division of the horde as promptly starts to wail
with humanitarian anguish over the terrible plight of the "oppressed" peasants and the "downtrodden" workers and to excite them to sedition and the futility of Jewish-managed
revolutions while simultaneously creating in feeble minds an
image of the Jews as great humanitarians whose huge and ten-

der hearts throb with compassion for the unhappiness of the poor. The crocodile of the fable never wept so hard while devouring his prey. The results of Jewish compassion are always the same. As General Fuller summarized the Jewish revolution in Russia in 1917-18: "They promised a paradise for the workers and they created a paradise for the bankers."

Under various names, Bolshevism has been a Jewish stock in trade from the earliest times, and such agitation of the proletariat in the nations of their victims must have been one of the first tricks perfected by the motley rabble of marauders that became a power that now is close to total domination over the globe on which it seems about to impose its "world government."*

In short, were the Essenes fanatics or agitators? And if the former, how do such fanatics fit into the Jews' strategy for world conquest so neatly? And, on another level, how does proletarian agitation, which manipulates the poor and the workers while swindling them, and which is now often carried on by professed atheists, such as Marx, complement or supplement the religious agitations on which the Jews have principally relied to conceal their actual power by enabling them to pose as "persecuted" by their victims? The Jews' need to whine piteously about "persecution" while they suck ever more blood out of the nations they are destroying is well-known, and, when the *goyim* do not provide enough pretexts, they sometimes arrange to "persecute" themselves, as today, when they occasionally bomb their own synagogues, partly to give them a chance to snivel in public as well as to provide a means of destroying insubordinate *goyim* under a cover of legality by bribing or overawing the judiciary of nations they have by the throat. Does their feigned concern for the poor

* The reader will enjoy Dietrich Eckart's essay, *Bolshevism from Moses to Lenin.* A reprint of the German text and an English translation are available from Liberty Bell Publications. On the career of Eckart until his death in 1923 after he was arrested by the Jews who then owned Germany, see William Gillespie's booklet, *Dietrich Eckart*, published by the author. Arm-chair strategists in politics may speculate about what would have happened, had Hitler taken the uncompromising position advocated in Eckart's "dialogue" with him.

among the despised goyim help the parasites seem "oppressed" themselves? And finally, is it possible that the Jewish mentality, which differs so fundamentally from our own, can believe its own shams? There is some evidence that, impossible as it seems, the Jews can make themselves believe in their own hoaxes. Such a mental process in an Aryan is simply insanity, and one does not wonder that Aryan psychologists sometimes conclude that paranoia or some other form of insanity is innate in the Jewish race, but that merely shows the folly of trying to understand alien mentalities in terms of our own.

About another aspect of the Essenes there can be no doubt. One of the "Dead Sea Scrolls" is the "War of the Sons of Light [i.e., Jews] Against the Sons of Darkness [i.e., Aryans]." It is a fantastic scenario, written, of course, long before the failure of the great Jewish outbreaks in the first and second centuries of our era, that describes the military operations by which the Chosen People, with some help from their Chooser, will smite the hated *goyim* and exterminate them, "so that none survive." But after the Jews have danced joyously on the enormous "mounds of the slain," lo! by some schizoid miracle, the *goyim* appear again, now in their proper status as slaves of the Jews. "Rejoice, o Zion, rejoice!... Keep the gates of Jerusalem and the other cities of Jews] constantly open that the wealth of all nations may be brought in to Zion, that their kings may be your slaves, and that all who have oppressed [*sic!*] you may bow their foreheads to the ground and lick off the dust of your feet!" And the ecstatic exhortation continues with the proclamation, "Israel shall rule the world forever."

Now it is a strange fact that when this document was first translated, quite a few Christians professed to be shocked by that glimpse of typically Jewish beatitude. I can only suppose that, as I have suggested before, they read their own holy book in a trance, for they must have read the same loving sentiments in their *Isaiah*, 49.23, where the same vision of "righteousness" (as Jews understand it) concludes with the promise that the kings and queens of the *goyim* shall become the household slaves of the Jews, and all the lower races "shall bow down to thee with their faces toward the earth, and lick up the dust of thy feet."

That vision of realized ambition is preceded, of course, by the usual drivel about how the world's destined owners are always persecuted for their "righteousness." I do not profess to be a psychiatrist, but I venture a guess that God's Race will feel oppressed and persecuted so long as there lives an Aryan whose tongue is not eager to lick their dirty feet.

THE HOLY HOAX

Since the publication of Professor Arthur Butz's definitive treatise, *The Hoax of the Twentieth Century*, there no longer remains even the faintest doubt about the "six million" Jews, whom Hitler is said to have exterminated before they crawled into the United States and other nations of the West as whining "refugees." That great swindle is, of course, a most impressive demonstration of the Jews' unique racial capacity for collective lying, but even Aryans who are now defying the Jewish Terror to expose it sometimes fail to see that it depends on a much greater hoax.

Suppose that the Jews' characteristically big lie were the truth—that the Germans really had made a desperate attempt to rid themselves of their parasites by killing six million of them. If the Germans had done that, what of it? Why should Aryans be concerned about that effort at national sanitation? By any objective standard, if the Germans had killed six million Jews, that accomplishment would have been only half as noteworthy as the undisputed fact that the Soviets, in just one of their many applications of "social engineering," exterminated at least twelve million Ukrainians. And in Aryan nations, from Sweden to Australia, no one seems incensed about that mass-murder, although the Ukrainian victims were largely Aryans, members of our own race. When the Ukrainians were murdered, Aryan journalists, gratefully gnawing the bones thrown them by their Yiddish owners, either concealed the fact from their readers or muttered platitudes about the need for breaking eggs to make omelets. And today, it has become a social *gaffe* even to mention in public something so trivial and ir-relevant as the murder of twelve million Aryans. But the Jews' hoax about the "six million" still makes feeble-minded Aryans yowl in "righteous" indignation.

The only explanation of that paradox is that Aryans, in their present self-abasement, do regard a Jew as far more precious than an Aryan. They take it for granted that the Jews are a vastly supe-rior race.

That immeasurable superiority must be accepted by Christians who believe their Bible, which tells them that during the greater part of human history Yahweh, the Big Jew in the clouds who cre-ated heaven and earth, was uniquely concerned for the welfare of his tribe and regarded other races as sheep, to be fleeced or butch-ered for their comfort. That conclusion is even stated quite frankly by some Bible-banging fakirs. I note that one Jerry Falwell, who is said to gross about twenty million dollars a year by vending holy hokum to the suckers, affirms that "God has blessed [!] America because America blessed the Jew, His Chosen People." And what is more insidious, the "modernist" shysters in the pulpits of all the established churches, who no longer try to make their customers believe the mythology, claim that what they call the "Judaeo-Christian tradition" represents a morality so sublime that it is an outrage even to question it. And that nonsense is generally be-lieved.

The infection has gone deep into the vitals of our people. A writer who discusses Western culture, whether historically or philosophically, will necessarily consider extensively the religion that dominated our race for a large part of its history. But I have yet to see a work on that subject which frankly describes that relig-ion as a disaster, comparable to the Black Death, which also pro-foundly changed the history of Europe. Serious writers on modern culture are not Christians: they would feel insulted, if you implied they believed the silly tales about Adam and his spare rib, the Yah-weh who graciously exposed his buttocks for the admiration and veneration of Moses, and the virgin birth of the son that Yahweh got by proxy. But nevertheless, when such writers mention the Jews, they describe them as a "uniquely gifted people," admirably "god-fearing," and chock-full of "righteousness," and they even credit the Jews with the invention of monotheism, which they suppose to be a "higher" form of religion. They may even go so far as Eric Voegelin, a learned and intelligent man, who began a multi-volume analysis of Western civilization with the Jews, whom he credited with an "epochal leap in being" that "establishes the order of man in his immediacy under God" (whatever that means) that thus made possible true civilization. Aryans commonly write or accept such bombast because Christianity, in which they no longer believe, so polluted the culture in which they grew up that they accept its claim to an enormous moral superiority over other religions. And so they naturally stand in awe of the wonderful race that invented such exemplary tales, even though the tales are false.

It is that superstition about a discredited superstition that prevents our people from recognizing a simple and indubitable historical fact. The Jews began as a petty tribe or band of marauders, mere bandits or pirates preying on the more civilized nations of the Near East, but, by centuries of selective breeding they made themselves into a race that has a unique racial cohesion and a unique genius for dissimulation, deceit, and fraud. They thus became a biological phenomenon for which there is no parallel, a race of human parasites, who dispersed themselves throughout the inhabited world, reaching even China by the first century B.C., and planting their colonies, much as certain species of wasps plant their eggs in the bodies of the caterpillars that will be the living nourishment of the larvae. When Jews sneak into a country to begin eating on its inhabitants, they ostentatiously parade an oddly barbaric religion, claim to be wonderfully "righteous" and "god-fearing," and whine that they are poor refugees, "persecuted" for their piety. How much of this they themselves believe is an irrelevant question: it makes no difference to their victims. The simple fact is that, thanks to their race's solidarity in dispersion and to their capacity for *collective* lying, the Jews have made themselves virtually the masters of the entire globe, from which they are determined to eliminate our race, a breed of cattle that is sometimes troublesome. As the disobedience of the German herd a few decades ago proved, the breed's capacity for rational thought cannot *always* be kept under control by the Christian doctrine of "Don't think: just believe!"

Although that capacity for rational thought is the characteristic of our race, it has never appeared in a majority of our people and it is commonly obfuscated or thwarted by their proneness to superstition. It seems to be no match for the cunning of the Jews, and at present the prospects are that the Aryan is a species that is not only endangered, but doomed.

THE RELIGION OF THE WEST

We must respect and honor the comparatively few persons today who have Mr. Clerkin's exemplary loyalty to our race while retaining their belief in Christianity. We must sincerely hope that, for the sake of a common cause, they will, by an act of truly heroic charity, forgive what must seem to them outrageous blasphemy. They have no need to be told what has happened to what was once the faith of Europe. And courtesy would be misplaced, if it estopped us from asking the crucial question about the terrible reality that we must face.

What suicidal superstition has besotted our race?

Our race is now the most degraded and despised species of mammals on earth.

If you doubt that, look about you.

Although Rhodesia is on their very doorstep, the Aryans of South Africa are pleasing Jewish financiers by kowtowing to the eternal savages. They are obsequiously squandering their resources to furnish the Blacks with "homelands," and have, for example, just announced that they will spend 1,000,000,000 rand ($1,400,000,000) to make just one of these squalid dens comfortable for the noble savages. White men are to have no rights in the "homelands," but the Blacks are to "participate" in the government of white men in the rest of South Africa, and to be "educated" free—obviously so that they can eventually take over, as in Rhodesia, although the Jews' stooges in the South African government haven't said so, as yet. And the Aryan population, which numbers about four million, has just been told that it will have to build twenty new cities to accommodate the twenty-one million Blacks who will swarm into its territory in the next two decades. And the dumb brutes accept their serfdom and chatter about the "prosperity" that their Jewish usurers have allowed them!

Now the significant thing is that the rudimentary minds of the Congoids perceive what the crazed Aryans refuse to see. The savages feel only wonder and contempt as they are flattered and loaded with gifts by a race they once thought intelligent. And they will tolerate the Aryans so long as the fools work hard enough for them and still have much to give. The savages are indolent and patient: they may tolerate the Aryan imbeciles for a decade or even longer before they proclaim *uhuru* and make South Africa another Congo, in which stupid white pigs will have only culinary utility.

In the Britain that was once great, now a little island that is being pushed steadily toward total economic prostration, where many Aryan parents are undergoing real privation to give their few children a decent education, the Aryans, according to a single despatch in the press, are handing out one hundred million pounds to the mongrels of Pakistan, 114,000,000 pounds to the mongrels of India, one hundred million pounds to the mongrels on Ceylon ("Sri Lanka"!), and eighty-two million pounds to speed up the raping and slaughter of the Aryan kinsmen whom they betrayed in Rhodesia. And not content with squandering their declining resources, they are importing Black and Oriental vermin from all over the world to destroy their children. One hour on a street in London should enable any observer—even a stolid Anglo-Saxon—to forecast accurately the future of Britain and guess how long it will be before the Aryans' children will wish they had not been born.

In the United States, there is a well-known proverb, "Give a nigger an inch and he will take mile." So Americans presumably know what they are doing when they coddle their millions of blacks and mulattos, shower them with gifts called "welfare," pay them to breed even faster, and even have white children hauled to "integrated" schools to be degraded to the animal level and usually raped and mauled. The Americans must know from long experience that their savages can understand such fawning appeasement only as a cowardly confession of weakness, and that the savages react as does a dog when he sees a fleeing rabbit. Not content with this, the Americans are importing at great expense more enemies: hordes of savages from Haiti, where the white population was exterminated more than a century ago; mongrel "refugees" from Cuba, chiefly males of military age; masses of mongrels from Mexico, who talk openly of "taking back" the southwestern third of the United States, which was once Spanish territory; and a flood of Mongolians, whose subtle minds are delighted by the insanity of the race from which they intend to take eventually the fertile lands of North America, Australia, and New Zealand. One can only assume that the Americans have a Christian urge to get to Heaven as quickly and painfully as possible.

All this is commonplace, of course, but few were prepared for the latest news from the "land of the free," where the dunces welcome to their bosoms and throats every race but their own. If the press is to be believed, five gentlemen from Belgium, who had come to visit friends in the United States, were hustled out of that country because a Jew thought that they had some "Neo-Nazi" thoughts in their heads. The propagandist who wrote those paragraphs in *Isaiah* was a prophet: the white curs are now crawling on their bellies to lick their masters' grimy feet.

Why speak of Australia, where a handful of Jewish gold has induced the same suicidal mania? Or of Sweden, where anyone who walks on a street in Stockholm can see, even if he looks only at faces that have light complexions, that the Swedes have already made themselves a minority in their own country?

Everywhere today, the average Aryan flinches when he hears

the word 'Aryan,' evidently believing that a respectful reference to his own race is the Unforgivable Sin Against the Holy Ghost. He will recite a statement that all races are equal, taking a Christian pride in believing what is patently false. He gabbles endlessly about "Christian charity" and a "Christian duty" to toil for the gratification of the rest of the world. He babbles about the "under-privileged" and "all mankind" and "underdeveloped nations" and "one world" and all the rest of the malodorous tripe that the Jews' newspapers and television feed the boobs every day.

The Aryans now take a Christian pride in their own degradation. They seem delighted to have not only the Jews, but all the vermin in the world eat and excrete on them. Unless you assume that Aryans really are a biologically inferior species, the only explanation of their madness, it seems to me, is that the cancer of Christianity has at last eaten into their brains. Is it too late for surgery?

THE JEWS AND THE
CHRIST-BUSINESS

THE JEWS AND THE
CHRIST-BUSINESS

Ralph Perier's article, "The Jews Love Christianity," in the August issue of *The Liberty Bell*, was given emphatic confirmation last Sunday in the magazine section of the *Telegraph*, Britain's largest "conservative" newspaper. It devoted a page to the Reverend Mr. Paul Oestreicher, an Anglican Vicar in Blackheath and a prominent member of the General Synod of the Church of England.

He began, naturally, with a paragraph about the awful sufferings of his fellow Jews under the awful Nazis, but explained that he wasn't gassed because his parents, who had lived in fear of "jackboots and long batons" and had hidden him in a cellar, "escaped" from Germany in May 1939. What he means, of course, is that they took a train from Berlin to France or Denmark, and that the Germans, if they noticed the departure at all, were glad to be rid of a pair of marranos and their tyke.

The Reverend Mr. Oestreicher rather indiscreetly gave the show away in the statement I will put in boldface. His parents had turned Christian before he was born, but he "grew up," he says, "proud of my Jewish background. Was not every Christian, every follower of Jesus of Nazareth, spiritually a Jew by adoption?" He goes on to claim that the holy Jews can "heal broken humanity," because "'Hear O Israel, the Lord God is one Lord. That is the overriding truth of Judaism and Christianity," two cults which he obviously regards as merely two sides of the same counterfeit coin.

By coincidence, *News of the World*, a Sunday newspaper which claims the largest circulation in Britain, devoted a whole page of its issue for 18 January to a Jew who has set himself up in the christ-business in India. He calls himself "Bhagwan Shree Rajneesh." His title implies that

The Jews and the Christ Business was (under the by-line "By Our London Correspondent") Dr. Oliver's contribution to, and was first published in, *Liberty Bell* for March 1981.

THE MASTER: Bhagwan

he is the incarnation of a god and his followers so regard him, but when talking to outsiders they usually give him the more modest title of "The Blessed One." This clever Kike runs a spiritual bucket-shop near Poona which attracts many wealthy and feeble-minded Aryan females, including even members of the British nobility, such as Lady Caroline, daughter of the Earl of Lauderdale, and Lady Zara, daughter of Earl Jellicoe and grand-daughter of the Admiral who commanded the British fleet at the celebrated Battle of Jutland (Skagerrak).

A recent American convert is the daughter of Congressman Leo Ryan, who was killed when the nincompoops who followed another holy man to Guyana staged a mass-suicide at "Jonestown" two years ago. Miss Ryan says of her six thousand fellow-converts in the nest of holiness near Poona that "if Bhagwan asked them to kill themselves, they would do it. If Bhagwan asked them to kill someone else, they would do it." She wasn't sure that she had quite that much faith in the Blessed One, although he is an "incarnation of Jesus or Buddha or Mohammed," who were probably the same god on different visits. She also reported that most of the six thousand half-wits are British, American, or German, and are in their twenties.

Males are also attracted to the Jewish messiah. Henry Frederick Thynne, sixth Marquis of Bath who was born in 1905, is probably the most distinguished male votary of The Blessed One and claims that, despite his age, he was "helped enormously." The most illustrious sucker was Prince Welf of Hanover, the nephew by marriage of Queen Elizabeth II. (He was the son of the sister of Prince Philip.) His pictures show him to have been a tall, handsome, and obviously vigorous man, but he died suddenly, reportedly after an exercise in karate, although some irreligious persons suspect that he may have died of disillusion

GATEWAY to the good life for pilgrims

and a wish to leave The Blessed One, who would not have been pleased by the defection of so prominent a worshiper. However that may be, Prince Welf brought his Princess and their daughter to share the joys of spiritual enlightenment and intensive copulation at God's shop near Poona and they are reportedly still there.

The boobs of the "jet set" who get holiness at the feet of The Blessed One enter the colony through a gateway where a sign informs that they must check their luggage *and minds* at the gate. They also leave their clothes, being given orange-colored Hindu dress for wear when they feel like it and leave their identities, being given new names. On the chance that someone may not have left *all* of his mind at the door, they are put through a session of three continuous days, during which teams of questioners incessantly force them to respond to the question, "Who are you?" When they are finally allowed to sleep, no shred of intelligence can be left, and they are ready for the elevating course in "primal screaming," in which the idiots howl like banshees until they are exhausted. That prepares them for life in a real kibbutz, in which the Saved have been freed of such silly inhibitions as a desire for privacy in bathrooms and bedrooms, which is contrary to the spirit of truly communal life.

The Elect sleep together in big rooms, but are routed from

CUDDLES: Happy hippies find togetherness in the Blessed One's camp

slumber at six A.M. every morning and set to jumping up and down while they yell "Hoo, hoo, hoo!" That, The Blessed One candidly told the reporter, "goes directly to the sex center" and their "energy starts to flow."

Much energy is needed to follow the Path to God, at least by the males of the colony. One great advantage of getting Spiritual Awareness at Poona is that when the Spirit moves you, you don't have to waste time by taking the female to a bedroom. All of the Righteous live in common, like the Adamites, Carpocratians, and other early Christian sects. So, when the Spirit of the Lord moves you, you just copulate with the female right then and there, for the edification and stimulation of other Pilgrims whose energies have been primed by yelling "Hoo, hoo, hoo!" in the morning.

There is, unfortunately, a limit to such godliness. The Spirit is, no doubt, always willing, but, as Jesus said, the flesh is weak. One male member told the reporter that after he copulated with "three or four women" in quick succession, he became tired and took a long rest. He was sure, however, that such exercises were "infinitely beautiful," although he admitted that Indian lice, Indian diseases, and Indian toilets were something of a deterrent to novices who have not yet become Spiritually Perfect and exalted above such worldly concerns.

Intensive copulation, according to the Yiddish Messiah in India, prepares the Elect to "find God by experiencing 'cosmic orgasm.'" What drug is used to help with "cosmic orgasms" is uncertain. The physicians whom I have consulted doubt that it is heroin, which seems to be a considerable part of The Blessed One's holy business.

One has to be fairly prosperous to enjoy Spiritual Rebirth at Poona. The minimum charge for Life with God is $125 a day. Three English females, a fairly well-known actress and two girls from the universities, whose funds were exhausted by prolonged godliness, were caught while smuggling heroin into France. They said they had to earn their keep in God's colony, and were given their choice of doing it by smuggling heroin into Europe or by public prostitution. Anyone who has seen and smelled the mongrels of India, where prostitutes are lucky if they can collect more than five rupees (sixty-five cents) from a customer, will not be astonished that the women chose the first alternative, but may wonder why the Spirit of the Lord did not benumb the inquisitiveness of the French customs inspectors. It may be that the three did not have enough Faith in their Saviour.

The Jew in Poona is much shrewder than was Dr. Wilhelm Reich, who set up an Institute for Sexual Politics in Germany to preach his gospel that sexual orgasms produce cosmic energy, which he called "orgone," and that the universe was malfunctioning because men and women were so inhibited they weren't having enough "total orgasms." He prudently escaped the nasty Nazis by leaving Germany a little ahead of the Reverend Mr. Oestreicher's parents. He reached the United States, via Denmark and Sweden, in 1939 and peddled to thousands of wealthy suckers his "Orgone Energy Accumulators," until he was sent to prison for fraud by a judge who must have been a "Neo-Nazi." The Jew from Vienna didn't think of bringing God into his act and posing as another Jesus. That's the sales-pitch that always works with nitwits who have been brought up as "spiritually Jews by adoption."

As the holy Jew in Poona could tell you, the christ-business is fine. It beats fire sales, Communism, and even usury all hollow.

APPENDIX A

A White Christian Racist
Defends His Faith
by Major Donald V. Clerkin

[The article by Ralph Perier in our August issue, "The Jews Love Christianity," has excited a great deal of comment, both adverse and commendatory. Since the question is fundamental to all racial thinking, we publish here an exposition of the Christian position by Donald Vincent Clerkin of the Euro-American Alliance (P.O. Box 2-1776, Milwaukee, Wisc. 55221).

We have sent a copy of this article to Mr. Perier and hope to have his comment on it in time for inclusion in our next issue.

* * * * *

In Appendix B you will find reproduced letters we have received—pro and con—in response to Mr. Perier's article in the August issue of Liberty Bell.]

* * * * *

The Jews Love Christianity is a brilliant exposition of a particular thesis. Mr. Perier is obviously well schooled in late Classical-Age history and the theological movement both of the period and during the previous centuries. Where I take issue with his thesis is in his overt prejudice against Christianity, which impeaches any attempt to appear objective, and in the fact that he seems to have forgotten that Christianity underwent a profound *metamorphosis* during its European sojourn of nineteen hundred years, the cultural alteration taking place during Europe's mediaeval era.

He approaches his subject from the viewpoint of a confirmed atheist: a more difficult position from which to argue for positive racism cannot be imagined. Perier forgets that if God did not create our superior Aryan race, then all we are and have accomplished throughout the ages is but a

"A White Christian Racist Defends His Faith" first appeared in *Liberty Bell* for October 1980.

product of chance. It stretches the imagination to ask us to believe that this people of genius might be, according to the odds associated with a roll of the dice or a turn of a card, no more intelligent and filled with constructive designs than a camp of Hottentots or Kaffirs.

Saying that the early Fathers of the Church were clever manipulators of a faltering Roman Imperium is one thing; to deny that Jesus of Nazareth actually lived is quite another. Still worse is the cruel reiteration of the Talmudic charge that all of Christendom have been worshiping the bastard son of a Roman or Greco-Syrian auxiliary by a whore of a Jewess. Simply because the Jews treat Jesus Christ and Bar-Kokhba in similar fashion in the *Talmud* does in no way prove that they were correct in their assessment of Christ; it merely shows the propensity of the Jews to hate roundly, even those who have attempted to serve their heinous purposes and have failed.

But it is in the infusion of Magian Christianity, formulated by Paul, who, in truth, was a renegade Pharisee, and developed by the early Church Fathers, many of whom may indeed have been Jews or allied Semites, into the Culture-stream of emerging Europe that Mr. Perier's argument falters. For whatever St. Paul or the Fathers may have contrived as a menace to Rome in its later days, a true Spenglerian *pseudomorphosis* did not take place over the Culture-organism of Europe. If indeed Mr. Perier is correct when he alleges that Christianity is but a hoax perpetrated by the Jews to deceive and destroy Rome, then one would be led to deduce that the Jews should have been clever enough to concoct a menace that could have stifled any possibility of an independent flowering of a peculiar European spirituality.

A study of history, especially Spengler's seminal *The Decline Of The West*, will prove beyond a shadow of a doubt that Europe was not smothered by a Magian *pseudomorphosis* of the Culture, the way that everything Semitic after Babylon stank of Baal. No, Mr. Perier, Magian Semitism did not change the face of Europe immediately after the fall of Rome: it was Christianity, Magian-Semitic at its birth, that took on a Gothic physiognomy.

Throughout the ensuing history of Europe—from 1176 A.D. to the Reformation, thence to the Calvinist 17th century and the Rationalist 18th century—Christianity was molded by the Culture-rythms of the European Spring and early Sommer. The center of Christian influence during these centuries was Italy, though to be sure an Italy no

longer of the Romans but of the Gothic tribes that came south to
plunder and stayed to rule. It is true that those Jews who swarmed over
the late Roman world threw off their togas upon the approach of the
Germanic tribes, hoping that the invaders would not confuse them
with the enemy Classical peoples: parasite Jews have always been hang-
ers-on to other peoples and civilizations. Jews, however, did not carry
Christianity to the Gothic peoples, for to have openly espoused the faith
of the latter Roman Empire certainly would have compromised the safety
of Jewry. Jews preferred to revert to full cultural status as a Middle Eastern
entity, something strange to the Goths, who viewed the Jews as a people
not of military virtue and therefore posing no threat to the new order over
Mediterranean Europe. The task of Christianizing the Goths was carried
out by the toilers in the monastic orders, who were hardly Jews, most being of the oldest Celtic blood. Rome had once conquered the Celts—the
Christian Celts prevailed upon then-*barbarian* northern and central
Europe to accept the faith of the New Rome, the papacy.

If there were Jews involved, and no doubt there were some in trading
and money lending *vis-a-vis* the early Church, especially in the Eastern
Empire at Constantinople, they certainly could not have been so influential in spiritual matters as Mr. Perier claims. Judaism as a practice, together with the promulgation of rabbinical exhortations to be found in
the *Mischna* and *Gemara*, was proscribed by order of the Church everywhere within its jurisdiction. Jews were identified as Christ-killers—de-
icides. Moreover, the feudal system of economics was not fertile ground
for the type of rape, cut-and-run business so well-beloved by the Jews.
That sort of swindle was not tolerated by the feudal aristocracy, the *Castle*,
united in cultural and spiritual ties to the Church, the *Cathedral.* It remained for the rise of Civilization during the late European Summer,
with the concomitant rise of great metropolises, to give the Jews a home-
base for their operations against the waning feudal system *and* the Gothic
Church. The Jew is indeed a world proletarian, but European Christianity
grew in aristocratic feudal-mediaeval soil; that is what motivated the Jew-
ish-promoted revolutions of the 18th, 19th, and early 20th centuries, up-
heavals which pulled down the Castle and the Cathedral.

It is no accident that Luther's North German revolt against the
open profligacies of the papal court, the expected reaction of the vi-
brant north against the decadence of the south, was perverted and pro-

foundly altered by John Calvin and his followers. Calvin, a 'French-man', was known in his own country as Jean Cauin and in Zürich as Johannes Cohen. Yes, Calvin-Cauin-Cohen was the veritable Jew under the Protestant-Christian bed. Mr. Perier is correct in his match of Calvin's peculiarly Jewish orientation of Scripture with the atrocities committed by his staunch English follower, Oliver Cromwell, especially against the equally staunch Roman Catholic Irish. Together with the fact that Cromwell undid the great work of Edward I and invited the Jews to return to England, offering a general amnesty even to those changelings who wished to throw off the pseudo-Christian cloak their ancestors had assumed for purely pragmatic reasons, we have a damning statement against Calvinism, an ideology of materialism masquerading as faith. Calvinism—Pharisaism and Talmudism in disguise—is responsible for the spawning of Freemasonry, which Adolf Hitler, a Catholic to the day of his death, rightly hated, and out of Freemasonry the hideous corruption of the B'nai B'rith. The founding society of *Illuminati* may have included atheists and deists, but there were just as many Calvinists operating against the Gothic Church and the Ancient Regime of Europe.

Even earlier the English, during the reign of the voluptuary, King Henry VIII, had witnessed the stamping out of the religious orders, with the confiscation in true Talmudic fashion of all monastic wealth. Henry's agent in this act of theft was Thomas Cromwell, a man greedy for personal gain, who swore that he acted in the finest traditions of John Knox, the thundering Scottish Calvinist who had called for the execution of Mary, Queen of Scots, a Catholic. Henry's argument ought to have been with the Calvinists: though time had worn on the monastic orders throughout Europe, still, the orders had proved their Christian charity and usefulness to the crowned monarchs, the nobility and the people of England for more than a thousand years. The attack on the Church was an act of gross ingratitude.

Though Europe struggled through the terrible fratricidal *Thirty Years' War* (1618-1648), that was an expression of separate emerging European nations jockeying for position during the Middle to Late Summer of the Culture. The rôle of the Jews is often hinted at as pushing both sides, Catholic and Protestant, forward into the fray. Those who argue from that position accord the Jews far more credit than they deserve. It could be logically argued that Mr. Perier's entire anti-Christian statement is nought but an offhanded salute to Jewish brilliance: the Jews, or so it would seem to the careful reader of Mr. Perier's work, are to be awarded the dubious prize for having schooled Niccolo Machiavelli in the fine art of political dissembling.

Cherchez le Juif has its profound meaning in both the French and Bolshevist Revolutions. Jewish Calvinism prepared the public mind of France for an attack upon the Church and the Bourbon State, and when it came, lo and behold, the Jew Maximilien Robespierre was the man to reckon with. The Enlightenment may have moved the intellectuals toward revolt, but that same Calvinism that struck Charles I's head off in Cromwellian England surfaced once again, this time in revolutionary France to lead the Mob against their betters.

We need but mention the names of the old Bolsheviks and their alter-egos the Mensheviks Trotsky (Bronstein), Litvinov (Finkelstein), Dan, Kerensky (Adler), *et al*—to realize the total Jewish underpinnings of the revolt against Christian Russia.

Claims may be made with acute accuracy that Kaiser Wilhelm II advanced the Jews too readily, so that they were able to stab Germany in the back in 1918. Few can successfully argue that Czar Nicholas II was the fawning benefactor of Jewry. His predecessor Czar Alexander II had made the grievous mistake of emancipating the Jews socially and politically: in 1881 his foolish kindness was repaid by an explosion of a bomb which took his life—the sordid plot having been hatched in the home of a Jewess. These emancipated Jews finished off the Romanovs and their Christian State in an ocean of blood: the Romanovs were the last truly Christian monarchs of the European blood; what remains are merely jet-set pretenders to the purple mantle of royalty— Jews of the spirit, if not of the flesh.

Mr. Perier is free to argue that the Jews love Christianity for its inherent weaknesses, that Christ was a hoax, that the Christian faith has been a useful tool and foil of the Jews. But if he knows anything at all about the life of Adolf Hitler, and it would seem that Mr. Perier leans toward Aryanism and National Socialism in his *Weltanschauung*, then he must accept the fact that Hitler himself espoused the type of racial and cultural Christianity I herein defend. Hitler, a Catholic to his last day on earth, called it positive Christianity to distinguish his faith from the *ersatz*-Christianity the *churchianity*—preached by the Jew-loving, liberal, *shabbas goyische* race and culture-distorting stooges and humbugs that have polluted Western Civilization in our century. In America we see their ilk in the form of the media-Christians—Fallwell, Robertson, Bakker, Van Impe, Graham, Schuller, Humbard, Roberts—who praise Christ out of one side of their mouths while giving material and moral support to the Antichrist Jews and their 'Israel'.

The American electronic-Church, our business interests, and our political establishment, as well as most organs of organized religion, are the province of the Calvinist *ethic*, which is why the Aryan poor in America are being thrown to the niggers via open *housing, busing,* and *affirmative action* fiats. But Calvinism is not Christianity: it is Pharisaism in pseudo-Christian garb; and it is unfair of Mr. Perier to apply this sheeny-Jew brush to all Christian fighters of the Aryan race.

Yes, Mr. Perier, with all due respect for your accomplishments as polemicist—and your powers of language and writing are truly prodigious—you have done yourself and all of us on the Aryan Right a disservice in your attack upon Christianity *per se.* Who do you suppose inspired the examples of Aryan greatness to be found throughout the pages of history? It certainly was not the Jews—nor was it *Nothing!* Those of us who fight on for our Race and Culture, and continue to believe in Christ because we believe our abilities to be ordained by God, we realize that there is no stony silence to be found in an atheistic world: without Jesus Christ we might be moved by the mad mutterings of the Jews. Consider also that no Christ would have meant no Bach or Handel, no Liszt, Franck, or, God forbid!, no Richard Wagner or Anton Bruckner. Can anyone who knows something of art, especially music, rationally argue that these masters were not influenced by a sense of personal piety arising out of a real and profound faith?

I wish to invite Mr. Perier and any of his following to offer proof that positive Christianity has had a deleterious effect on the struggle for the victory of the Aryan race. The Euro-American Alliance and Brigade have built their foundations on faith in Christ. We intend to carry out our mission in the manner of Knights of the Cross. Without Christ as our exemplar what cause would be served by fighting on? Do we fight for money? No. Do we fight for land or bread? No. We fight to preserve the aesthetic beauty of the Aryan *Geist*, which takes the physical form of the White race and its works.

APPENDIX B

The following are letters we received
in response to Mr. Perier's article,
"The Jews Love Christianity,"
which appeared in the
August 1980 issue of
Liberty Bell:

Dear Mr. Dietz: 30 Sep 80

Today the AUGUST *LIBERTY BELL* arrived. Technically it is getting better all the time. But ideologically I feel a word of caution may be called for. I read through the article, "The Jews Love Christianity." It has some interesting and some good information. But it suffers from the heresy of Freethinks, which is that Christianity is an obstacle to civilization and development.

If this were true, how does it come that virtually the only nations that have good plumbing are the ones that have the most Christian churches? Cardinal Faulhaber once reproved those who prefer the old Teutonic Pagans to the modern Christians, admittedly imperfect (sinful) though they still are. Faulhaber said, "Until the Christian Monks came to civilize them, the old Saxon Pagans lounged around clothed, if at all, in the hides of bears, and the women folk did all the domestic work." Even the old Greeks, before they were Christianized, had more slaves than free men, their wives were chattels, and their social life was homosexual.

Good luck. Hope all is well.

A.A., Md.

☆ ☆ ☆

Liberty Bell: 3 Oct. 80

Enclosed is $4.50 to cover 1 copy of "The Jews Love Christianity" and one copy of "Germany Must Perish".

Was glad to see you print the article on "The Jews Love Christianity".

Do you know where I could get *The Jews and Modern Capitalism,*

219

by Werner Sombart?

Sincerely, Mrs. J.S.G., Virginia

Dear George: 8 Oct 80

Please send me your C-60 cassette, "Jewish Entertainment mit der Telephone" and a picture of the Führer. Please find a check enclosed.

As a very active 20-year member of the Mormon Church, I have become quite concerned about the recently surfacing articles by not-so-authoritative authors, indicating that the Jews were the creators of Christianity, and that this was just another master conspiracy of theirs to subdue, and eventually destroy the great Aryan Gentile Nations. I can't bring myself to be severely harsh on these writers, but your Christian readers who have been distressed by these materials can feel assured that his particular theory is completely false and incorrect. It is true that the Satanic Jewish malignancy has severely crippled the development of the Church, beginning even before the death of the Savior. Anyone with a mind to think and eyes to see, must be aware of the tremendous degree of apostacy and degeneracy with which Catholicism, Protestantism, and their myriads of fellow travelers have undergone within the last 1800 years. It is no wonder that intelligent people can recognize the black imprint of the Jewish Anti-Christ on todays' Christianity.

Not only now, but in all preceding dispensations it has been the goal of the pharisees to destroy any vestige of our Savior's kingdom here on earth and they have been highly successful at it. But, be assured that Christ has also been equally undeterred in restoring his truths among his people wherever they even possess a spark of ability to receive it.

I suppose these critics can be partially justified in labeling Christianity as just another fabrication of the Jews, because that is what it has evolved into, at least up until 1830. Unfortunately, the vast majority of the Christian world is totally unfamiliar with the tremendous storehouse of restored scriptures, documents, and translations that have proven conclusively that Christianity in its pure and undefiled form is the oldest religion known to civilized man. Your readers might like to know that for more than 30 years, Papal and Hebrew translators have combined their efforts to intentionally hinder and suppress the translations and publication of ancient archeological manuscripts that demonstrate conclusively that Christianity existed hundreds if not thousands of years before the birth of Christ. These scholars know that to make these works public would precipitate the drying up of the very fountain whereby their own apostate creeds draw sustenance.

At the present time I am considering writing a paper comparing the similarities between Mormonism and National Socialism. These two institutions are probably the greatest potential forces for good that have ever existed among men, and that's why the Jews have carried on their relentless struggle to destroy them. If only a catalyst could be developed to act as a uniting agent between the two, it would guarantee not only the survival of the White Aryan Race, but the leadership and organization needed to safeguard all the world's population against the pernicious Jews. By far the vast majority of Mormons have no knowledge of the Jewish conspiracy and I'm afraid if I go public with this, even my own people will put me away!

George, do you think that this world which is so completely addicted to lies and falsehood can tolerate anymore truths???

R.D., Oregon

Dear George: 10 Oct 80

I was especially delighted by the article, "The Jews Love Christianity." It was an excellent expose of what Jewish Christianity really is. After all, Christianity was created by the Jews for the purpose of "diddling the *goyim.*"

Anyone who has taken the time to study the History of the Jews and the History of the origins of Christianity is forced to accept the fact that Jewish Ebionite Christianity defeated all rational forces in the Roman Empire and fastened the Doctrine of the Trinity on the Western World. The Jews should be proud of Christianity because they created it.

There is one mystery though that is hard to explain. Since the New Testament is an incredible book of forgeries, deletions, and additions, why did they not remove from the New Testament the sayings of Jesus that obviously showed his hatred of them. Jesus, if we can believe the synoptics at all, definitely despised the Talmud (the tradition of the Elders, *Matth.* 15) and held in complete contempt the pharisees, who are today our modern Jews.

Unfortunately the *goyim* choose to ignore the sayings of Jesus that indicate his hatred of the Jews and instead, today, the Jews have so diddled the *goyim* that they foolishly say that Jews are God's Chosen People. Weird, isn't it?

Whether the *goyim* will ever straighten up and act rationally, is a good question. But it is certain that as long as fossil religions continue to dominate the minds of the masses we tetter on the edge of an abyss. The Bible, the Koran, and the Talmud must be relegated to the scrap heap or mankind will continue to have a hard way to go.

Sincerely, L.H., Ph.D.

Dear Mr. Dietz: 10 Oct 80

I have just read the article "The Jews Love Christianity" by Ralph Perier in the August *Liberty Bell* and cannot understand your purpose in printing such a devastating attack on Christianity. Who is Ralph Perier? If he is an American, I would like to remind him that the great men of the White race who built this country were Christians. In carving a great nation out of the wilderness—as they fought their way westward claiming new territory—the first thing they built in each new settlement was their Christian church. Their first prayer in the United States Congress was a Christian prayer. Our great inventive geniuses (Thomas Edison, Henry Ford, etc.) were Christians.

If the descendants of our great Christian Founders have become so brainwashed and Judaized by the race-mixing media that they now comprise a nation of idiots, that does not alter the fact that the great country we had built for us was built by White Christians—not by atheists, "Odinists" or Jews.

Mr. Dietz, you cannot reach the White people of this country by attacking Christianity. It is one thing to point out how far astray they are being led by their Judaized race-mixing so-called leaders and quite another to tell them that Christianity, the faith of the builders of Western Civilization, is a stupid rotten religion.

P.K.

Dear George: 12 Oct 80

Received the August issue of *LIBERTY BELL*. Interesting as usual. However, I am somewhat surprized that you permitted the publication of Ralph Perier's "The Jews Love Christianity".

Whereas it DID contain much truth and justified condemnation of what Christianity has become, it did not have grounds to be as rabid as was the case. The article, in short, was quite distorted. It was primarily guilty of the same error that so many Christians are: associating Hebrews/Israelites with Jews.

But, above all, with you being such a devotee of National Socialism and the man principally responsible for it, A. Hitler, it was surprising you sanctioned the Perier piece. Hitler, by his own testimony, was a staunch Christian. Thus, he, too, must be an utter idiot for honoring that faith. And, "idiots" are just about what the "sophisticated" Perier called Christians! So, YOU either believe what Perier did or what A. Hitler did. Which way is it?

On another matter, may I order one of those "Communism is Jewish" stamps? Check enclosed.

Thank you, J.M., Tennessee

☆ ☆ ☆

Dear George: 13 Oct 80

I have just read "The Jews Love Christianity" and it says very well my opinion that the Communists cannot be dealt with because Christianity is their best protection. If the White race is to survive we must reject the Jewish, Christian propaganda and adopt something which is at least true—like the pre-Christian Vikings believed.

Please send 10 copies of "The Jews Love Christianity", 10 Vol. 1 The International Jew and 2 "Nature's Eternal Religion". Check enclosed.

Yours truly, G.G., Washington

☆ ☆ ☆

Dear George: 17 Oct 80

It is with a great deal of pleasure that I am writing this brief note to you. The reason for it is the outstanding article in your August issue of The Liberty Bell by Mr. Ralph Perier titled "The Jews Love Christianity".

Mr. Perier is not only an exceptionally good writer, but he manages to inject a bit of humor into a very difficult and serious subject. This article will stand for a very long time as a standard of excellence, good research, common sense and therefore the truth. I am sure in due time it will be widely disseminated, read and admired.

Both you and Mr. Perier deserve to be congratulated and should be very proud to have written and published such a landmark article.

Best regards, F.M., New Jersey

☆ ☆ ☆

Dear Mr. Dietz: 18 Oct 80

I read the August, 1980 issue of THE LIBERTY BELL with mixed feelings. On the one hand I was pleased because it was the meatiest issue in a long time, with some truly first-rate articles. But on the other hand, I was dismayed because you may have unnecessarily alienated the Christian segment of your supporters.

In his autobiography, George Lincoln Rockwell stated that he left the matter of religion to the individual conscience of his followers. I believe he was wise in that decision. Wrangling over religious matters only causes needless strife among the very people who should be united against the common enemy. I am reminded of the situation in Northern Ireland; although the roots of the conflict go much deeper than just religion, Catholics and Protestants are fighting over something as irrelevant as the nature of God—White men killing other White men even as hordes of blacks and Asians swarm into Britain.

Ralph Perier's article, "The Jews Love Christianity", was an excellent article, I must admit. I enjoyed reading it and I agree with most of what he said. My personal feeling about Christianity parallels that of one of your former co-workers who stated in an issue of WHITE POWER REPORT a few years back that our barbarian ancestors should have made drinking cups out of the skulls of the missionaries who penetrated the dark Northern forests. Certainly there would have been far less pernicious Semitic influence on our culture if we had continued to worship Wotan and Donar in the sacred groves.

However, the fact remains that a vast percentage of our rightwing brethren consider themselves Christian. They perceive any attack on Christianity as the work of the Devil, the Antichrist, or Communism. Despite its dreary origin in the deserts of the Levant, Christianity has been a part of the warp and woof of Western culture for so long that the rightwinger is constitutionally unable to dissociate it from the other values he cherishes and wishes to uphold and defend. In fact, I believe that Professor Revilo P. Oliver has argued that Christianity has necessarily molded itself over the centuries to fit the racial personality of its believers. Certainly it would be hard for a visitor from another planet to believe that the coldly austere grandeur of a German Lutheran service and the frenetic whooping and heaving hysteria of a South Side Chicago Negro Baptist ceremony were manifestations of the same religion.

To the rightwinger, Christianity is a blanket that neatly covers everything he holds dear. Attack Christianity, and he feels you have attacked himself, his wife, his children, his country, and his way of life.

Just the other night, I saw a television interview with the Imperial Wizard of one of the Ku Klux Klan factions. The Wizard (whose name was Wilkinson, I believe) was quite insistent on the point that he was a Christian and that the Klan as a whole was a Christian organization. Wilkinson came across as a sympathetic, affable fellow, and was softspoken with a pleasant southern drawl. He seemed sincere, dedicated, and good-hearted. To him, Christianity summed up everything he was for. He is probably no different from most other rightwingers. Attacking his religion would alienate him completely.

It occurs to me that several excellent tactical reasons exist for the Klan to emphasize Christianity. One is that it automatically excludes Jews. Wilkinson readily admitted that the man interviewing him (Jay Levine) could never join the Klan for just that reason. In a country as enormous as the United States, in which much of the white population has had no experience with Jews at all (other than seeing hooknosed "comedians" on television make incomprehensible jokes about life in Brooklyn using strange words found only on delicatessen menus), emphasizing the religious aspect of the distinction between Christian and Jew is the only way to make the Gentiles understand what a Jew is. The more subtle biological difference (Jews as economic parasites, cultural distorters, unassimilable aliens, etc.) are less readily understood. Christianity is also a unifying agent. Whites by and large still have little concept of themselves as a race, which is why white men could kill white men in the Civil War so black men could be free and why white men could kill white men in World War II so Jews could operate department stores in downtown Berlin. While whites don't think racially yet, they do think of themselves as Christians. Whites who can't be reached by an appeal to them as white people can often be reached by an appeal to them as Christians.

Mr. Perier mentioned that one of the worst products of religion is the idea of a "holy war." I agree, and our problems are exacerbated by the root cause of holy wars: doctrinal intolerance. "God is not mocked," say the fundamentalists, and vigorously attack even midly critical presentations of sacred matters. Freedom of opinion is not one of the virtues encouraged or even tolerated by this god. His worshipers seriously believe their chances of heaven depend solely on holding the correct beliefs, despite the fact that few believers even agree on what those beliefs should be and lustily squabble with each other about them. In the rightwing press, this has the result of stifling rational debate on religious matters (Wilmot Robertson has occasionally run letters in INSTAURATION from readers threatening to cancel their subscriptions in outrage over articles mildly critical of Christian belief, for example). Because the Christian takes his beliefs seriously (he'd better, or St. Peter will turn him away from eternal bliss), he refuses to listen to different points of view.

I quite agree with Mr. Perier that Christianity is utter nonsense. Its emphasis on sin, suffering, guilt, redemption, and salvation, if taken seriously, is enough to make moral neurotics out of all too many of its followers. Enormous amounts of productive energy and talent go to waste arguing over superstition. Even though Christianity has been warped and bent to adapt it to the Northern European racial personality, the fit still isn't any too exact, and millions of our fellows suffer from trying to live according to a code of ethics that is impossible to live by. Insistence that the Bible is the "inspired Word of God" has retarded science, as otherwise intelligent churchmen over the centuries have preferred to believe in the literal truth of the ludicrous marvel tales of a primitive tribe of ignorant desert barbarians instead of the observations and conclusions of scientists like Galileo and Darwin.

However, as would-be reformers, crusaders, activists, or revolutionaries, we are stuck with the reality of the situation. The people we have to reach ARE Christians and will resent any challenge to their faith. We have a monumental task before us just persuading our fellow whites to realize that they are whites. If we attempt to tear down Christianity, too, it will make the job impossible by alienating potential supporters completely before they ever hear the rest of the message. Part of th eproblem is that we don't really have an alternative. Something basic in human nature seems to hunger for some kind of a religion. Perhaps a revitalized Odinism, as some have suggested, could serve as a substitute for Christianity, although none of the Odinist groups I've seen so far look as though they are very close to taking off. I've heard that one of the reasons Christianity caught on with our distant forebears was because the old Nordic paganism was dying of old age at the time, so perhaps reviving it would be useless now. A brand new religion? I'm not familiar with all the tenets of Pastor Miles' faith, but what little I've heard about it suggests that he has developed something closer to the European soul than Christianity. Still, the problems inherent in converting millions of people to a radically new religion are enormous. Whites have been Christians too long to willingly give up their "traditional" faith at the drop of a hat. Moreover, the effort to convert the masses would drain time, energy, and talent from more pressing problems.

For the activist, it is indeed frustrating to realize that our fellow whites are passively content to watch kosher "entertainment" on television and in the movies, and listen to singing Congoids on the radio without a whimper of protest, but are galvanized to action over an issue as ridiculous and trivial as prayers in the schoolroom. Worse yet, the liberals were right on that one: compulsory prayer in a public school probably does violate separation of church and state. But conservatives saw the decision to eliminate prayers as an attack on traditional values, and rose to the defense. In a way, I sympathize with the well-meaning conservatives, but it was the wrong issue at the wrong time. I've also often wondered if daily rote recitation of the Lord's Prayer really does make better citizens out of children befuddled by its rococo language.

Despite the recent flurry of "born-again" religion, old-style Bible-believing is far less common today than a century ago. Advances in science have shown God, if he exists at all, to be either very remote or very subtle. Fundamentalism may well die out on its own accord, given another century. Unfortunately, the very people otherwise most receptive to racialist ideas (namely the ones least corrupted by the less scientific dogmas of modern education) are something of a vast repository of unquestioning belief in the teachings of the Bible. No wonder the Jews themselves laugh condescendingly at the antics of the "hicks" and "yokels" south and west of New York City, and make allegedly funny movies about Protestant evangelists (to name two, OH, GOD! and IN GOD WE TRUST). There is, of course, no need to ask what would happen if some *GOYIM* made a movie satirizing the more moronic aspects of Jewish fundamentalism, the Hassidim). Still, truth exists independently of race. Some born-again Christians of my acquaintance were profoundly shocked when Jewish astronomer Carl Sagan announced on his television program COSMOS that "Evolution is a fact; it really happened." Sagan may be Jewish, but he is also correct about that. Further, it should have occurred to the Bible-believing Christians that here was a Jew denying the literal truth of the very storybook his own people wrote (or compiled, if you accept the idea that the stories in the Bible were largely lifted from the mythologies of other peoples).

Nonetheless, Christianity endures as a unifying factor for our people, even among those who don't take it seriously or never understood it. It is the closest thing whites have to an ethnic religion. The Jews, of course, are something more than a religion. They are an ethnic group, a distinct gene pool. Their religion has given them a rallying point over the centuries and helped provide them with a sense of identity. Judaism as a religion, however, has evolved into an uninspiring mishmash of sterile, arid philosophy and traditions whose point or usefulness was outlived millenia ago. Judaism does not actively seek converts. Rather, it is content to hold its own as the spiritual expression of a limited, select group of people. It is probably the last surviving tribal religion in the civilized world. I sometimes wonder if the doctrine of the "Chosen People" began when some thoughtful rabbi suddenly realized that if the god of the Jews created the world, he must presumably be the god of the Assyrians, Babylonians, Egyptians, and everyone else. Yet the Holy Writ indicated that God was apparently lavishing the Jews in particular with a great deal of attention and concern, even at the expense of his other children. How else to explain God's inordinate interest in the Jews but to say that he had selected them for some great purpose? As the saying goes, how odd of God to choose the Jews. With the passing of the old indigenous European paganisms, however, Christianity has been the only binding force OUR people have had.

In its better moments, Christianity has inspired Europe's noblest music and art. It may be argued that music and art inspired by the extinct Germanic religion would have been even better (Wagner's operas may be a hint of what could have been), but we'll never know for certain. Christianity has also given our people a focal point: the local church has always been a kind of community center. It has also encouraged the common decencies, such as fidelity to one's spouse, honesty in dealing with one's fellows, and contributing to the welfare of the community as a whole. Most of this was already present in the European tradition and grafted on to Christianity bodily. ANY religion might have lent itself to such functions. The reality we have to live with is that it happens to be Christianity that won out in Europe.

Mr. Perier admirably laid out Christianity's less desirable features, such as its numbing universalism and its defiance of the reality of race. I can name a few more, such as its adoption of the Jewish mentality in regard to women (from their formerly free and independent place in pagan Europe, women became little more than cattle in the Christian era), and the concept of Man as a contemptible, helpless little worm to be ground in the dust by God's feet, in sharp contrast to the pagan attitude of Man as potentially a heroic and noble being. (Perhaps one thing that helped kill paganism was the fact that too many legends had the gods acting less ethically than the average human being.) Finally, as Mr. Perier emphasizes, the worst aspect of Christianity is the false glory it confers on Jews in general, helping them gain access to our society and culture.

How can Christianity be dealt with, then? I can offer a few suggestions.

1. We must deal with it somehow. It isn't going to disappear very soon.

2. We must be very careful in dealing with it. Too many potential supporters take it very seriously, indeed, and are easily alienated.

3. Rather than attempting to destroy it, we must learn to live with it.

4. We must isolate and neutralize Christianity's drawbacks. Christian supporters should be encouraged to be wary of philo-Semitism.

5. Christian sects that attempt to read the Jews out of Christianity should be supported and encouraged. I include here such things as British Israel, Identity, Christ-Was-an-Aryan-Not-a-Jew cults, and similar movements.

6. Alternatives to Christianity, whether entirely new religions that are racially healthy, Odinist revival movements, or rational atheism, should be encouraged.

7. Matters of religious doctrine must be left to the individual conscience. Freedom of religion should be encouraged. No one religion should be supported over all others by any political movement. Supporters should be warned of what happened to Germany during the Protestant Reformation (Central Europe was laid waste by battling armies of various Catholic and Protestant factions) and reminded that it is suicide for white men to be fighting other white men over questions of faith when the enemy is at the gate.

8. Finally (and this may be the most hopeless goal of all), Christians should be encouraged to learn to tolerate white men with different opinions about the Almighty.

Yours truly,
Keith Jensen, Minneapolis, MN.

☆ ☆ ☆

Dear George: 20 Oct 80

I just received my copy of Liberty Bell, so forget my last letter, this month's issue is just great. Ralph Perier 's article is magnificent. This is the type of revelation which must be disseminated. Unfortunately his thesis will mostly fall on deaf ears.

Please send two copies of it plus a copy of Oliver's "Christianity and the Survival of the West".

Thank you, P.A., New Jersey

☆ ☆ ☆

Hello, George: 21 Oct. 80

I hope you and your family are well and, though it is a long time since I canceled my sub, I hope you have no hard feelings toward me, for I certainly have none toward you. Only the best, as a matter of fact; and am more strongly involved in the cause than ever.

I still read LIBERTY BELL, when I can, Sam W. is always kind to pass his issues on to me. The subject of this letter, in fact, has to do with an article in the August, 1980, issue thereof. I will not pretend that Sam did not bring it to my attention, he did. I do not write in criticism of it because he asked me to do so, but because of my honest thoughts about the matter. The article under examination is "The Jews Love Christianity", by Ralph Perier.

Why the continuing (though not continuous) attack on Christianity, George? I realize that most churches leave a lot to be desired (like true Christianity); I realize that quite a bit of "conservative (whatever that is) Christianity", like the Falwell humbuggery, is jewized nonsense; but the Identity (Gospel of the Kingdom) Message is the strongest Rightist movement going. The Jews know the Identity has "gottem" because it tells the world that Christ was not a Jew, and that jews aren't Israel.

George, my purpose is not to comment on your religious conviction, or lack of it, whichever; that's strictly your affair and not mine. Nor will I tell you how to run your magazine; you've been doing an excellent job of it, on your own, for a long time, now. But the Jews do not love Christianity. They hate it and they fear it, in its pristine form, just as they hated and feared its holy founder.

Keep up the good work and please believe me that I am,

Very sincerely yours, H.S., Texas

☆ ☆ ☆

Dear Mr. Dietz: 21 Oct. 80

Letter writing is not my line but I feel I must let you know how disappointing and absurd THE LIBERTY BELL August issue is. Especially I'm referring to the article "The Jews love Christianity" by Ralph Perier. Such a writing reveals the lack of wisdom and understanding of the author. It was hard to believe you would print such material for it certainly is not in reason with THE LIBERT BELL message until now.

"The fool has said in his heart 'there is no God'." Without God man is competely lost in the jumble of life. Don't undermine the faith and hope of your fellow man by forwarding this type of reasoning. Man cannot get away from his creator!

Sincerely, Mrs. A.S.

☆ ☆ ☆

Dear Mr. Dietz: 29 Oct. 80

The articles you have been printing to expose the Old Testament and "Christianity" as a whole have been fantastic! About a year ago, the falseness of the "Holy Bible" was revealed to me in a vision in which I saw the words, "Hoax of the Centuries" appear on the Bible.

Religion is the strongest stranglehold an enemy can use to destroy an empire or race. It can take the strongest mind and make it pulp and, thus, obedient to the inferior mind by the use of superstitions FEAR and GULLIBILITY. This, the deceitful, scheming Jew knew and took advantage of centuries ago when their psychopathic minds produced the "silent" killer known as the "Holy Bible".

Why did the powerful WHITE Roman government fall? The Jews, by "creating" Christinaity, had taught the valiant, gullible Romans to "resist not evil", "turn the other cheek" and "love your enemies". Over a period of time, the battle was won subtly by the Jew from within the government itself. A great empire fell!

I have just finished reading NATURE'S ETERNAL RELIGION by Ben Klassen which is on your booklist. (I received my copy from A.E.) It is MUST reading for every white man, woman and child. It fully explains HOW Christianity destroyed empire after empire by destroying the white man's ability to use sound reasoning and good judgement. The subtle means as mentioned above were applied.

Today we see the results: a sick white race decaying under the burden of guilt for every woe that has ever happened in the world. But there is hope! It is found in the white man himself.

Keep up the good work. Keep truth coming.

Sincerely, Mrs.D.C., Arizona

☆ ☆ ☆

Dear Mr. Dietz: 31 Oct. 80

The August issue of Liberty Bell was excellent. The article "The Jews Love Christianity" was outstanding. Some of the things in the article I already knew and some I only suspected, but the article tied it all together. I wish I knew how to get more people to read it. Thank you for publishing it.

H.G., Texas

☆ ☆ ☆

Dear George: 22 Nov. 80

Liberty Bell just gets better and better. The August issue was spectacularly enlightening. And then Ronald Hand's follow-up in September. By all means let him write more. His insight is profound. Only when whites throw off the shackles of corrupted "Christianity" can the race flourish again.

Yours truly, P.A., New Jersey

☆ ☆ ☆

Dear George: 10 Oct. 80

If I didn't know your intentions I would think that the article by Ralph Perrier was written by some nut in lower Slobovia or Madylyn O'Hair or some other Jew trouble maker. I don't understand your purpose.

Enclosed are two articles that may be used to make up for that catastrophe. [The articles enclosed were, *The Point of Return Through Jesus Christ, The Son of the Living God,* by the Word of Christ mission, and *Christian Persecution and Genocide,* by William S. LeGrande.]

Best regards, S.W., Texas

Dear Mr. Dietz: 3 Dec. 80

...The two booklets that your correspondent sent you are trash, but of somewhat different quality. The one from the "Word of Christ Mission" [*The Point of Return Through Jesus Christ, the Son of the Living God*] is disgustingly ignorant, illiterate, and mendacious. "Historians [!] think that it was as late as 200-300 A.D. that a Judaean became [!] to be called a Jew for short"!! That, of course, is just drivel, derived at third- or fourth-hand from the early writing of Benjamin Freedman, and one has to be spectacularly ignorant not to know that 'Jew' is simply the English form of the word of which I will show the derivation:

יהוד > יהודאי *(Aramaic)* > 'Ιουδαῖος > Iūdaeus > *(Old French)* Juieu > *(Middle English)* Juwe > Jew.

The booklet by Le Grande [*Christian Persecution and Genocide*] is literate and shows considerable reading (some of it misunderstood), but it is just more of the "British Israelite" fantasy, which is so ridiculous historically that it isn't even good for a laugh. I do feel sorry for the many persons who try to salvage their Christianity and their race at the same time, but they are attempting an impossibility. It is not only preposterous historically, but absurd socially. "The Christian Israelites of European descent must first attack the false teachings of the church and correct them"! They have as much chance of doing that as they have of playing in a celestial harp-ensemble post mortem.

Best wishes, R.P. Colorado

Dear Mr. Dietz: 12 Dec. 80

After reading one of your articles "How the Jews Love Christianity" I have to draw a conclusion that your philosophy would have to be the same as the destroyers of our American Heritage that say there is no God. This is the same philosophy that has promoted communism, infiltrated our schools with evolution and humanism and all forms of liberalism into our society. My Bible tells me "The fool hath said in his heart, there is no God. They are corrupt, they have done abominable works, there is none that doeth good."

I am continually amazed when I find so-called defenders of our Aryan race that are blinded to the truth that God has used this race for the fulfillment of all His prophecies. The Adamic race was created for the pwrpose of bringing forth civilization on earth. Out of this race came all of the civilizations of the past and the final end-time promise to Abraham, Isaac and Jacob of a great nation and a multitude of nations.

Errors are made, today in the use of the term "Jew" as representing the people of the Bible. This term did not even come into existence until 1775 A.D. and is the English pronunciation of a word from German that stands for Judaism or the followers of Judaism. The second error that is made is that the "Old Testament" is the Jews' book. The Jews' Torah didn't get accepted by the Jews until 1775 when Moses Mendelssohn, translated the first five books of the "Old Testament" into Yiddish. Young Jews were deserting Judaism so the Torah was brought in to clean up the Talmudic act and keep the Jews from fleeing from the control of the Talmudists. So our Bible has nothing to do with the Jews, but is now and always has been the religion of the Aryan race.[!]

At the time of Christ, God's Kingdom had been taken control of by the enemies of our race, the Edomites. Esau was Edom. Esau sold his birthright to Jacob and married cannanite wives (of the mongrelized stock of Ham). The Edomite has been attempting throughout the ages to regain the Kingdom from God's people, the true Israelites (Aryans). Edom also means RED (isn't it interesting that Christianity's enemy, communism, calls itself RED).

Most of the Jews today are eastern-Europeans called Khazars. They refer to themselves as Ashkenazim. Isn't it interesting that one of the sons of Gomer, the son of Japheth was called Ashkenaz? (see Genesis 10:2) These people were never Israelites but are the ones today claiming the promises of God to the Israelites.

God is truly working out His plan with His people, the white race. Any that cannot see it are purposely blinding themselves from truth and are serving the enemies of our race. I would hope that you would come to a knowledge of God's Word and recognize the need to teach the truth of God's Word to our white brethren in God's Kingdom today. By the parable of the wheat and the tares (Matth. 13:24-30) and in the explanation of it in Matth. 13:37-43, we are told that the Kingdom is in the world and that Jesus will return to cleanse His Kingdom of all things that offend. The Book of Obadiah is the prophecy of the removal of Edom from the Kingdom in the latter days.

"How the Jews Love Christianity" is as Talmudic oriented as articles written by the Jews themselves. If you would like a conter part to the article, write to The Abelard Reuchlin Foundation, Kent, Wa. and ask for their booklet "The True Authorship of the New Testament" authored by Hevel V. Reek.

Other articles imply that those teaching the "Identity Message" are supportive of the Jew. Obviously the authors of such articles are not too familiar with the majority of Identity ministers. Most teach that the white race is Israel and that the Jews are Edom. The Edomites rejected Jesus Christ at His first coming and have been the enemies of true Christianity throughout the age including the present. I refe you to the enclosed booklets written by Pastor Sheldon Emry of Phoenix, Arizona.

Sincely, R.E.R., Washington

☆ ☆ ☆

Mr. Dietz,   11 Dec. 80

Your last few issues of The Liberty Bell have been more than I can stand. Your constant attack on Identity and British Israel Christians I can tolerate no longer. Even the man you worship, Adolf Hitler, was a good Christian believer. You are right in your condemnation of the denominational churches (99.9% of all Christianity is Judaism), but your hatred of the true Christian doctrine makes you an enemy of Christ (an Aryan, not a Jew). Christ said that "HE WHO IS NOT FOR ME IS AGAINST ME." I suggest you get the Dec. 1980 copy of Christian Vanguard and read the expose of you and this idiot Ralph Perrier.

[A copy of the Dec. issue of Christian Vanguard was sent to us by a reader in Texas who remarked in the margin of the paper, "Shame on you for attacking the JEWISH Vanguard. I believe these people are trying to create a class of WHITE JEWS. Also, you should attack the Old Testament as sheer fabrication. Encl. some booklets, (The Great Jewish Masque and A Real case against the Jews). Send a copy of your article. Thanks, W.F.B., Tx. - The same correspondent yesterday (Dec. 20) ordered 50 copies of "The Jews Love Christianity and a subscription to THE LIBERTY BELL!]

As for your "resident theologian", Reinhold Dunkel, I have read many of his replies to Christian Identity people (letters) and he has shown his total ignorance of the word of God by his replies and remarks. Much has been written by Christian Patriots on the trickery and treason of Robert Welch and his Birchers on his atheism and humanism, as expounded in his famous "Blue Book", but I will repeat one of their accusations here, "You can't expect to fight or defeat atheistic and Godless Communism when you are atheistic and Godless yourself." I have one or two issues of the Liberty Bell left on my subscription, after that, take me off your mailing list. I would continue to subscribe to your magazine, if your vicious smears of our beliefs would stop, but the last few issues have shown only an increase in them with no sign of a let-up. I am going to write or contact all in the Patriotic-Christian movement that I can [*in good, Christian fashion— und bist du nicht willig, so brauch' ich Gewalt!*], and try to encourage them to stop any financial aid to you as well. This may sound harsh [*No! It doesn't! It just sounds typically Christian!*] or "Un-American", but our God's holy law demands DEATH to all his enemies [*this demand of your God's holy law was presumably the reason for millions of 'unbelieving' Germans having been slaughtered during the 30-Year-War, all in the name of your Saviour, Jesus Christ!*], who would not let him reign over them (Luke 19:27). This would have to include Anti-Christian ARYANS [*naturally! 'Good Christians' did not hesitate one moment when they were urged on by their 'Christian' leaders with slogans like "Onward Christian Soldiers", and "Let's make the world safe for democracy", to kill millions of their fellow white men on Europe's battlefields, and, most particulary, during terrorist air raids on defenseless women, children and old men, who most likely thought themselves to be 'Christian', too,—and all in the name of your 'Saviour', Jesus Christ!—balderdash!*], as well as Anti-

Christian Jews and coloreds and all his other enemies [*Does that include all Moslems, Hindus, Buddhists, etc. also?—Well, your Savior has his work cut out for him to keep his (minority) followers from being exterminated!*]. I would ask that you repent of your errors (sins) and turn and serve the God of White Christian Israel [*Heaven forbid! Neither you nor anyone else is going to turn me into a white Judaeus honoris causis!*], and be saved from the hell ahead in store for our nation, because in that period if the niggers and heathen don't get you and you live through it, the death sentence (or banishment) [!] will have to be carried out by the Christian saints [*!—No, thanks! If that is what your God's law says, I'll take my chances with the heathens!*]. You will be caught between two fires, the Anti-white red heathen on one side, and the white Aryan Christians [!] on the other. Choose this day who you will serve! Christ or Anti-Christ, God or Mammon!

Lyndle J. Gharst,
117 West Main Moweagqua, IL 62550

☆ ☆ ☆

Dear Mr. Dietz: 15 Dec. 80

Before my order I must say that I thank you for your heroic stand for our race and for the inspiration it provides for thousands of White Nationalists...

Thank you, A Racial Comrade,
B.S., California

☆ ☆ ☆

Dear Mr. Dietz: 16 Dec. 80

Please renew my subscription for two years.

With respect to the Perrier articles: I don't think it is wise to put down Christians and their beliefs on such a scale. The arguments seemed to emanate from or are similar to those put forth by the Grand Orient masonry and Jewish philosophical sources. Read "The Plot Against the Church" by Pinay [*a Catholic Priest, no less!*]

I believe there is no hope for Western civilization or the White Race without an aroused and aware Christian populace. They must be made aware of the deceit that has crept into the religion. The church is more than some bad priests and people who do not live to the fullness of their faith. We need unity not divisiveness.

Sincerely, J.S., New York

Dear Mr. Dietz: 20 Dec. 80

I am sending with this note a twelve dollar money order for a year's subscription to The Liberty Bell.

I became acquainted with Your magazine through the August 1980 issue, which was given to me by P.W. This is easily the best magazine I've ever read. "The Jews Love Christianity" and British Israelism articles were fantastic and have liberated several friends from the toils of Christian Suicidal thinking. Please rush my copies of the next twelve months. More correspondence will be forthcoming.

Thank you, T.R.G., Florida

☆ ☆ ☆

Dear George,   19 Dec. 80

All this material on religion lately reminds of a little ditty we used to sing as kids. It is sung to the tune of "I am Jesus' little lamb." "I don't care if it rains or freezes, I am safe in the arms of Jesus, I am Jesus' little lamb, Yes, by Jesus Christ I am." Best wishes and merry Christmas to you and yours,

B.G., Pennsylvania

☆ ☆ ☆

Dear Mr. Dietz: 29 Dec. 80

Major Donald Vincent Clerkin's excellent article, "A White Christian Racist Defends his Faith", was certainly a breath of clean, pure air after the two previous issues of The Liberty Bell. That is, after Ralph Perrier's "The Jews Love Christianity" in August and Ronald Hand's "Summary of New Testament Studies" in October.

One gasps upon being informed that Mr. Hand is an ordained minister. What is Mr. Perier's background? His distortion of the Sermon on the Mount has a nice, Talmudic twist. As does his reference to St. Athanasius as a "bull-headed holy man." St. Athanasius was bull-headed, if you will, in defending the Divinity of Christ against the Jew, Arius, who in the 4th century, spread the same blasphemy that the 20th century Perrier rehashes in the August Liberty Bell.

Mr. Perier, in attempting to pit reason against faith, takes a lot on faith himself. He does not prove there is no God or that Christ was not Divine. This blasphemous smear of Christianity is only his belief, his persuasion his FAITH, if you will. But smearing is not proving.

Sincerely, Mrs. B.M.C., Texas

☆ ☆ ☆

Dear Mr. Dietz: 21 Dec. 80

If some of your readers want to believe in Christianity and White racism simultaneously, that's their business. But they are quite mistaken when they assert that Adolf Hitler was a Christian. Nothing could be further from the truth!

It is true that Hitler never formally left the Roman Catholic Church, and that in the earliest days of his political career he made some superficially pro-Christian statements. However, in both instances he was motivated solely by the political realities with which he had to deal, and was not reflecting his own personal religious convictions.

In his private conversations, Hitler revealed what he really thought of Christianity:

(Eve. of 11-12 July, 1941)

"The heaviest blow ever struck humanity was the coming of Christianity. Bolshevism is Christianity's illegitimate child. Both are inventions of the Jew. The deliberate lie in the matter of religion was introduced to the world by Christianity. Bolshevism practices a lie of the same nature, when it claims to bring liberty to men, whereas in reality it seeks only to enslave them. In the ancient world, the relations between men and gods were founded on an instinctive respect. It was a world enlightened by the idea of tolerance. Christianity was the first creed in the world to exterminate its adversaries in the name of love. Its key-note is intolerance..."

(October 14, 1941)

"The best thing is to let Christianity die a natural death. A slow death has something comforting about it."

(Eve. of 20-21 Feb., 1942)

"Since my fourteenth year I have felt liberated from the superstitions that the priests used to teach."

(27 Feb. 1942)

"Our epoch will certainly see the end of the disease of Christianity. It will last another hundred years, two hundred perhaps."

(10 Oct. 1941)

"Christianity is a rebellion against natural law, a protest against nature. Taken to its logical extreme, Christianity would mean the systematic cultivation of the human failure. "

(Night of 19 Oct. 1941)

"The reason why the ancient world was so pure, light and serene was that it knew nothing of the two great scourges: the pox and Christianity. Christianity is a prototype of Bolshevism: the mobilization of the masses of slaves with the object of undermining society. Thus one understands that the healthy elements of the Roman world were a proof against this doctrine. Yet Rome today allows itself to reproach Bolshevism with having destroyed Christian churches! As if Christianity hadn't behaved in the same way towards the pagan temples."

(Midday, 21 Oct. 1941)

"It's striking to observe that Christian ideas, despite all St. Paul's efforts, had no success in Athens. The philosophy of the Greeks was so superior to this poverty-stricken rubbish that the Athenians burst out laughing when they listened to the apostle's teachings. But in Rome St. Paul found the ground prepared for him. His egalitarian theories had what was needed to win over a mass composed of innumerable uprooted people."

(Midday 14 Dec. 1941)

"Kerrl, with the noblest of intentions, wanted to attempt a synthesis between National Sociaiism and Christianity. I don't believe the thing's possible, and I see the obstacle in Christianity itself.

"Pure Christianity—the Christianity of the catacombs—is concerned with translating the Christian doctrine into facts. It leads quite simply to the annihilation of mankind. It is merely whole-hearted Bolshevism, under a tinsel of metaphysics."

(Eve. of 14 Feb. 1945)

"...For Christianity is not a natural religion for the Germans, but a religion that has been imported and which strikes no responsive chord in their hearts and is foreign to the genius of the race."

All of these quotations are from "Hitler's Private Conversations", which were written down by Dr. Henry Picker, a secretary of Martin Bormann, on Bormann's orders. Both men were present during these conversations.

(It is interesting to note that the last passage quoted above has been deleted from the edition of THE TESTAMENT OF ADOLF HITLER, published by Sons of Liberty. This is the only selection of the Bormann documents still in print.)

These quotes are merely random samples of Hitler's thoughts on Christianity. I could go on for pages and pages. Instead, let me close with a quote from Peter Stahrenberg, founder and leader of the American National Socialist Party:

"My religion is National Socialism. That's the only religion I believe in. Christianity is bunk." (1938)

Sincerely, R.G., Virginia

[Editor's Note: We have in our possession a copy of Hitler's Secret Conversations 1941-1944, which was first published in English in 1961. The above quotations correspond with those in the original, and we are now endeavoring to obtain a supply of this book—if still available, or reprint it, if permission can be obtained from the Copyright holder. This is a magnificent book, indeed an EYE-OPENER!]

☆ ☆ ☆

Dear George: 21 Dec. 80

The following is a quotation of what Martin Bormann had to say about Christianity:

"National Socialist and Christian concepts are incompatible. The Christian Churches build upon the ignorance of men and strive to keep large portions of the people in ignorance because only in this way can the Christian Churches maintain their power. On the other hand, National Socialism is based on scientific foundations. Christianity's immutable principles, which were laid down almost two thousand years ago, have increasingly stiffened into life-alien dogmas. National Socialism, however, if it wants to fulfill its task further, must always guide itself according to the newest data of scientific researches."

"The Christian Churches have long been aware that exact scientific knowledge poses a threat to their existence. Therefore, by means of such pseudo-sciences as theology, they take great pains to suppress or falsify scientific research. Our National Socialist world view stands on a much higher level than the concepts of Christianity, which in their essentials were taken over from Judaism. For this reason, too, we can do without Christianity."

"No one would know about Christianity if pastors had not crammed it down his throat in his childhood. The so-called loving God by no means reveals the knowledge of his existence to young people, but amazingly enough, and despite his omnipotence, he leaves this to the efforts of a pastor. When in the future our youth no longer hear anything about this Christianity, whose doctrine is far below our own, Christianity will automatically disappear."

"It is also astonishing that prior to our own era nothing was known to mankind about this Christian God, and even since then the great majority of the inhabitants of our earth have known nothing about Christianity. Because of this, according to the arrogant Christian dogma, they are damned from the outset."

"When we National Socialists speak of a belief in God [Gottgläubigkeit: Non-Christian theism], by God we do not understand, as do naive Christians and their clerical beneficiaries, a man-like being who is sitting around in some corner of the spheres. Rather, we must open the eyes of mankind to the fact that in addition to our unimportant earth there exist countless other bodies in the universe, many of them surrounded, like the Sun, by planets and these again by smaller bodies, the moons. The force which moves all these bodies in the universe, in accordance with natural law, is what we call the Almighty of God. The assertion that this world-force can worry about the fate of every individual, every bacillus on earth, and that it can be influenced by so-called prayer or other astonishing things, is based either on a suitable dose of naivete or on outright commercial effrontery."

"In contrast, we National Socialists call upon ourselves to live as naturally as possible—that is, in keeping with the laws of life. The more thoroughly we know and attend to the laws of nature and life, the more we adhere to them, the more do we correspond to the will of the Almighty. The deeper our insight into the will of the Almighty, the greater will be our success." (1942)

Best regards, R.G., Virginia

☆ ☆ ☆

Dear George: 26 Dec. 80
   I read the article published in Christian Vanguard Dec. 1980, and in my opinion, concerning Christian National Socialists (I call it Judeo-Christianity) James Combs is a nut case, and his facts are often wrong to boot—as this man never lived in Germany and experienced National Socialism during the Golden Age.

Best regards, H.H., Minnesota

☆ ☆ ☆

From *Christian Vanguard,*
James K. Warner, Editor, December 1980.

Anti-Christianity Betrays Phoney Conservative Groups
by James Combs

   Most CHRISTIAN VANGUARD readers regard themselves as Christians. What even many of these unusually-aware patriots do not realize is that a large body of patriots deny Christianity. Indeed, these latter people hold the faith in bitter contempt.

   Ralph Perrier is an anti-Christian spokesman who had published in 1980 an article which strongly and articulately denounces our religion. In "The Jews Love Christianity", which appeared in one conservative journal, Mr. Perrier offered a lengthy argument against the faith.

   The gist of that author's opposition is that "Christianity was a Jewish invention" which Jews now use to control us. He sees no positive value to Jesus' mission to us, feeling that—if there was such an actual man, Jesus was only one of several "Jewish agitators and miracle mongers".

   Mr. Perrier gives reluctant credit to "British Israelites" (and presumably the Identity movement); but, he then says, "Unfortunately, their doctrine is historically preposterous ..."

In recognizing and then rejecting the Identity followers, Perrier reveals his basic ignorance of church history. This, despite the contradiction of indicating that he is well read on the subject. The Christian-critic, e.g., labels Jesus "a Jew" and totally confuses Hebrews/Israelites with Jewry. He either ignores or does not know about the mongrelized, demonic development of Jewry.

This error on his part is, ironically, the same one suffered by the vast majority of churchgoers today. In considering Hebrews/Israelites and Jews as being one and the same, confused Christians come to commit the crimes against their faith and the White race for which Mr. Perrier holds Christianity in such disdain. Our unaware kindred have been misled by satanic influences to virtually honor the Jews, thinking of them as "God's chosen". In so doing, the Jews, with impunity, have been able to foment massive-radical troubles for the civilized world. If any Christian-Whites show resentment and resistance, they are disarmed by pacifying propaganda to the effect that "we mustn't oppose God's own".

Thus, Ralph Perrier is justified in speaking unkindly of Christians when they suicidally let the Jews deceive them into acting like blind "sheep". If our people in the main are guilty of any character faults, they would have to include gullibility and laziness. They put too much credence in what they are told by Jews or Jewish stooges and are too indolent to search out the truth. What results is an unobstructed path for Jews and their scheme to control the world.

Mr. Perrier is quite correct when he states that "Jews love Christianity". That is, Jews "love" the Christian faith in its present conduct. Thanks to vast "brain-washing" campaigns—via seminaries, Sunday school and other church literature and con-men "evangelists"—Jewry has Christianity under social and political subservience. Perrier gloatingly demonstrates some instances whereby Christians have been duped by Jewry with twisted "religious" manipulation. Christian-Whites being maneuvered into the World Wars is one example. What occurred was horrid harm to the White race and its culture.

It is one thing, though, to discredit our faith when Christianity is ill used; it is another to revile Christianity down to its very foundations. Perrier, as other critics, state the religion is a myth, created by Jews and has been from its beginning a disservice to the White race.

These admitted enemies of Christianity detect nothing but evil in it. Perrier typifies this element by disregarding reality and suggesting the religion has only detracted over time from White culture. However, one has only to observe the magnificent cathedrals of Europe and to admire the splendid Christian art-works in our museums to recognize the line of this reasoning. Great men, monuments and movements— all to the glory of Whites—trace their inspiration to Christianity.

Perrier resorts to every tactic in his attempt to insult our faith. As other anti-christs, he even tries to use sick-sex: "...the early Christian sects.... taught that Jesus had revealed that the only road to salvation lay in male homosexuality or, conversely, in umlimited promiscuity". We, indeed, can find such sexual deviation even today with those who base their "religion" on abused sexual practices. But, as thoughout the history of Christianity, these misled sinners do *not* represent the far-greater majority of us. Yet, critics, as Perrier, will latch onto something of this disturbed sort as "evidence" Christianity is a "false" belief!

A significant example in Mr. Perrier's article which testifies to his fundamental ignorance is seen in a distortion of the gospels. He refers to "144,000 male Jews who despise women" (those who are selected by God in the crucial "final times"). In truth twelve-thousand male "virgins" from each of the 12 Tribes of Israel are to be chosen as dedicated strugglers for our people. Mr. Perrier is, indeed, uninformed as he fails to differentiate between "Jews" and the people of biblical Israel. In so doing, he—as others like him—pass-off the evil of Jewry to the Hebrews/Israelites and, thereby, belittle both the Old and the New Testaments (in short, the Holy BIBLE).

When this writer reads or hears of anti-Christian "theories" and "facts", it is wondered what manner of faith, if any, do the critics have? If Christianity is so unhealthy, so unredeemable, then what would these men replace it with?

It is surmised that Mr. Perrier may have a leaning toward the old Nordic or "Aryan" religion (Odin, Thor, etc.). If so, there is no question that considerable criticism could be made also of this now bankrupt belief. If it is so "worthy", why did it fail?

Although Perrier would appear to be strongly anti-Jewish, he, nevertheless, finds himself as vulnerable to criticism as do misled Christians, foolishly doing Jewry's evil work. Here Mr. Perrier is, crucifying a religion in a manner not unlike the way the Jewish TALMUD does. He expresses the basest vituperation for our people, indicting them as veritable morons. One ponders why he would try to sway and disillusion them from their "myth" if they are such dullards? He, at best, can be viewed as an arrogant and self-righteous "know-it-all".

Does he see himself as an "intellectual" atheist, one too sophisticated to indulge in a "fairy tale" as Christianity? How, then, does he account for our creation? "Evolution", possibly? And, if he feels our religion is too far-fetched for acceptance, how can rationalize absurdity "evolution"?

Some remarks of Mr. Perrier suggest he is pro-Nazi German. If so, how does he reconcile his feelings of nausea for Christianity with the devotion Adolf Hitler had for the same faith? If we Christians are so dense for believing in the "Jew myth" of Christianity, then does this not mean Hitler was an idiot also? Hitler was a Christian. One is reminded of him saying: "My feeling as a Christian points me to my Lord and Savior as a fighter ... not a sufferer but as a fighter ... How terrific was the fight for the world (by Jesus) against the Jewish poison" (THE MIND OF ADOLF HITLER, Walter C. Langer, Signet, 1972, p. 44).

Were Perrier understanding of Christianity, he would know that there are *two* of the belief which he so severely castigates. One is the Jew-designed fraud he correctly rages against. The other is the bonafide faith, one that—as Jesus—detests the satanic Jews and their corrupting works. Mr. Perrier's failure to fully differentiate between the two accomplishes nothing more than to weaken patriotism, to bring doubt within our people's midst. He is *not* "enlightening" us; he, rather, divides us.

It is true that the counterfeit part of "Christianity" direly needs exposure. "False prophets" as the Billy Grahams, Jack Van Imps, Jerry Falwells, etc. *should* be revealed to Christian-Whites as the Jew-owned conmen they are. We *should* be made aware of how Jews have used a distortion of the BIBLE to manipulate the uninformed members of our people. As Perrier accuses, there likely are some misinterpretations or mistranslations of the Holy Testament, which results may have narrowed our social conduct.

The man-made shortcomings in the religion deserve attention. But, taking a "broadside" at our entire faith without serious effort to find any good in it is not warranted! Such total condemnation even .

leads one to question the motive of the condemner.

What has Perrier gained? Is the White-patriotic movement better for his vicious assault? Are Christian-Whites' morals and morale improved by such partial truth and perverted information? Who really benefited from his abuse

Christ and His followers? Us or the Jews?

This group is obviously made up of American Nazis, not Christian National Socialists as they were in Germany. There is a tremendous difference in basic ideology.

(Editor's note: The publication that Mr. Combs refers to is "The Liberty Bell" published by George Dietz, a confirmed, self-admitted atheist. He is a Johnny-come-lately in the American Nazi movement. He was born in Germany, moved to America and became quite prosperous in the real estate business. Some six or seven years ago he bought out Revere Press, a small, but very good patriotic book publisher. He now has a very extensive book list, mostly by reprinting books of other publishers without permission. For the past eighteen months he has revealed his true colors, a devout and dedicated ATHEIST, by publishing several anti-Christian, atheist articles in his monthly magazine "The Liberty Bell" with different authors' names. This latest one, the worst by far, is supposedly written by a Ralph Perrier. We do not know if a Ralph Perrier exists; it may be a pen name for George Dietz.

Just for example, Dr. Warner spent several thousand dollars on three trips to Europe picking up rare out of print booklets and pamphlets from collectors and paying exorbitant prices for them. We advertise it and within two or three months Mr. Dietz is selling our book. We have not mentioned this before because our prime interest is spreading the truth but when he adds insult to injury by attacking The Identity Movement and all Christianity in general, THAT IS GOING TOO FAR.)

(*Liberty Bell Editor's Note:* The reader who sent us the above article (in December 1980) wrote the following in the margin:

"Shame on you for attacking the *Jewish* Vanguard. I believe these people are trying to create a class of *White* Jews. Also, you should attack the Old Testament as sheer fabrication. Enclosed 4 booklets. Send a copy of your article.—Thanks."

APPENDIX C

A Summary of
New Testament Studies
By Ronald S. Hand

The big question for the reader of historical interpreters of Christianity today ought to be centered around the matter of assessing the documents of the Christian faith; assessing them for their reliability, authenticity, and historical correctness. This latter element is significant, in that correctness in historical matters is the great weak point of all believers in a particular dictum, philosophy or creed. So that whenever a controlling idea can assert itself, it finds its way shaping, molding, and altering facts to suit the individual, or else producing false facts to fit the case in point.

Another most significant area for examination is the use of the early Christian church of certain apocalyptic (revelatory) portions of the Old Testament. The church believed that the end of the world was "at hand" and the wind-up of history was in process. Today, however, we see evangelical Christianity in a similar situation. Many people are waiting for the second coming of Christ. In the popular imagination, this hoped-for event will be the panacea for all of the world's problems. Simpson, in his book *Which Way Western Man?*, has little to say about Christian or Jewish Apocalyptic literature which is a potent weapon of the Jews.

During the eighteenth century, New Testament scholars began to study the texts in Greek and comparative texts were examined for variations. Many of these were found to exist, but scholars became an isolated, unpopular and reclusive type of literary technologist. Meanwhile, the trend in religion took shape based primarily upon favorite proof-texting of famous Bible quotations. Homespun theology was the order of the day. But the biblical scholars made some solid ground and carried much weight among the intellectual class. Eventually German scholars were carrying literary and historical criticism to great lengths and they reached remarkable conclusions. The Bible, to them, was no different than any other book of anthologies, letters, philosophical treatises, or other compositions. The Bible fit into a certain literary genre characteristic of all the world's religious writings, and followed certain identifiable types, subjects and purposes. William Gayley Simpson does not inform us of scholarly progress at all. He does conclude very much like the consensus of scholars do, which is all well and good, but fails to provide the National Socialist inclined person with specific Biblical knowledge.

Few persons in the Christian Charismatic Movement, or Bible fundamentalists, have any conception of the following facts:

1. That the Old Testament writings called the canon (39 books of the Jewish Bible) were not even decided upon until about the year 110 A.D., some seventy years after the death of Jesus.

2. That the New Testament was not completed, and its content determined, until after 325 A.D., three hundred years after Jesus, and two centuries after the death of the apostles.

3. That the number of New Testament books was limited to 27 because of numerology based on the trinity (3x3x3=27). That the creeds of the church, in their present form, were determined by ecumenical councils dating from 325 (Nicea), and 457 A.D. (Chalcedon), in which unpopular ideas and notions were laid to rest under the heavy dictum of heresy.

4. That the New Testament quotations of the Old Testament are not exclusive of questions from other disapproved and later non-canonical literature. (Jesus' saying about the moon turning to blood, is a quotation from a pamphlet entitled The Assumption of Moses, written by a Pharisee from 0-25 A.D.)

5. That certain motifs, such as the title "son of man", were only later applied to Jesus in order to suggest his divinity. That title is of dubious origin, for Ezekiel uses "son of man" as a synonym for serf, while Daniel uses it with respect to the future messiah.

6. That some of Jesus' discourses are rewritten accounts of Plato, such as his night meeting with Nicodemus, when he discusses the prospect of being born-again. This term "Born-Again" is a favorite of Socrates, to be found in Plato's *Phaedo* in which "Born-again" meant

to be literally reincarnated through the natural birth process.

7. That the same evangelist, John, uses the term love as did Socrates, for St. John borrowed the assertion "God is Love", from Plato. 8. That most predictions of the prophets were fulfilled not by the historical Jesus (who was quite different from the Christ of the Gospels), but by the fictional Jesus Christ who was a creation of the imagination of certain Jews who crept into the church at a later time, such as Paul.

The prophecy-fulfilling events in Jesus' life were elaborated after the fashion of theological scheme, based upon guesswork and creativity in the furtive minds of the literary guild of the converted pharisees. So it happened that the militant Jesus who said "and he that has no sword, let him sell his garment and buy one" (*Luke* 22:36), was converted into a passive Jesus who said "it is enough", when the disciples showed him two swords. Then Jesus heals the ear of the servant of the high priest after Peter cut it off with the stroke of a sword. It is most interesting to see how the writer had edited out the real facts and substituted the fictional account. Jesus is converted from a Social Justice revolutionary who blasts the extortion of the Pharisees for taking widows' houses, into a docile monk who encourages people to "pray lest ye enter into temptation." So we see that side by side remain some of the original sayings of Jesus, interspersed with whole rewritings of hodgepodge confusion, and deliberate distortions of the man's real purpose. Jesus says in *Luke* 12:49 "I am come to send fire on the earth; and what will I, if it be already kindled?" But the next verse is a midrash which converts the fire into a baptism. "But, I have a baptism to be baptized with; and how am I straitened till it be accomplished." In verse 51 we read of another midrash on these words, "Suppose ye that I am come to give peace on the earth? I tell you Nay; but rather division." The midrash (commentary) which follows reduces the saying from a Weltanschauung (world view - "Peace on Earth") to a Volkishschauung (family view, "Far from henceforth there shall be five in one house divided, three against two and two against three.")

There is a method whereby the critic may obtain ground floor knowledge about the historical Jesus. One is by comparing the gospels and contrasting them. Allow the contrast to glare. When we do, the following picture emerges in the resurrection accounts: Mark has one boy at the tomb; Matthew has one angel; and Luke has two angels, while John has Jesus himself. A perfect example of the growth and development, or evolution, of the "Son of God" concept. However, we read also that in Mark the boy in the tomb tells the women to expect Jesus in Galilee, while in Luke the two angels tell the women that the disciples must remain in Jerusalem until they are endowed with power from on high. This is a redaction of the most glaring type. The Pharisee has altered the pro-Galilean bias of the early Christians to a pro-Judean one, in which Jesus is robbed of his integrity, and has been repatriotized. Also, we read in John that the women are not allowed to touch the risen Lord till he ascends unto the Father. However, in Matthew they held him by the feet; evidence of clumsy editorial work. These contradictions make the resurrection stories seem grossly fictitious.

In the nativity scenes we have even more to amuse us. A triangle love affair develops when Joseph takes the pregnant Mary as his wife. The Jew soap opera makes Jehovah out to be the third party in a lustful story. How might Mary's virginity be accounted for?

And was Joseph jealous of the divinity who overshadowed her? (This reminds one of the story of Rosemary's Baby, in which the devil overshadowed Rosemary to produce a son of the devil). This amusing account of Jesus' birth obsessed the minds of 8th and 9th century theologians who speculated on Mary's perpetual virginity. Some argued *prepartum*, for example, that her hymen was intact until Joseph broke it so that Mary would be ready for childbirth. Others argued *contrapartum*, for example, that Jesus broke her hymen at birth. But most of them insisted upon *post partum*, that is to say that it never did break, but was miraculously preserved, through elasticity, so that Jesus had no discomforts, and to protect Mary's virginal qualities. This seems so inappropriate in the light of the visitation of the virginal shepherds who, naturally, had no spouses, but lived idle days on the hillsides with their pet ewes. The almost universal reputation of shepherds carrying syphilis makes the whole account of "Jesus' birth" ridiculously absurd. First, God is the third party in a love triangle, then, Mary has a supersized vagina (Jewish pornography), and the visitation of animal incestors. What a triptych this would make for a Flemish painter!

But this scene is absent from Mark and John. Neither contains a nativity scene. The reason is obvious. Mark allows Jesus to be a Galilean, from Nazareth or Capernaum. John, on the other hand, is most fantastic as he predates the flying saucer enthusiasts by many centuries, in suggesting that Jesus had no natural birth but merely descended to earth from the sky (*John* 3:13, "And no man hath ascended up to Heaven [Elijah, Enox ??] but he that came down from heaven, even the son of man which is in heaven."). Thus all the vagaries of the virgin birth are dispensed with in a single stroke, and Jesus is now the Bread of Heaven bred in heaven. Such discrepancies cannot be glossed over, for they give us a picture of the antagonistic, pretended, and delusive efforts of the Jew-Christian scribes to hammer out of nothing a glorious fable.

The uses of Jewish apocalyptic are certainly illuminating on the subject of Jewish literature. Basically, apocalyptic refers to literature of a very symbolic kind. It is allegorical and uses symbols of animals and objects to illustrate other "ideas" about which they really speak. In so doing the secretive writer of political exigencies can allude to things he abhors in his Roman or Greek occupied country, and lambast their customs and ways through Jehovah's vindictive fury. Thus we have pictures of an evil Anti-Christ who is only superseded by a more evil Jewish Messiah who will right everything in the end for "chosen people."

As is usually the case in apocalyptic, the irrational element reigns supreme in the imagination. Thus the "smoke of their torment ascends upward night and day forever and ever," even though "the lake of fire" was on earth which passed away from "him who was on the throne" to disappear into nothingness. Thus: Hebrew melodrama—but in the ancient world! The Eternal Jew! He works the same way, with or without New York and NBC!

However, there are elements in apocalyptic which tantalize the mind. Some expressions could be updated to the present and made to seem like real divine inspiration. Thus in *Rev.* 17, the ten kings that rule one hour with the beast are taken to be ten nations of the modern European Economic Community which will go into oblivion with Christ's second coming. Strangely enough, Europe has gone into many oblivions since and because of Christ's first coming. The thought never occurs to these biblical fanatics that the ancient Roman empire had ten dioceses while still in the day of the apocalypticist. The ten kings were the ten governors of the provinces of Rome. The hour in which they would reign with the beast (Rome) was an indication that the apocalypticist hoped for a short day for the empire. The short day dragged on for several hundred years however. The rebuilding of the Temple in Jerusalem is presupposed in *Rev.* 11. This scene is occupied by two prophets, probably Moses and Elijah, who return to earth to witness against unbelieving humanity and punish them with fire from their mouths. They are killed, however, and the whole of the world's population sees their dead bodies in the streets of the great city while they celebrate their death. The key to futurism here is in the word "sees". For, say the proponents of the futuristic school, the advent of Television has now made even this possible; an unsuspecting *goy* may be deceived by Jewish poetic license.

Let us compare for a moment what the writer of *Acts* has to say about the feast of Pentecost as to its universality. *Acts*, chapter 2, has it that 16 countries had representative Jews visiting Jerusalem during the holy season. When Peter and the apostles speak in tongues, these diaspora Jews from sixteen regions comprise the Jews of the "whole world". "And there were dwelling at Jerusalem Jews, devout men, out of every nation under heaven." The Jewish universe at that time certainly didn't include the western hemisphere. But that did not constrain the writer to make ambitious claims for Israels omnipresence around the world. To the Jew: the only world that counts is the Jewish one. But, the lesson applies to the "seeing" of *Rev.* 11. For everyone sees the two witnesses as they die and are resurrected 3 1/2 days later. Can anything less be said of this in the light of apocalyptic phraseology than that exaggeration, misrepresentation and poetic fervor have displaced technical facts, usurping those facts with insane or exotic Eastern images? The strange fancy or unreal imagination of the fanatical Jew is as ridiculous today as it proved itself to be during the Greco-Roman times. The filthy unblown nose of the Jew intrudes itself into the serene and perfect-seeking cultural essence of our Western Civilization.

Yes, more can be said, but not in the scope of this paper. That Jewish hopes were based upon glowing visions and hallucinatory experiences explains only part of this general phenomena. It can be aptly stated that the Jews have used the psychology of the Gypsy long enough to learn the fatal weak-points in the mind of Indo-European peoples. But as always, through our long history, the Jewish people still turn their primitive psychic energy against Aryan mankind—in every possible way, and in every possible place. In ancient Rome they used every trick possible to unbalance the mind of that solid race of men; in modern America they will use every trick possible in order to unbalance the minds of three generations of young people. The Jewish theme has always been: Destroy, destroy, and crush out of existence, all that which is Superior, all that which is fine and good in our human nature.

Everywhere it is the same old story. When will we Aryans learn the truth of treacherous Jewry? A Renaissance man arises in Germany about 1933—a rebirth of our culture and civilization becomes possible. And so world Jewry organizes to smash a character called: Adolf Hitler. Or a great Admiral of the Sea is presented to the world. What does the busy Jew then set upon doing? To Nuremberg, and sent that courageous hero of the German Navy to ten years in a humiliating prison. This sordid picture is repeated in dozens and dozens of cases. As Americans we know too well how our best minds and best characters are effectively destroyed—here in the United States. I list here only Hitler and Doenitz because they are so widely known even to the illiterate American.

And so for Bible lovers, and men of good reason, let us hold the Bible in our hand for its positive virtues: but let us beware of its poisonous aspects, characteristics which as Nietzsche once reminded us: "Ok, let us study this Bible, it should be studied, but let us first put on a set of white gloves before picking it up." Excellent advice, from the dimensions of philosophic mind. But do not let the Bible become an intoxicant, do not allow an ancient "television script" so much scope as to cause a derangement of Nordic mentality. Our instinct is more in areas of building boats then in clever effeminate rationalizations for virginity; we should rather love One Leader, or Six Philosophers, or Twelve poets, or One Hundred writers—than to sit still and hate a given civilization, or to act like sick priests and poison the minds of the young against all high and manly virtues.

So we find Simpson to be only slightly deficient for the National

Socialist reader. In support of Simpson, at least one reader concludes that his philosophical approaches and descriptions about our own racial awareness remain valuable. National Socialism, without firm insight into the Racial Question, is not National Socialism at all—for culture and civilization stem from nothing else in this universe, but from superior mind and character.